Rancière and Film

Edited by Paul Bowman

EDINBURGH
University Press

© editorial matter and organisation Paul Bowman, 2013
© the chapters their several authors

Edinburgh University Press Ltd
22 George Square, Edinburgh EH8 9LF

www.euppublishing.com

Typeset in 11/13 Adobe Sabon by
Servis Filmsetting Ltd, Stockport, Cheshire, and
printed and bound in Great Britain by
CPI Group (UK) Ltd, Croydon CR0 4YY

A CIP record for this book is available from the British Library

ISBN 978 0 7486 4736 1 (hardback)
ISBN 978 0 7486 4735 4 (paperback)
ISBN 978 0 7486 4737 8 (webready PDF)
ISBN 978 0 7486 8474 8 (epub)

Contents

Acknowledgements

I would like to express my deep gratitude to Jacques Rancière for contributing an afterword response to the essays that make up this collection, despite having to contend with many serious matters in his life at the very time that I was asking him to read and respond. The fact that he did so is a testament to many different things, including his commitment, his integrity, his professionalism and, indeed, passion for film and for thought.

This book would not have happened were it not for the kind invitation of Ian Buchanan and the generosity of all of the contributors, Nico Baumbach, Rey Chow, Abraham Geil, Bram Ieven, Mónica López Lerma, Patricia MacCormack, Mark Robson, Richard Stamp, James A. Steintrager and, of course, Jacques Rancière.

Rancière and the Disciplines: An Introduction to Rancière before Film Studies

Paul Bowman

All men are intellectuals, one could therefore say: but not all men have in society the function of intellectuals . . .

This means that, although one can speak of intellectuals, one cannot speak of non-intellectuals, because non-intellectuals do not exist . . . Each man, finally, outside his professional activity, carries on some form of intellectual activity, that is, he is a 'philosopher', an artist, a man of taste, he participates in a particular conception of the world, has a conscious line of moral conduct, and therefore contributes to sustain a conception of the world or to modify it, that is, to bring into being new modes of thought. (Gramsci 1971: 9)

Introduction: Politics before Film Studies

The question of the relation 'Rancière and *film*' quietly presupposes another relation: 'Rancière and film *studies*'. This leads to a bifurcation: what is the character, status and significance of Rancière's work on *film*, and – quietly – therefore also, the character, status and significance of Rancière's work in relation to the discipline or disciplines of film *studies*? I say 'disciplines' because film studies both is and is not *one* discipline. No discipline is univocal. No discipline is singular – other than in the eyes, or the fantasy, of the most reductive, taxonomical and exterior gaze – a gaze from outside of the field in its heterogeneity. Nevertheless, the name exists, the institutional and discursive entity exists, even if what passes for film studies here is very different from what passes for film studies there. In short, film studies exists within and as a part of disciplinary discourse – even if, to echo one of Jacques Rancière's formulations about disagreement, what one person might understand by the term 'film studies' will be very different from what another person might understand by the term.

It is not my aim to try to adjudicate on which type of film studies is 'best'. Nor do I want to propose or define a Rancièrean film studies (although I think that there is such a thing – or a few emerging interpretations of such a thing). Rather, I want to interrogate a fundamental problematic subtending the relation 'Rancière and film' and its quiet – but not sleeping – partner 'Rancière and film studies'. This is the question of Rancière's work (whether on film, or on politics, aesthetics, ethics, philosophy, history or literature) in relation to *discipline*. For if there were one thing that Rancière's work would aspire not to be, that one thing would be *disciplinary*. In other words, my argument is that Rancière's politics, his ethics and his aesthetics are *anti-disciplinary*, through and through. Therefore, the big question to be tackled in an academic/intellectual context such as this is that of *Rancière's relation to discipline*.

For the sake of argument (but, really, because to propose as much is eminently verifiable, and in terms of all different kinds of evidence – evidence that there is neither time nor need to set out), let us propose that film studies is a discipline. Film studies is disciplinary. It is an academic and intellectual exercise that is perfectly comfortable and entirely at home within the university. Indeed, it is hard to imagine anything like it existing outside of the university. It has no necessary politics and no problem at all with being merely, simply or entirely academic. Nevertheless, in many respects doubtless this is a simplification and a defamation. Doubtless there are many who 'do' film studies who have political aspirations and orientations, informed rigorous critiques, theorizations, explorations and problematizations. (One need only note the power of *feminism* in film studies or *postcolonialism* in film studies to perceive this.) However, as a field, film studies is not characterized or defined by even the problematization of disciplinarity. Rather than in film studies, the problematization of disciplinarity emerged most fully and most forcefully (in the Anglophone academic world, at least) with the development of cultural studies. This was fuelled and furthered by the critical force of 'French' poststructuralism, which was waging its own wars on institutions and status quos at the same time, and often for broadly the same reasons, as Anglophone cultural studies.

This is a significant point to make *here* because it draws attention to the fact that the interventions of Jacques Rancière and those of cultural studies are almost the same age. Moreover, both have always challenged 'discipline', through ethical and political

critiques of discipline's partiality and bias and through a prin-
cipled (unprincipled) advocacy of various forms of indiscipline.
Both actively critique institutional bias, conventions, hierarchy
and inequality. And both might seem to be different manifestations of the same impulse, or to be part of the same 'discursive
formation'. But does this mean that Rancière and cultural studies
are allies, or partners? This question *matters*, I think, because
exploring it casts light on the relation of Rancière to discipline, to
politics and, both tangentially and essentially, to film studies.

Despite their proximities, cultural studies has often been organized by the very paradigms that Rancière has most challenged:
Althusser, Bourdieu, Habermas, Derrida; and by problematics that
Rancière has little if any time for: gender, sexuality, queer studies,
abjection, alterity, technology . . . Nevertheless, recent years have
seen the rise of a Rancièrean paradigm not only in film studies but
also in and around cultural studies. And even if this can be said to
be hardly the fault or concern of Rancière himself, a Rancièrean
cultural studies paradigm nevertheless raises wider issues – not just
about cultural studies, but also about any of the many disciplinary
spaces into which Rancièrean work has intervened (politics, ethics,
philosophy, aesthetics, art, history, sociology and, of course, film).
So, posing questions about the relations between Rancière and the
disciplines raises and also casts light on fundamental aspects of
the relations between academic work and political or social and
cultural intervention (Bowman 2007; 2008b). This may not be
of importance to any and every type of film studies, but it would
seem to have to be a component of any Rancièrean film studies.

So, before looking at the relations *between* disciplines or fields
and their others (other disciplines and fields and other places and
practices), let's first consider the effect of Rancière's interventions
into the field of cultural studies. In one sense, Rancière's relationship with cultural studies (and vice versa) is not new. (He has,
for instance, long been friends with figures formative of cultural
studies in the UK and the US.)[1] But still, it can be said that the
recent widespread engagement with Rancièrean perspectives in
cultural studies (as his work has been translated into English)
has precipitated some significant reconceptualizations of politics,
aesthetics, film, subjectivity, spectatorship, pedagogy and power.
Yet this has not amounted to a paradigm shift or a paradigm
revolution, in Thomas Kuhn's sense (Kuhn 1962). Cultural studies
remains, as it always was, interested in issues of politics, aesthetics,

film, subjectivity, spectatorship, pedagogy and power. Film studies
too. So, in Kuhnian terms, Rancière's recent emergence does not
amount to a kind of revolutionary science. It is more a kind of
innovation into the ongoing concerns of normal science.

Of course, by discussing Rancière and cultural studies in terms
of discipline, science and paradigm, I may be accused of having
overlooked, forgotten or of having fundamentally misunderstood
both Rancière's and cultural studies' shared critiques – indeed,
shared rejections – of *disciplinarity*. This is a critical rejection
which boils down, in Stuart Hall's formulation, to the essential
difference between 'academic work' *as scholarship* and 'intellectual work' *as a political practice*, or as *aiming for/aspiring to
intervention* (Hall 1992; Bowman 2007; 2008b). In other words, I
may be accused of having forgotten both that cultural studies has
always insisted that it is *not* a discipline and that Jacques Rancière
has always targeted disciplined and disciplinary orientations in his
polemical interventions. Rancière targets disciplines because they
are instrumental in establishing who can and who cannot speak
(Rancière 2008a).

However, it is precisely in the light and because of these shared
critiques of disciplinarity that I formulate it in these terms;
because my question is this: given the fundamental critiques of
disciplinarity as power in cultural studies and in Rancière, what
is the significance and impact of the emergence of a Rancièrean
paradigm within cultural studies? In other words, if one question
of both cultural studies and Jacques Rancière has long been not
just 'what happens when education happens', but 'what happens
when disciplinarity happens', I want to ask: What happens when a
Rancièrean paradigm happens?

Rancière and the Disciplines

Rancière has been read as a theorist (and polemicist) of politics, of
aesthetics, of film, of pedagogy, and even of sociology and philosophy; he has also been read as a historian, an archivist, a theorist
and philosopher of workers' history, and so on. And this is all
fine. But it is also only half the story. The other half is the consistent factor which runs through and unifies Rancière's work. Many
people have identified this as an insistent focus on the problems
of equality and inequality. And this is also correct. But I would
prefer to point out that there is another constant factor and focus.

And it is this: all of Rancière's key interventions have been directed towards the matter of academic disciplines themselves, or towards the phenomena and forces of disciplinarity. Rancière's target is the disciplines. Not discipline itself but rather, *the* disciplines: institutional, academic, intellectual disciplinarity.

Althusser was critiqued because he exemplified the hierarchical, almost aristocratic, logic of discipline (Rancière 1974; 2011a). What was rejected was the injunction to respect, defer to and emulate the masters. Bourdieu was critiqued because his theoretical orientation was regarded as based on a similar tacit or unconscious presupposition of inequality: that there are those who know and those who don't know, and so on (Rancière 1991). There are similar critiques of philosophers, of political theorists and of various sorts of cultural theorist, specifically those concerned with the cinematic apparatus and agency (Rancière 2009a).

They are all similar in the sense that Rancière discerns in many approaches to many topics the same inegalitarian presuppositions. So this is unsurprisingly what most people get from Rancière: the idea that we should not accept inequality and be vigilant against inegalitarianism, both in the status quo and in thinking. We should not regard any 'other' as ignorant, as unknowing, as needing the help of the teacher, the experienced or the expert; because this presumes that there are those who *really do know* and those who *don't know*, and that those who don't yet know need those who do know in order to learn, in a never-ending game of catch up which, although not necessarily asymptotic (like a Zeno's paradox of movement), always keeps some people lower and some people higher, some people in and some people out, some people up and some people down (Rancière 1991). In reading Plato and Aristotle, Rancière calls this the geometrical world view: the view of the world as naturally or ideally hierarchical (Rancière 1999a). Democracy is the threat which could screw this up for those who are in and up. Which is why those who are 'in' or 'up' all hate and fear democracy (Rancière 2006b).

However, when it comes to his writing on education, pedagogy, teaching and learning, Rancière could be said to have little to no interest in *what* is being taught or *what* is being learned. Or, if he has, it is incidental and not essential to his argument. Rather, what Rancière is interested in is what is happening in the pedagogical *relation*. In other words, Rancière is not saying that teachers do *not* know, or that they arrogate their expertise. Rather Rancière is concerned to show that, in traditional pedagogical relations, what is being taught is deference to the status quo: that the master's or the discipline's version of what to do and how to do it is what is to be deemed best, right and proper.

Disciplined Intervention

Ultimately, Rancière is consistently concerned to show that disciplines *discipline*; that discipline *disciplines*; that discipline happens; and that it *imposes* ways of thinking, ways of seeing, ways of doing, ways of sharing. To translate Rancière's concerns into another register: Rancière's primary 'target', so to speak, is therefore arguably the disciplinary gaze – wherever it attempts to assert itself and institute itself as institution. This is because the disciplinary gaze is a disciplining gaze and it has material effects, first on perception and second on processes, practices and procedures; and these are reciprocally reinforcing. Contingent ways of thinking, making, doing and being are instituted as propriety or even necessity. Hierarchy and inequality ensue. And so on.

However, it deserves to be noted: hierarchies are not essentially '*bad*' in and of themselves. Hierarchy is not a dirty word. Rather, hierarchy *becomes* 'bad', in Rancière's thinking, when a contingent hierarchical formation or state of inequality comes to be passed off as necessity, and particularly when a state of imposed subordination or stultification is enforced as necessity.

Because of his own discipline-phobic gaze, Rancière's 'target' is predominantly not so much this or that state of inequality 'out there' (so to speak), 'in the real world' (as it were); but rather the inegalitarian disciplinary gaze 'over here' (so to speak), 'in thought' (as it were). As such, Rancière was not necessarily *against* Bourdieu or anyone else who has ever claimed to care about or who has ever tried to intervene into inequality 'out there'. Rather, Rancière has simply always been keen to point out the moments and ways in which this or that social policy was based on a particular theory or orientation, one that has itself been based on or organized by the very presumption of inequality that it sought to eradicate.

Given this 'interrupted' focus – a focus that is never 'simply' or 'directly' focused on the outside world – Rancière's style of intervention might be deemed 'theoretical', in a pejorative sense (as in, 'it's not *really* a *proper political* focus'). But this is only tenable if one remains blind to the relations between academic work and anything (or maybe even everything) else. Rancière does not overlook this disciplinary or institutional dimension; which is why I would prefer to think of his orientation as 'alterdisciplinary' (Bowman 2008b) – that is, as an attempt to alter disciplinary orientations, especially in terms of the ways in which disciplines theorize and practise intervention into and engagement with the 'great outdoors' (or the 'outside world', the 'other' of the university) that is their object.

Specifically, this means that, without *doing* sociology, and without seeking to intervene into the outside world that is the object of sociology, Rancière nevertheless at one time sought to alter sociology. This was not just for its own sake, but precisely because certain sociological paradigms were articulated with and came to inform state educational policies and programmes in France at that time. As such, Rancière's strategy of intervention is to be regarded as tactical and alterdisciplinary, rather than strategic or disciplinary. It has been called 'polemicizing' (Arditi and Valentine 1999), but its polemics are aimed predominantly at academic discourses. In this sense it is typically neither *obviously* nor *directly* political. Rather, it is gauged as an intervention into precise disciplinary sites – sites of the production and partition of the sensible, perceptible and intelligible. These need to be recognized for what they are: fundamental sites of the production, maintenance and circulation of *discourse*. Such disciplinary sites are of course multiply consequential: first, in terms of their production of what Rancière terms the *partage*; and second, in terms of their direct or mediated relation to other sites and scenes, and their relationships with many of the practices and procedures of culture and society.

In other words, although Rancière uses a different vocabulary to either many of his French contemporaries or the Anglophone cultural theorists influenced (or hegemonized) by the work of Antonio Gramsci, Ernesto Laclau and Stuart Hall, Rancière clearly accepts the complexity, the lack of obviousness and the inevitable circuitousness, the multiply-mediated lack of directness of the hegemonic entanglements (articulations and reticulations) of different social, cultural, state and other apparatuses and processes. Like many figures in cultural studies, postcolonialism and even poststructuralism 'proper', Rancière is evidently much more invested in the sociological and the institutional than the philosophical or ontological. This is what led Alain Badiou to propose that Rancière should be regarded therefore as neither 'doing' philosophy nor 'doing' politics (Badiou 2005: 116): Rancière doesn't do philosophy properly, says Badiou, because he prefers to talk about politics; but, he adds (with a twist of the knife), even though Rancière likes to go on about politics, he isn't really or actually doing politics, is he? However, I think that Badiou has missed the point. For it seems to be the case that Rancière has consistently chosen to engage at length with matters such as Bourdieuian sociology while not bothering so much with questions of ontology because the connection between *that* discipline, *there and then*, *mattered* in a *political* sense much more than any philosophical exploration of questions of ontology did anywhere at that time. (Which is not to say that theoretical questions of ontology don't matter politically, or that they never will; it's just to say that they didn't matter politically, there and then.)

So, Rancière's intervention there, as elsewhere, should be regarded as an intervention aimed at the site of the *production* of the partition of the sensible, the perceptible and the intelligible. These sites are disciplinary. His interventions seek to draw attention to and ideally to subvert and transform inegalitarian disciplinarity, to change the practices within disciplines. This focus on disciplinary production is not an abnegation of or abdication from social or political responsibility. It is aimed, instead, at precisely the points of the formation of disciplinary orientation and hence at the bases of the determination of strategies and types of intervention by particular disciplinary paradigms into what is still most easily thought of as 'the real world', 'out there'. Because of this, Rancière's approach can be thought of as a kind of crowbarring open of selected disciplinary paradigms along their lines of inequality; or of attempting to throw a spanner into the works of existing orientations, by repeatedly pointing out their biases and investments in inequality.[2]

And this is an important and admirable orientation. But where are we to place Rancière 'himself'; or rather, how are we to characterize his own way of seeing (if it is simply 'his'), his own perspective, the partitioning he has available to him in his perceiving? With whom or with what does Rancière share his vision? From where does it come and with what implications?

It could be argued – and despite any protestation from Rancière himself – that there *is* a Rancièrean paradigm, and that its own key coordinates can be discerned in his deep investments in the texts, issues and perspectives of modernism. Such an observation may be taken by some to suggest that 'therefore' Rancière's insights are of limited relevance. But then there is his investment in the notion of equality. In terms of this, perhaps Rancière's (contingent) investment in modernism is incidental.

Police Politics

Equality is Rancière's claim. Indeed, it seems that equality is Rancière's claim to universality – even if he himself may claim to make no universal claim. Nevertheless, Rancière's claims about equality are 'verified' by him in case after case, example after example, taken from ancient to modern to postmodern context. As such, it seems clear that this claim about equality is not local, particular, singular or contingent, but is to be regarded as universal.

Moreover, therefore, equality also always involves a nonreferential dimension. Equality is not a referent. It is a proposition in need of verification. But the means of verification are not objective or referential either. They are not simply there in advance. They themselves have to be invented or performed in the process of verification (Arditi 2008). Hence contestation is irreducible, and hence also Rancière is necessarily closer to Lyotard, Derrida and even Butler than he would ever care to concede. But, in any case, the point is this: viewing the world through this lens enables Rancière to perceive a remarkable consistency subtending all manner of political impetuses and police responses.

And there are always police responses. In Rancière's paradigm there are police impulses and there are political impulses. There are political responses and there are police responses. But – as he famously insists – it is only very rarely that political impulses and responses gain the upper hand and prevail (Rancière 1999a). In fact, Rancière repeats, politics will not 'prevail'. Rather, from time to time, and essentially unpredictably, politics may emerge, erupt, as an event; there will be occasional convulsions, *but politics will not prevail*. Police stabilizations will always arise and will always tend to prevail. (In Gramsci, in Ernesto Laclau, in Stuart Hall, in Judith Butler and in many other places, even in Derrida, this is called *hegemony*.) In Rancière, a crucial issue is that both politics and police are in a sense *imminent possibilities*. Politics is the *threat*; the threat that policing works to deter in advance, to ward off; and to rein in, to redirect and to rewrite. Policing works for – indeed as – indeed, it is – the status quo, the extant, the established, the proper. Politics is only ever a momentary eruption along fault-lines between instituted entities and (or about) uncounted potentialities, caused by subterranean tectonic forces. Policing is everything that will work to try to predict, prevent, manage, play down, tidy up, rewrite and write off moments of the real or possible eruption of politics.

One might see this conception of politics – no matter how specific and unique a flavour it has – as bearing a very historicizable family resemblance to other conceptions of politics, whether modernist, Marxist, poststructuralist, or all of the above. But this is not necessarily a criticism, and Rancière has always insisted that his work does not try to deliver a new theory of anything. Indeed, when one simply reads Rancière, it deserves to be said, his works seem strongly driven by a desire to deflate, to simplify and to recast and reorientate, along simpler conceptual lines than one finds in many theorists, thinkers, writers and (political) philosophers. Very often in Rancière one finds moments in which he explicitly seeks to point out the way that other – often very popular – approaches seem to be contrived, jumbled, confusing and confused.

This in itself suggests why Rancière is increasingly popular across disciplines across the globe. His work offers clear commentary on and critique of other major classic and contemporary figures – Foucault, Derrida, Debord, Habermas, Lyotard, Bourdieu, Arendt, Deleuze, Agamben, Plato/Socrates, Aristotle – according to a clear and yet very novel and suggestive conceptual paradigm.[3] Moreover, Rancière's motivation itself, and his key themes – power, politics, police, democracy, oligarchy, equality, inequality, pedagogy, stultification, and so on – could not be said to be anything less than dominant concerns in cultural studies, cultural theory, continental philosophy and beyond. As Robert J.C. Young put it over twenty years ago, the political perspective, the political paradigm, emerged as the increasingly dominant 'architectonic' of knowledge in the arts and humanities throughout the twentieth century (Young 1992).

Rancière himself may have rejected the hyper-politicizing approach of the deconstructionists, the postmodernists and (implicitly) cultural studies, by proposing a counter-argument to their hyper-politicizing (Rancière replies to the argument that 'everything is political' by saying that if this is so then therefore nothing is). But still, his insistent focus on the question of politics associates him with this academic/intellectual formation and impulse. And moreover, it is within these contexts that Rancière has received his warmest welcome.

Which produces some paradoxes. For if, on the one hand, *politics* is indeed to be associated with eruption and disruption, and if, on the other hand, *police* is to be associated with stabilization, then what are we to make of the diverse disciplinary hospitality to and embracing of Rancière's interventions? Might it mean that, despite its own intentions, Rancière's work is closer to *police* work, that is, to the disciplines and hence to discipline, than it is to *politics*? This may seem to be a terrible irony. For all that Rancière seems to have ever wanted to do is to stir things up, to alter disciplinarity along egalitarian lines, and to do so because of the connections of academic institutional discourses with wider cultural and political scenes and discourses.

But, given that – as Sam Chambers has argued – in Rancière, the word 'police' is not ultimately negative (Chambers 2011), then maybe to associate Rancière with 'police' is not so bad. For, even though Rancière wants to preserve his polemical binary (politics–police), it must be the case that there can be a *better* police and a *worse* police – without 'politics' happening at all. This is why the impetus in Rancière is that of a more agitating drive towards demanding equality where there is currently inequality, even if that agitating is in and of itself neither politics nor the precipitation of politics.[4]

But if Rancière's police or disciplinary status is 'vindicated' by being 'politics-orientated', there is still the question of his relation to the policing that is academic disciplinarity. In other words, if we can vindicate or validate Rancière *because he is interested in politics*, then this means that we can do so because what he is doing *passes muster* according to the protocols that police a disciplinary scene organized by a disciplinary or police demand *to be politics-orientated*.

Perhaps I am being hyperbolical. But my point is in *any* and *every* case, it is clear, Rancière would not want to be disciplinary. He is avowedly an advocate of 'indiscipline'. As he puts it:

> [indiscipline] is not only a matter of going besides the disciplines but of breaking them. My problem has always been to escape the division between disciplines, because what interests me is the question of the

distribution of territories, which is always a way of deciding who is qualified to speak about what. The apportionment of disciplines refers to the more fundamental apportionment that separates those regarded as qualified to think from those regarded as unqualified; those who do the science and those who are regarded as its *objects*. (Rancière 2008a: 2–3)

But then, if Rancière is so critical of the disciplines because of their ordering, validating, hierarchizing and excluding effects on voices, entities, identities and bodies; if instead he advocates adopting an 'indisciplinary gaze' and stance, in order to *see* disciplinary partitioning and hierarchizing in action; then what is to be made of his popularity in so many disciplines? What does it signify? And accordingly, is his strategy really capable of 'breaking' the disciplines – and which ones? And if so, to what end? One answer – one set of answers – suggests itself.

Rancière and the Postdisciplines

First, the adoption or incorporation of Rancière into so many disciplines suggests that disciplines 'themselves' are perhaps no longer quite what they used to be. It is clear that they are no longer the institutionally and discursively scaffolded, often hermetically sealed or stringently policed enclosures that they may once have been. They are today perhaps neither Foucault's fields nor even Lyotardian or Wittgensteinian self-enclosed experimental 'paralogies' (Lyotard 1984). Their social relations, reticulations and articulations are now utterly transformed – so much so that the dystopian predictions of the denuded and dilapidated 'university of excellence' that Bill Readings described in the mid-1990s is now a manifestly true and lived day-to-day reality, in more and more locations (Readings 1996).

We could justifiably spend a lot of time unpacking what this transformation or translation may mean. In a very concise paper, posted online, in note form (on Google Plus), Simon During has proposed that we start to think of the contemporary university not in terms of disciplinarity but rather in terms of postdisciplinarity (During n.d.). Postdisciplinarity, he proposes, has many features, including a fluidity of investments, processes, attachments, activities and orientations. Academics in more and more fields are now less likely to be beholden to or to identify with traditional disciplinary orientations and protocols, or to connect their activities with canonized methodologies, and are more likely to have their thought organized by particular proper names ('Foucault', say, or 'Deleuze', or indeed, 'Rancière').

Other indexes of postdisciplinarity, During suggests, include the fragmentation of the field and the rise of the 'centre': the research centre, the teaching centre, the centre of excellence, what Derrida once represented as the externally funded and non-philosophical (business, military, private or state) supplements to the university; supplements demonstrating that, always and already, but increasingly palpably, 'the university' is not 'one' (Derrida 1983; 1992b). Along with the rise of the 'centre' (as index of the balkanization of disciplines), the proliferation of subjects with the suffix 'studies' is the other well-known characteristic: cultural studies, media studies, literary studies, gender studies, computer studies, management studies, sport and leisure studies, hospitality studies, and so on and so forth. Some of these suffix-studies arose in a sense 'politically' (cultural studies, gender studies, queer studies, and so on), while others arose according to a rather more corporate, pragmatic, utilitarian or profit-orientated logic. All of these logics intertwine in the eternally returning annual scramble for students and/or research grants.[5]

Given the increasing transformation of universities and their functions from being public institutions providing ostensibly public services into private enterprises increasingly offering obviously consumer goods, services and 'investments', there has been an attendant transformation of the activities and orientations within erstwhile disciplines (which are themselves housed now within more or less managerialist enterprise centres). Disciplines (or postdisciplines) are less driven and governed by fixed/policed procedures and structures. They have become more 'fluid' or 'perforated' discourses – intertwined, overlapping and enmeshed, rather than discrete and paralogical. Because of this, disciplinary 'partition' and 'policing' become much less straightforward. As Bill Readings famously put it, it no longer matters *what* you do as long as you do it excellently (Readings 1996). And if what you do is frowned upon or rejected by one journal or conference, you can always just go and do what you so excellently do somewhere else. Performative transgressions can no longer be reined in or disciplined even if stalwarts want it.

In other words, surely the disciplines are already well and truly broken. At least some of them. Or perhaps the partitions that were once between them have moved elsewhere. Where once there were famous fights about the presence and effects of disciplinary boundaries – as when the likes of Derrida and Rorty spearheaded the acquisitions and mergers process between literature and philosophy – it seems now that the former differences between subjects, disciplines or fields have not only been eroded but have upped sticks and gone. Where they remain, the question is whether they have the status of fetishes, spectres or, to use Barthes's expression, 'figures in the carpet'.

In such a context – or such a proliferation of contexts – one might question the extent to which the logic either of mastery, or of disciplinary or pedagogical stultification, or indeed of police, supervenes or perseveres or is hegemonic in the university at all.[6] It is true, one might search for it, ask where it is, seek it out, hunt it down; but this kind of implies that the old despotic master is already on the run. One might also therefore question the tactical, strategic, politicized or otherwise interventional value of championing, any longer, 'indiscipline' (as Rancière has done), or cross-, inter-, ex- or anti-disciplinarity (as cultural studies has done) – especially when the entire institutional geography or DNA of the university seems more and more guilty of the charge once levelled so uniquely at cultural studies: that it is a 'mishmash', a 'ragbag' and a 'hodgepodge', a ramshackle bricolage of mutually incompatible and incoherent voices.

All of this might be put rather more polemically: are the fundamental cultural studies and Rancièrean critiques of disciplinarity anything more than critiques of the past? Is *The Ignorant Schoolmaster* (Rancière 1991) *any longer* an allegory about the problems of power as exemplified in pedagogy? Is it now simply a story about how things *used to be* in schools? Are *The Nights of Labor* (Rancière 1989), *The Philosopher and his Poor* (Rancière 2004a), and other similar books now anything more than treatises on the way class-focused intellectuals *used to* think (reductively) about the objects of their concern? Is *The Emancipated Spectator* (Rancière 2009a) correcting anything more than some old elitist, modernist and Marxian orientations?

While this is a possibility, and may well be partially true, I do not think that this reading does justice to the situation. A postdisciplinary context is not free from the fraught logic of disciplinarity. Moreover, a postdisciplinary context becomes one in which disciplinary orientations and projects are 'up for grabs', going to the highest bidder, precisely because disciplinary identifications and anchorages have been so shattered, fractured or dislocated. And such is the landscape of the posthumanities. This is how the land lies after the battles between the disciplines and the antidisciplines. This is what it looks like after what was technically a 'victory' for cultural studies. But this was a victory which, as many different voices have observed in different ways, perhaps signals the death, demise or exhaustion of the 'project' of cultural studies. To paraphrase John Mowitt: the problem with cultural studies today is that it has been a victim of the success of its own paradigm (Mowitt 2003). If everybody's doing it, then who needs cultural studies as such? Jameson's notion of the vanishing mediator seems pertinent here: an agent, agency, force or practice which enables a change or blazes a trail and then recedes (Jameson 1973).

Portable Politics

Needless to say, establishing such a landscape in the arts, humanities or university is surely not what anyone in cultural studies ever believed the project was about, in any register. The intervention of capital and state, specifically in the form of the neoliberalist deregulation and expansion of markets, played a decisive role – which is doubtless why Marxism has returned to politicized academia with such a vengeance (see Johnson 2012). But does this mean, after the fracturing or desiccation of the disciplines, that all the poststructuralist and cultural studies critiques of disciplinarity, institutional power and micropolitics should simply give way to the macropolitical perspectives championed by the increasingly popular Maoist and Leninist positions propounded by the likes of Badiou and Žižek? In the face of political challenges and in the wake of all the lessons of poststructuralism, is there really no alternative but to become revolutionary Marxists? This all strikes me as a regression and a forgetting of some important lessons.

Rather than this, Jacques Rancière's insistent focus on many forms of *relation* and many forms of *event* in terms of the question of *equality* seems to offer a position that does not regress from the legacies and lessons either of poststructuralism or from the key impulses of emancipatory Marxist and other egalitarian projects. Rancière's lessons about what happens when certain sorts of lessons happen, about how and why and where and when inequality emerges when relationships form, and so on and so forth, all seem to be lessons that always need to be learned.

Rancière has been criticized for being simplistic – for instance, for obdurately affirming the simple (perhaps untenable) binary politics/police (Marchart 2007), or for seeing everything or reducing everything to 'class', and so on. And this might always prove problematic for cultural studies. Moreover, the Rancièrean lessons about equality and of democracy are arguably much easier to learn than the complex critiques of disciplinarity and hegemony that form part of the cultural studies canon. In fact, to pick up and redeploy one of Rey Chow's observations, Rancière's lessons are eminently *portable* lessons (Chow 1993: 146). You can pick them up, you can take them with you. You can apply them anywhere. And you should. Whichever way you look at it, you should. Nor does 'understanding', 'grasping', 'comprehending' or 'feeling able' to voice such lessons require anyone to 'perform' either the role of or an empathy with what Rey Chow calls '*portable oppressions* and *portable oppressed objects*' (Chow 1993: 146). And this has got to be a plus.

Moreover – and finally – given the absolute university insistence these days on specifying aims, objectives, 'learning outcomes' and 'transferable skills' in education (in teaching and even in research), I can think of few more important 'learning outcomes' and few more important 'transferable skills' than the ability of as many people as possible to sense, perceive, formulate, express and critique inegalitarian hierarchies, institutions, partitions and distributions. In this sense, Rancière's portable – *almost sound-bite* – paradigm perhaps offers a more productive paradigm for political thinking, political engagement and possible intervention than most others currently in circulation in cultural studies and many other postdisciplines. For Rancière's is a portable paradigm that can be picked up as a tool or weapon by any in the humanities who want to fight to try ensure that the posthumanities do not simply 'roll out' in such a way as to become the inhumanities.

It is in terms and in light of this backdrop that I believe Rancière's love and study of film is to be best approached.

Notes

1. I discuss Rancière's relationship with a 'marginal' yet nevertheless 'instrumental' figure of British cultural studies, Adrian Rifkin, in a forthcoming paper entitled 'Autodidactics of Bits'.

2. In this respect, the mode and manner of *intervention* chosen by Rancière can be read as equivalent to that of Derrida. Both of which, I would argue, imply a strong affinity with a Gramscian world view – especially a Gramsci read *after* Foucault and after Ernesto Laclau. But that is another discussion. And I do not want to digress too much into a kind of disciplinary cartography, in which I try to attribute to Rancière a position and a value in relation to other landmarks, coordinates and supposedly fixed points in the turning world. Rather than position Rancière on some kind of map of disciplinary discursive space, it seems more appropriate – given Rancière's relentless implicit and explicit critique of disciplinarity – to continue to pose questions about Rancière and disciplinarity. There are many possible questions. For instance, Rancière points out the premises, presuppositions and ensuing practices and procedures entailed by what might be called various disciplinary paradigms – Althusserian, Aristotelian, Bourdieuian, Jacototian, Wordsworthian, Derridean, Debordian and so on. But is that pointing out itself *paradigm-free*? Is Rancière's vision itself somehow free, universal, neutral, objective or natural? Does Rancière offer or constitute a new or old paradigm for this or that discipline? Even if he doesn't explicitly offer a paradigm for others to use, surely his thought must be regarded as constituted by some contingent mode or manner of thought? What partition of the perceptible does it presume?

3. So in this sense I think it seems reasonable to affirm that Rancière can be regarded as offering the coordinates of a paradigm shift, akin to the sense given to the term 'paradigm shift' by Thomas Kuhn – albeit, in this case, in the arts, humanities and social sciences, rather than the hard or physical sciences. Evoking Kuhn's work on the structure of scientific revolutions may seem excessive or inappropriate here. However, at least one thing seems pertinent, even if there is no conceptual or practical similarity between paradigm shifts in the arts and paradigm shifts in the sciences. It is this: in Kuhn's account, paradigm shifts are inextricably connected with controversy, scandal and resistance; with redefinitions of 'normal science' or 'normal everyday disciplinary activity'; with what is proper activity and with what is discredited and obsolete. As such, they are even associated with job losses and departmental closures, arising from the radical redefinitions and reconfigurations of the field and of the activities within it. (Even if things do not happen so dramatically or starkly in the arts, humanities and social sciences – even if people are not fired because their activities suddenly become obsolete – and even if the fields are

much more obviously organized *politically*, into camps, groups, schools of thought – I think that the force of 'paradigm shifts' can be felt and play themselves out at the other end: not in terms of firing, but in terms of hiring.)

But, if Rancière's *is* a paradigm shift, it is a very quiet one. It does not seem to have attracted all that much controversy. I doubt whether the fate of university schools and departments hangs in the balance around it. I doubt even whether it could be said to have precipitated a syllabus crisis. But, given their discursive nature, perhaps paradigm shifts in the arts and humanities have always operated according to different temporalities to the hard sciences. Or perhaps it's something else. For, unlike in cases such as Marxism, Freudianism, Lacanianism, Derridean deconstruction, Mulveyan film theory, Deleuzean philosophy, Habermasian theory, Laclauian theory and so on, I have never even met anyone who got particularly hot under the collar about Rancière's arguments. I can only think of a handful of people, in fact, who have taken issue with Rancière – and even then, the taking of issue was not particularly heated: a couple have questioned the Rancièrean replacement/displacement of the Heideggerian and/or poststructuralist terms 'politics' and 'the political' (or 'le' and 'la' politique) with 'politics' and 'police'; another has argued that Rancière offers a gross simplification and effectively a kind of defamation of Derrida; another has said to me that, whatever the worth of Rancière's critique of Bourdieu, he'd still rather be in bed conceptually with Bourdieu than Rancière; while another has criticized Rancière for not being Žižekian enough . . . There would also be a (Lacanian, at least) criticism of Rancière's fundamental Jacototian claim that children learned their first languages by themselves.

Of course, to reiterate, Rancière has never said that he has a new paradigm or that he ever even wanted to precipitate a paradigm revolution. At most he could be said to offer a reconfiguration of the ways that we think about politics, art, film, education. However, I raise all of this here – in an essentially hyperbolical way – in order to draw attention to the almost fluid 'acceptance' of or accommodation to Rancièrean insights, Rancièrean challenges, polemics and provocations, *in Anglophone academia*. I emphasize the Anglophone here, because I know that the story of Rancière in French and in France is different. I also know that the story of the rhythms, logics and choices of the translation of Rancière from French into English is itself a complex and noteworthy narrative. Sam Chambers has reflected on this process of the literal (and disciplinary) translation of Rancière into English, and I refer you to his discussions of this in his book, *The Lessons of Rancière* (Chambers 2012).

4. According to Oliver Marchart (2007), this makes Rancière's rejection of the ontico-ontological difference (the difference between le and la politique, or politics and the political) untenable.

5. But, During (n.d.) suggests, whatever their origin and orientation, in the place of a strong sense of unique disciplinary method, postdisciplines tend to 'share' common figures, common names. To Simon During's argument about the emergence of postdisciplinarity, I would add an important point made by Robert J.C. Young (1992: 111–12). Young reads the history of the historical changes in the dominant paradigms of knowledge – the changes in the type of 'truth' that have been sought or established in the university – from Religious, to Artistic, to Utilitarian, to Political – over the 200-odd years of the modern university's grown in Europe, Britain and beyond. Young notes that what he calls the dominant 'architectonic of knowledge' today is nothing other than 'political truth'. *The* dominant paradigm – *the* questions that need to be engaged in order for work to be deemed valid or validated – are the questions of politics. This is because, in Young's terms, political truth is the dominant form of truth within academia today. The trail was blazed for the emergence of this paradigmatic orientation with the institution of cultural studies in the UK in the 1960s, along with a wide array of cultural, political, intellectual and theoretical processes: 1968, civil rights, feminism and postcolonialism, to name some key players. We could add other forces and players to this list. But the point relates to the sense in which politics and the political can be regarded as the emergent and in places dominant paradigm of new disciplines, interdisciplines, antidisciplines and postdisciplines. Viewed accordingly, the crossdisciplinary appeal of Rancière, like many other figures before him, perhaps, can be viewed as the enrichment of what in Thomas Kuhn's vocabulary would be termed 'normal science'.

6. One might wonder whether, in being against the strictures of disciplines, orientations such as those of 'traditional' cultural studies and/or Jacques Rancière are against anything other than the past.

2

What Does It Mean to Call Film an Art?

Nico Baumbach

The origins of this essay derive from the attempt to make sense of a certain resistance to Jacques Rancière's work that I have encountered at film studies conferences in the United States. As I see it, this resistance can be traced to what is seen as a tension or contradiction between Rancière as the self-proclaimed amateur advocating for universal equality on the one hand, and what are perceived as the trappings of cultural distinction that mark his writings on cinema on the other – specifically the familiar auteurist pantheon that makes up the films he focuses on and, perhaps more significantly, the fact that he discusses cinema as an art.

To the extent that American academic film studies has been concerned with the egalitarian or democratic potential of cinema, it tends to insist on the separation of film from the category of art especially insofar as the category of art is thought to derive from the discourse of aesthetics as it emerged in German Idealist philosophy. In the US, until recently, studying film in terms of art or aesthetics tended to persist only in more traditional departments that emphasize either film appreciation or formalist analysis and reject the more explicitly political forms of film theory and criticism that helped establish the field in the 1970s and 80s by foregrounding class, race, gender and sexuality. But increasingly aesthetics is making a comeback, as are other methods of inquiry of the sort that might once have been thought to have been outmoded by the more cutting-edge currents in critical theory and cultural studies. Today it is not rare for theory and cultural studies to be perceived as outmoded, as humanities departments seek methodological (and financial) support from the sciences and a foundation that is not marred by the taint of politics.

It is perhaps symptomatic of this state of affairs that even within more theoretically and politically inclined enclaves of film studies, the question I have encountered more than once in relation to Rancière's work is how do we *use* Rancière? What are the practical applications of his claims or theories? I have attempted to take the question seriously and apply it directly to the question of teaching. How and why might we teach Rancière or how might Rancière influence the way we teach cinema? This question necessarily splits into two because it means confronting both Rancière's writings on film but also on pedagogy in general. In thinking directly about not only how we might teach Rancière, but also how Rancière's work might allow us to think differently about teaching film in general, I hope to address this question of why Rancière's ways of thinking about film as an art are often met with resistance from people who might otherwise be most receptive to his project. The goal of this essay, then, is not simply to explain how we might resolve this perceived tension in Rancière's work, but rather to use the tension between Rancière's work and certain preconceived ideas in US film studies to look more closely at what it means to teach film as an art or not as an art. I take it that, if Rancière's work is useful to us in Anglo-American film studies in any way, it is not because he solves any of our problems. On the contrary, he creates new ones that may be useful to us precisely because they don't allow for as easy solutions as the old ones.

Before discussing what lessons we might draw from Rancière about how to teach film in particular, a few words about Rancière on pedagogy in general are in order. In *The Ignorant Schoolmaster: Five Lessons in Intellectual Emancipation* Rancière confronts the reader with a series of propositions about intelligence, equality and instruction that may make professors rethink the value of appearing in front of the room as experts who presume to provide access to knowledge that we have and that our students do not. Methods of teaching that take the goal of study and the proof of intelligence to be the progressive acquisition of knowledge and skills through a determinate method are one example of what Rancière calls 'stultification'.[1] This stultification is redoubled by the idea that this progress is realized not just through the student's encounter with texts, but through the mediation of the professor who is necessary to lead the student on the path to knowledge. The ignorant gain knowledge through the mediation of one who counts as knowledgeable by virtue of the authority of a degree and an institution, and the transmission is thought somehow to require the physical bodily presence of the master for it to take place.

In opposition to this logic, Rancière, following the forgotten nineteenth-century French pedagogue Joseph Jacotot, offers the slogan of intellectual emancipation: everyone is equally intelligent. Similar sounding claims – while they may not have much place in institutions of higher learning – are not necessarily uncommon. We often hear that everyone is intelligent in his or her own way, that all opinions are equally valid, or the relativistic claim that there are multiple intelligences that are merely different with no criteria to evaluate their differences. But this is not what Rancière (or Jacotot) means by the equality of intelligence. He does not mean that we each have equal capacity, whereas some of us have just had less chance to exercise it, because this reinstates the logic of progress which places some in the position of having knowledge that others are expected to acquire. He means that there is, as he puts it, 'a single intelligence' to be affirmed axiomatically. There is only one intelligence because intelligence in the 'opinion' of the ignorant master has no meaning outside the verification of the equality of intelligence. As he puts it, 'Equality was not an end to attain, but a point of departure, a supposition to maintain in every circumstance' (1991: 138). At no point should a hierarchy be instated between one who knows and one who doesn't. The consequence of this logic is that one cannot teach what one knows; one can only teach what one doesn't know. As Jacotot realized, this idea of intellectual equality could not be converted into a method that could be institutionalized without undermining its very principle. Ultimately, Rancière tells us, 'he refused all progressive and pedagogical translation of emancipatory equality' (1991: 134). It would seem that to be an emancipated pedagogue is not to be employable.

Rancière's 2004 lecture 'The Emancipated Spectator'[2] sought a link between the idea of pedagogy preached by Jacotot and discourses about theatrical spectatorship. 'What the pupil must *learn* is what the schoolmaster must *teach* her. What the spectator *must see* is what the director *makes her see*. What she must feel is the energy he communicates to her. To this identity of cause and effect, which is at the heart of stultifying logic, emancipation counter-poses their dissociation' (Rancière 2009a: 14). In other words, the theatrical spectacle that seeks to show spectators how to become active is analogous to the master explicator who guides the student to knowledge. Focusing specifically on the theatre itself as *dispositif* and not on the teaching of theatre, let alone film, the essay is nonetheless readily adaptable to a commentary on the pedagogue who teaches cinematic spectatorship. The film professor can show the student that what she saw is not what she thought she saw, that what she felt is not what she should have felt. Proper access to the film is only by way of a professor who becomes a gatekeeper, either confirming the ways of seeing prescribed by the film or thwarting them – showing how the film doesn't say what it thinks it says. The egalitarian inversion, it might be argued, is to affirm the equal validity of all students' responses as somehow more authentic than the resentment-fuelled interpretation of academics and critics. But the authenticity of the experience of the ones who don't know compared to the inauthenticity of knowledge in the hands of disciplinary power again presupposes two different intelligences and reinstates another hierarchy. How do we get out of this deadlock?

The answer comes through recognizing that the professor/student relationship is not binary; rather, between the professor and the student there are written texts and, specific to our topic, films. And in this case, rather than teaching how to read and write a new language (as Jacotot did), the kinds of knowledge and skills to be acquired in a film studies class are less defined in advance. This is often a source of anxiety for those invested in demonstrating that film studies is a legitimate discipline, but we might see it as an opportunity rather than a problem that needs to be solved. So rather than asking directly how we might think of a teaching method in general in such a way as to avoid reproducing this relationship of hierarchy, and then get to cinema, I'd like to look at things the other way around and ask whether there is an approach to cinema that may allow us to think about what it might mean to teach in a way that allows for intellectual emancipation. How can the professor use cinema to teach the student and herself about equality?

Here we can turn to Rancière's writings on cinema. Whatever may be new or surprising or emancipatory about Rancière's approach to film in his two books devoted exclusively to cinema, *La Fable cinématographique* (2001) and *Les Écarts du cinéma* (2011), he seems to reproduce a familiar canon common to the intellectual cinephile that we might tie back to the old Henri Langlois Cinemateque and *Cahiers du cinéma* up through Deleuze (see Rancière 2001a; 2006c; 2011c). This line arrived in modified form in the US by way of Andrew Sarris's *American Cinema*, which provided a hierarchical taxonomy of auteurs adapted from the lessons of *Cahiers*. In both the American and French contexts, Hollywood was central and it should be remembered that claiming cultural and artistic status for a mass medium and authorship for directors working within the rigid confines of a commercial studio system was itself a challenge to certain currents of mainstream intellectual snobbery that refused to admit that film was on a par with the more traditional arts or saw only more literary or socially conscious (and typically foreign) films as worthy of serious consideration. Sarris's 1968 book exhibits the ambivalent relation to cultural distinction of the emergent cinephile intellectual culture with its marked rebellious spirit in elevating certain B-movie genre films over prestige films of more obvious artistic pedigree, while at the same time dismissing 'the pernicious frivolities of pop, camp, and trivia' (Sarris 1968: 15). It helped to codify for an American audience the tradition of cinephilic taste that can no longer be thought to be on the margins, a variation of which can be found in Rancière's choice of films. It connects the auteurs of classical Hollywood celebrated by *Cahiers* in the 1950s (Rancière writes on Nicholas Ray, Anthony Mann, Vincent Minnelli and the American films of Fritz Lang) to the significant precursors to the kind of modernist filmmaking represented by the *Cahiers* critics when they became filmmakers at the end of the 50s and became known collectively as the French New Wave (Roberto Rossellini, Robert Bresson are two prominent examples that Rancière writes on) to the films of the New Wave filmmakers themselves (Rancière writes on Godard, Rohmer and Marker) to the more formalist radical filmmaking celebrated by *Cahiers* following its post-68 theoretical turn and the contemporary filmmakers indebted to this tradition whose work is rarely seen or promoted outside of international film festivals (Rancière writes on Jean-Marie Straub, Béla Tarr and Pedro Costa). Rancière's choice of objects and broadly auteurist and largely text-based approach might suggest that he reproduces the hackneyed model of French intellectual cinephilia that was given a withering feminist critique by Geneviève Sellier in her book *Masculine Singular: French New Wave Cinema* (2008).

The complex histories of French and American cinephilia are beyond the scope of this essay. What I wish to highlight here is the extent to which the success of this tradition has coincided with the acceptance of film as an art. Sellier, in her critique of the culture of French cinephilia, takes inspiration from English-language gender studies that she argues have been effectively ignored or marginalized in France, where a highbrow culture invested in a universal (and gender-neutral) concept of art still dominates (Sellier 2010: 103–12). In the US, by contrast, a common cinephile complaint is that American academia ignores film as an art on behalf of social or political categories such as class, race and gender (see Bordwell 2011; see also my response to Bordwell: Baumbach 2012).

In the 1930s Walter Benjamin famously proposed that the question should not be whether film and photography are arts, but whether they have changed the very nature of art (Benjamin 2008: 28). While today few would dispute film's claim to be 'an art', what is meant by this tends to remain remarkably vague. To confuse matters, 'art' has in many arenas (not least the academic discipline of art history) continued to be associated with what appears on museum walls or, in other words, with the idea of art that Benjamin thought was disappearing, and not film or even (with some exceptions) music, drama, literature or poetry. Given this semantic confusion, the question should be not only whether the category of art is applicable to the study of film, but also what is meant by art and how is film understood when it is not understood as an art.

Therefore, to further pursue the question of what Rancière might tell us about cinema that can help us think about teaching, I'd like to start by asking not what films we might teach but first what we might *teach film as*. I'll address this question by way of two sub-questions: first, if we do not teach films as art what do we teach them as? And secondly, what are the different ways that film gets taught as art?

In regards to what we can *teach film as* if not art, two possibilities present themselves. To be clear, these two possibilities do not necessarily preclude also seeing some films as art, as I will explain below, and they are not always necessarily mutually exclusive, but nonetheless they are common relatively distinct ways of identifying film as something other than art.

1) The first category I'll propose is seeing film *as ideology*. I use the word ideology as shorthand here, but in this category I wish to include seeing film as 'commodity' as well as seeing film as 'myth' in the Roland Barthes sense, while acknowledging that neither commodity nor myth are strictly equivalent to ideology. Nonetheless, what unites this category is the logic of demystification or the

'hermeneutics of suspicion', an approach that Rancière has criti-cized for reproducing the position of mastery and the logic of inequality (see Rancière 2004b: 50).

One needs to be careful here, of course, because Barthes did not wish to conceive of myth as something that could be unveiled, and we might add that this is true of much of the more sophis-ticated forms of ideology critique, especially that derived from Louis Althusser's concept of ideology, which takes ideology as an a priori condition of daily life not to be confused with false consciousness (see 'Myth Today' in Barthes 2012; and Althusser 1971). The 'hermeneutics of suspicion' as defined by Paul Ricoeur, which starts with Marx, Nietzsche and Freud, has from the very beginning been suspicious of the hermeneutics of suspicion itself (Ricoeur 1970: 32–6). Nonetheless, the tradition of ideology cri-tique must retain the notion that theory can say something that the film itself cannot – that, as Laura Mulvey put it, theory can be 'a political weapon' against the unreflective pleasures offered by film (Mulvey 1986: 198). Or as Metz put it, theory can wrest film from the imaginary and win it for the symbolic (Metz 1982: 3). Seeing film as ideology presumes that film is first an imaginary or idealist phenomenon and that one can extract meaning from the text of the film that it simultaneously contains and seeks to obscure.

2) The second way of seeing film as something that is not art I will call seeing film *as culture*. By this I mean asking how film or films function culturally without necessarily treating them as ideol-ogy that needs to be demystified or art that needs to be appreciated. I do not intend this category to be strictly correlative to the work done on film by writers and academics that identify with the tradi-tion of cultural studies, but obviously there is overlap. By seeing film as culture I mean a way of seeing film that is committed to retaining as its object the ordinary ways that films are received and experienced without (necessarily) denouncing or unveiling them on the one hand, or championing them on the other. It means a way of approaching films less in terms of how meaning inheres within the film text than in terms of how films take on or acquire meanings.

I'd now like to turn to the different ways of seeing film as art. The first way I'll call the *Romantic Model*, though it has certain variants that may sound more modernist than romantic.[3] The paradoxical logic is the following: film is an art like any other, that is, the seventh art, because film is an art like no other. In other words, I want to say that the logic behind the titles of both

Rudolph Arnheim's *Film as Art* and V.F. Perkins's *Film as Film*
would fall into this category (Arnheim 1957; Perkins 1972). In this
model not all films are art and teaching films as art means teaching
representative masterpieces to show how they use the specificity of
the medium to transcend the medium.

The second model I'll call the *Utilitarian Model*. We could
also call it the poetic model, not in the sense of romantic poetics,
but because it sees art as *poiesis* or in terms of ways of doing or
making. Here I am thinking of the popular American textbook
Film Art by David Bordwell and Kristin Thompson. Bordwell
and Thompson insist that when they refer to film art, pedigree is
not an issue. They are using a concept of art that does not require
transcendence, but rather acknowledges the wide variety of types
of films and audiences. Cinema is an art, they tell us, because it
offers filmmakers ways to 'design' experiences that viewers find
'worthwhile' or 'valuable'. They tell us that we can analyse cinema
as an art because it is an intentional formal construct (Bordwell
and Thompson 2008: xviii, 2–3). The criteria for art are then three
things: a) analysable form – patterns are discernible as are innovations within available patterns; b) authorship – the effects of
these formal constructs they tell us are not accidental; we analyse
cinema as art because we attribute design or intention to it; c)
identifiable positive effects – effects that Bordwell and Thompson
call 'worthwhile' or 'valuable', though these adjectives are left
vague because they are meant to encompass an enormous range of
effects. What is key in this model is that art is not pure means, but
has identifiable ends.

The third category I propose is what I'll call the *Didactic Model*
of film art. This category is meant to be a supplement to the category that sees film as primarily ideology. In that model film can
become political when it becomes art or vice versa. Art is understood here in an avant-garde or political modernist sense as that
which breaks from film as ideology.[4] Those who teach film as
ideology often reserve film's power as art to its critical capacity,
its politics. Political film is not film about politics but film that
uses film form to disturb our normal relation to film through what
Althusser called a knowledge-effect. This argument is perhaps
most explicit in Jean-Louis Comolli and Jean Narboni's seminal
1969 essay 'Cinema/Criticism/Ideology' (Comolli and Narboni
2009), and it can also be found in many of the most influential
essays published in the British journal *Screen* in the 1970s.

The fourth category I'll call the *Sociological Model*. It corresponds to the category that sees film as culture. As I suggested, seeing film as culture goes against seeing film in general as art, but what it recognizes is the *art effect* of a certain category of film. It is from this category that we get not the syntagm 'film art', but that of 'art film', which is to say that 'art' when applied to film refers not to its practice in general or its exceptional instances but is more like a genre or mode of film practice with a specific institutional history and specifiable codes and conventions that appeal to a specific elite cultural milieu. According to this model we can read film as art only to the extent that it circulates as art. This category need not be evaluative but it is available for the Bourdieuian critique of discourses about art cinema or the 'festival film' and so on.

This leads us to our fifth category of seeing or teaching film as art, which after Rancière I will call the *Aesthetic Model*. What the other models all share is a logic that assumes that the operations of art have specifiable effects. Like the ignorant master, the emancipated idea of art dissociates cause and effect. What aesthetics means in Rancière's analysis is the suspension of the rules of appearance that define the difference between art and non-art. But the suspension of those rules is not their overcoming. Art in the aesthetic regime is art to the extent that it thrives on an ambiguity or paradox and here lie both its limitations and its egalitarian dimension.

Rancière does not wish to defend aesthetic theory as a specific discipline or branch of philosophy engaged in the science of the beautiful, but rather to return to the original paradoxical construction of the term to combat the ways in which the critique of aesthetics (like the institutionalized concept of aesthetics it is rightfully against) has been in the service of the neutralization of the politics of aesthetics. He agrees with certain critics of aesthetics that he is otherwise arguing against when he claims that '"Art" is not the common concept that unifies the different arts. It is the *dispositif* that renders them visible' (Rancière 2009b: 23). But he emphasizes the political dimension of the modern *dispositif* of art over and against its domestication in modernist *doxa*. To think of film as art in the aesthetic sense as advocated by Rancière is to tie it back to the history of a form of experience of sensible being that is not strictly equivalent to its function as an object of culture or ideology, even if it is imbricated with these functions. The significance of understanding film as art in this sense is not simply a rescuing of film for art against its debasement as mere entertainment, but also a rescuing of art from its impoverishment as being understood as merely a mark of cultural distinction. Rancière's investigations into regimes of art have consistently disclosed that the history of modern art in what he calls the 'aesthetic regime' does not leave us with an either/or decision between art's sovereignty and autonomy on the one hand or the dissolution of art at the hands of culture, technology, media or commodity on the other. Cinema emerges in a moment in which it can be recognized as art, because art has already been understood as something which does not specify its intentions or effects, and to understand it in this context is to revive its egalitarian potential.

As discussed, Rancière rejects the Didactic Model, but not for the same reasons that it is rejected by the other models we have discussed. The logic of demystification it follows has typically been directed at film's commodity character and the critique of it has been to affirm cinema as a popular cultural form. If the professor is to refuse the role of master who explains to students what they should have seen in the film he has shown them – which is to say either its ideology or its art – then he should, it would seem, embrace the cinema that already speaks to the student. This is the approach of the Sociological Model that tends to assume that what is already familiar and available to the student will invariably condition what the student is capable of appreciating.

It is time to return to what is particularly mystifying about Rancière to many in Anglo-American film studies: how is it that someone on the left insisting on the interdependence of aesthetics and politics today can defend the Kantian idea of disinterested taste against Pierre Bourdieu's critique of 'distinction' – of the way that the bourgeois idea of universal judgement masks the forms of domination exercised by cultural capital? Rancière argues,

> Aesthetic experience eludes the sensible distribution of roles and competences which structures the hierarchical order. The sociologist would like this to be nothing more than the illusion of the philosopher, who believes in the disinterested universality of judgments concerning the beautiful, since it ignores the conditions which determine the tastes and the manner of being of the worker. (Rancière 2006c: 4)

But as Rancière discovered through the journals of workers, this 'ignoring' is not only the privilege of the philosopher or the petit bourgeois aesthete but of the worker himself. And it is not a lack of knowledge, but a suspension of it; it is a refusal of the idea that only the bourgeois is capable of aesthetic pleasure, a refusal that is denied by the sociologist who insists on the power of knowledge to expose all aesthetic pleasure as illusion and to deny it to the worker. The scientific critique of institutional power reproduces that power by insisting that any deviation from its efficacy be seen as only an illusion.

In *The Nights of Labor*, Rancière quotes the journal of a worker during the era of the 1848 Revolution: 'Believing himself at home, he loves the arrangement of a room so long as he has not finished laying the floor. If the window opens out on a garden or commands the view of a picturesque horizon, he stops his arms a moment and glides in imagination toward the spacious view to enjoy it better than the possessors of the neighboring residences' (Rancière 1989: 81). This evidence of the worker's aesthetic reflection is not so much an appeal to the authenticity of worker experience against the academic attempt to define it for him in advance. Rather it is more complicated because it challenges equally Rancière's attempt to find an authentic worker's discourse; the worker's discourse, as he discovered it, defied what it was supposed to be. The worker's experience of the work that goes into creating the home of the one who hires him is meant to expose the lie of the kind of disinterested appreciation that is supposed to be made possible only by the luxury of ignoring the labour that went into it. For Rancière, this example signifies the way that aesthetics can mean a displacement of the idea that there is a discourse proper to the worker and another discourse proper to the man of leisure. What interests Rancière about this example is not the universality of aesthetic sensibility, which speaks even to a lowly worker, but rather how aesthetics – in a specifically modern sense – can mean the suspension of the distinction between those who are condemned to work with their hands and those who have the luxury to live the life of the mind.

This point re-emerges in the final essay of Rancière's most recent collection of writings on cinema, *Les Écarts du cinéma*. In the essay entitled 'Politique de Pedro Costa', Rancière describes a scene in Costa's *Colossal Youth* (2006) in which Ventura, an immigrant labourer from Cape Verde and a denizen of the slums of Lisbon, is seen walking through a museum that we learn later was where he suffered an accident while working on its construction. Here it is not a question of the worker admiring the paintings on the wall, participating in the kind of disinterested reflection thought specific to the privileged classes, but nor is it a question of aesthetic sensibility being denied to the worker. The paintings on the museum walls echo the still lives Costa's camera has made out of the light and arrangements of objects in Ventura's run-down home. What Costa's film reveals, Rancière argues, is the richness of Ventura's world, and the failure of the museum is its stinginess in this respect. It does not, like Costa's film itself, offer 'an art commensurate with the experience of these travelers, an art that emerged from them and which they themselves can enjoy' (Rancière 2006e). The museum is indicted not because its grandeur contrasts with the misery of the inhabitants of the slums but, on the contrary, because it withholds and limits its idea of art, whereas Ventura's everyday world displays the beauty, grandeur and sensory richness of art understood in a more expansive and generous way. As Rancière argues,

> This politics is a stranger to that politics which works by bringing to the screen the state of the world to make viewers aware of the structures of domination in place and inspire them to mobilize their energies . . . The politics here, rather, is about thinking the proximity between art and all those other forms which can convey the affirmation of a sharing [*partage*] or shareable [*partageable*] capacity. (Rancière 2006e)

The politics of the film is, then, not simply its stance on oppression, on the economic and political history that is responsible for the miserable conditions of those living on the margins of society. The politics is rather found in a politics of aesthetics or a politics of cinema, which means a different way of looking at the world and the experience of a group of individuals whose lives and environment are typically only shown to signify misery and incapacity. Rancière continues:

> The politics here is about being able to return what can be extracted of sensible wealth – the power of speech, or of vision – from the life and decorations of these precarious existences back to them, about making it available to them, like a song they can enjoy, like a love letter whose words and sentences they can borrow for their own love lives. Isn't that, after all, what we can expect from the cinema, the popular art

of the twentieth century, the art that allowed the greatest number of people – people who would not walk into a museum – to be thrilled by the splendor of the effect of a ray of light shining on an ordinary setting, by the poetry of clinking glasses or of a conversation on the counter of any old diner? (Rancière 2006e)

He poses the last line as a question for a reason, because Costa's films are not shown in multiplexes, and to the cinephiles who discover them at small international film festivals or acquire the DVDs after reading about them in *Artforum* (or in a book by a French philosopher) they are not recognizable as examples of what most people think of when they think of movies as a popular egalitarian art accessible to everyone. Pedro Costa, perhaps not unlike his protagonist Ventura, seeking to do justice to the singular worlds of individuals not usually granted access to the media and attempting to make that world shareable, becomes, in Rancière's words, something of 'a sad monk' confined to the ghetto of the art world. As films are increasingly made and marketed to particular demographics, to make a film for anyone is perhaps to make a film for no one.

Here again we come up against the ironic history of film's relation to art. To claim that a Chaplin film was art could be seen as a democratization of art. According to Benjamin, Chaplin's films, unlike modern painting, were experienced by the masses in terms of 'an immediate, intimate fusion of pleasure – pleasure in seeing and experiencing – with an attitude of expert appraisal' (Benjamin 2008: 36). But at the same time as cinephilia claimed for art the egalitarian pleasures of mass entertainment, it also became available for a new code of distinction that drew divisions between the auteurs who count and those who do not, the knowing cinephiles and the ordinary mass of fans. As knowing the difference between the right and wrong Hollywood auteurs became a sign of cinephilic distinction, soon cinephilia also became associated with the kind of highbrow culture it once stood against. Nonetheless, as Rancière's essay on Pedro Costa attests, the same way that films for the masses can be claimed as art, so too can so-called art films be claimed for the masses. Rancière's stance on cinephilia corresponds to his stance on aesthetics – to read within its paradoxical discourse for its egalitarian dimension and to indict the indictment of it that attempts to close off its possibility by reifying its most problematic exemplars.

In *Les Écarts du cinéma*, he champions 'la politique de l'amateur' – a play on 'la politique des auteurs' – the term used by Truffaut that once set the agenda for the cinephilic cause (Rancière 2011c: 14). The position of the amateur can be adopted by the professor as well as the fan. By dissociating cause and effect, the policy of the amateur allows films to participate in a shared inquiry into ways of making, watching and thinking about the combination of moving images and sounds and by extension ways of seeing, saying, acting and being in the world. The Aesthetic Model, as I have called it for the purposes of this essay, means teaching film as art and teaching art as something available to anyone.

Notes

1. See *The Ignorant Schoolmaster*: 'The new explication – progress – has inextricably confused equality with its opposite. The task to which republican hearts and minds are devoted is to make an equal society out of unequal men, to reduce inequality indefinitely' (Rancière 1991: 133).
2. The lecture became the title essay of a book published in French in 2008 and translated into English in 2009.
3. Rancière has argued that so-called modernism is an especially restrictive interpretation of a new way of understanding art in what he calls 'the aesthetic regime of art' that goes back to at least the late eighteenth century and includes the history of Romanticism (see Rancière 2004b: 10–11).
4. For many examples of this logic in 1970s film theory see Rodowick (1994).

3

After the Passage of the Beast: 'False Documentary' Aspirations, Acousmatic Complications†

Rey Chow

The Paradox of Sound

In his classic *Introduction to Documentary*, Bill Nichols writes that a great deal of the persuasiveness of documentary films stems from the soundtrack, which he equates more or less with the spoken word (Nichols 2010: 26). Of what does the audience need to be persuaded? – the truthfulness, authenticity and plausibility of what is presented. This association of sound with a rhetorical function (persuasion) underscores sound's relation to the image in documentary film as one of support. Working in a subordinate role, sound, it is thought, enhances and consolidates the tasks set by the image; the soundtrack is simply *part* of the general imagistic plan of work. Although this may at first seem like a specialized set of issues (sound) within a specialized genre (documentary), it is, on closer examination, an interesting lead-in to fundamental questions about the evolving politics of modernist artistic representation. With reference to a number of Jacques Rancière's concepts, I would like, in this essay, to examine the ramifications of sound's distribution, that is, the ways it participates or is particularized in what, strictly speaking, is an audiovisual situation.[1]

Although he does not discuss sound per se any further in his book, what Nichols goes on to say about how the image works and does not work offers us something valuable to think with. 'Images lack tense and a negative form', he writes. 'We can make a sign

† This essay was originally conceived for a forum on documentary and sound. I am grateful to Paul Bowman for encouraging me to amplify the many theoretical connections it bears to Rancière's work. A German version of the essay, trans. Claudia Kotte, is included in *Ton. Texte zur Akustik im Dokumentarfilm*, ed. Volko Kamensky and Julian Rohrhuber (Berlin: Verlag vorwerk 8, 2013).

that says, "No Smoking", but we typically convey this require-
ment in images by the convention of putting a slash through an
image of a cigarette . . . The convention of a slash mark through an
image to mean "No" or "Not" is very hard to adapt to filmmaking' (2010: 28). The image, by this account, has a privileged – one
might say an a priori – relation to existence; its positivistic mode is
much more conducive to the suggestion of something being there
than to the suggestion of non-existence, absence and negation. For
Nichols, this is the reason sound (in the sense of speech or narrative) is needed:

> Whether it is through what we hear a commentator tell us about the
> film's subject, what social actors tell us directly via interviews, or
> what we overhear social actors say among themselves as the camera
> observes them, documentaries depend heavily on the spoken word.
> Speech fleshes out our sense of the world. An event recounted becomes
> history reclaimed. (Nichols 2010: 28)

Nichols's notion of 'fleshing out' is thought-provoking, not least
because sound is, in fact, seldom conceived in such concrete corporeal terms. Even so, this is not the most important point he offers.
Rather, the most important point is that there is a structural relation at work in the meaning-making apparatus of documentary,
and that, because of the positive form of the image, anything that
works alongside it, such as sound, would probably occupy a place
like the slash mark, which serves as a negating force that, in turn,
enables the meaning of the images to come into being. To complete
the logic of Nichols's observations, we can say that in relation to
the image, sound tends to occur by way of a hollowing-out, an act
of subtraction that, paradoxically, has to be added to the image. In
relation to the image, sound functions at once as a cut – an incision
into a continuum – and as a supplement, an excess.

The Question of 'What'

This structural relation between sound and image may have much
to do with their individual semiotic tendencies, but in the context
of documentary films this relation and the tension it generates are
made acute by the (scientific and moral) imperative of realism, that
is, by documentary's claim to be, and assumed status as, a truthful
record, transcript or repository. To be effective, conventionally,

realism needs to hold out the promise that there can be a coincidence or correspondence between reality and documentation, and
that what a documentary provides is *evidence*.[2] As a consequence,
it also requires that the discussion of documentary revolve around
the question of 'what', which is the question of content: what is
recorded, transcribed and stored?[3] As Dai Vaughan writes, the
medium itself is an essential part of the consideration:

> Where fiction uses film in much the same way as it had already used
> words or marionettes or the bodies of live actors, documentary
> represents a mode of cognition which may scarcely be said to have
> existed before 1895. The only precedent which suggests itself is that
> of *a hunter who, without laborious inference, reads into the spoor the
> passage of the beast*. (Vaughan 1999: 85; my emphasis)

How might what Vaughan calls 'the spoor', a word that bears ety-
mological kinship to the German word *Spur*, be discussed in relation to sound? Indeed, can the question of 'what' – 'the passage of
the beast' – be discussed in sonic terms, when 'spoor', like trace,
track, mark, imprint and all such figures, conjures a kind of reten-
tion involving space and visibility? Where and how in the passage
of the beast is sound to be found, if it is not simply reduced to
rhetorical support?

These questions call to mind the way sound is typically perceived. Unlike the way an image appears, which is usually in a spa-
tially locatable spot, as an exterior and a (sur)face, sound typically
comes to or comes at us from multiple directions, in a manner that
is more a matter of emanation than manifestation.[4] Even when
a specific cause or source can be pinpointed, sound tends to be
perceived in a twin process of gathering (in) and dispersing (out),
as though it is coming from and then vanishing into a general surround. As a phenomenon whose key feature is its fugitivity, its
exit from itself or movement through time, sound creates impressions that are the opposite of a sense repository in stable, spatial
or surface (one might say 'facial') terms: the moment one grasps
(hears) it, it is already off, deferred and referred somewhere else.
Unlike the image, sound does not operate with the architectonics of
graphs, planes, frames, screens, windows, doors, edges and similar
constructs, and thus frustrates interpretative endeavours that rely
on the pictorial illusionism produced by such architectonics –
illusionism such as closing and opening, covering and uncovering,

scrolling up and down, left or right, for instance – for purposes of sense-making. This is perhaps why it is so difficult to talk about sound in relation to documentary except in the aforementioned terms of rhetorical support. By virtue of its claim to being a record of something, documentary realism implicitly conjures the onto-logical, formal and often didactic demarcation of an inside from an outside.[5] Sound emission, on the other hand, transcends such a division, because perceptually sound does not make its mark (of being heard) without at the same time straying off. Jean-Luc Nancy puts it in terms of an intrinsic difference between the ear and the eye: one functions by 'withdrawal and turning inward, a making *resonant*', while the other functions by 'manifestation and display, a making *evident*' (Nancy 2007: 3). As sound does not (become) sound, as it were, by staying put or holding still, it poses a fundamental challenge to the notion of indexical 'thereness' that defines the physical trace or imprint left by something. Rather than the indexicality of 'what' and 'there', sound bears much greater affinity to the *ephemerality* of the passage, the passing, of the beast. For precisely this reason, when sound is involved in the depiction of such ephemerality, whether in a documentary or fic-tional mode, special designs need to be adopted to prevent sound from stealing the show.

A 'False Documentary': *Hiroshima mon amour*

To elaborate my discussion, it would be interesting to consider some examples of such sonic designs. How might the difficulty posed by sound determine the conception of an intradiegetic economy? As I would suggest with the classic *Hiroshima mon amour* (1959; dir. Alain Resnais, screenplay by Marguerite Duras), films that deal with sharply bounded situations involving a before and an after, such as a catastrophe, a tragic loss or the encounter with a foreign culture, are especially difficult, as the filmmakers are confronted not only with the task of capturing the passage of the beast but also with that of presenting such a passage as a lived experience. In such a context, the questions of what counts for interiority and how are often acute, and sound, because of its tran-scendence of the division between interiority and exteriority, easily becomes a conceptual problem. What kinds of sonic distributions are possible? What parts or participation can sound have in this type of situation? Above all, how might sound, itself ephemeral, be particularized in relation to the *rivalling* ephemerality of the beast?

Hiroshima mon amour is of unique relevance because it was consciously conceived against the conventional documentary mode. After the release of *Nuit et brouillard* (*Night and Fog*, 1955), the trend-setting documentary about the Nazi concentration camps, the director Alain Resnais was commissioned to make a short documentary on the aftermath of the atomic attack on Hiroshima. Reportedly, after spending months collecting archival footage, he declined the project on the grounds that it would simply be a remake of *Nuit et brouillard*. Instead, he suggested a fiction feature with Marguerite Duras as his collaborator. The result was the renowned *Hiroshima mon amour*.[6] As we shall see, this shift in genres from documentary to fiction – what Duras calls a false documentary – has deep resonances in post-war European debates about the ethics of representation, of what can and cannot be represented, especially in the aftermath of a catastrophe such as genocide.[7] Not the least of these resonances is, quite literally, the critical but often neglected part played by sound.

As many readers will remember, the story is simple. A French actress, known in Duras's text only as Elle (She), is making a film about peace in Hiroshima; she has a brief love affair with a Japanese architect (known as Lui or He) and in the process recalls the traumatic events triggered by her love affair with a German soldier in Nevers, France, her hometown, during the Second World War. On the eve of their planned elopement to Bavaria, where they are to get married, the German is shot. The woman arrives on the scene only to witness him slowly die. She is treated as an object of contempt by her village community, which sees her as a national traitor. She becomes temporarily mad, is confined to a cellar by her parents until she recovers and is sent off to Paris. News about Hiroshima arrives then, and the war is over.

What actually happened? The necessity of posing this question and the intimation that it may, nonetheless, be unanswerable are in many ways what make this film so powerful to watch even more than half a century later. This predominant feeling of life becoming unanswerable – and for some, unrepresentable – is, of course, the rationale that underlies Gilles Deleuze's volumes on post-war cinema, in which he portrays a fundamental shift in the modes of intelligence encrypted in the film image before and after the Second World War. While film images before the war have to do with the communicability of physical actions and movements, after the war they increasingly take on the qualities of contemplativeness and indirection typical of reflective consciousness, to become what Deleuze calls time images (Deleuze 1986; 1989).[8] To this extent, *Hiroshima mon amour* is an exquisite dramatization of the shift argued by Deleuze, as the action of the entire film is emotional and open-ended rather than direct and resolved. This is a film not of acts but of acts of remembering, in which time, in the form of an intermixing of the past and the present, mediates states of subjective association and cathexis.

In the synopsis she provides for the screenplay, Duras expresses her disapproval of the documentary mode in this manner:

> Toujours leur histoire personnelle, aussi courte soit-elle, l'emportera sur Hiroshima.
>
> Si cette condition n'était pas tenue, ce film, encore une fois, ne serait qu'un film de commande de plus, sans aucun intérêt sauf celui d'un documentaire romancé. Si cette condition est tenue, on aboutira à une espèce de faux documentaire qui sera bien plus probant de la leçon de Hiroshima qu'un documentarie de commande. (Resnais 1960: 12)

> Their personal story, however brief it may be, always dominates Hiroshima.
>
> If this premise were not adhered to, this would be just one more made-to-order picture, of no more interest than any fictionalized documentary. If it is adhered to, we'll end up with a sort of false documentary that will probe the lesson of Hiroshima more deeply than any made-to-order documentary. (Duras 1961: 10)

In this false or anti-documentary spirit, then, the film begins by establishing a tension between what can and what cannot be seen. After the famous inaugural images of naked arms first embracing in the midst of ashes and then in sex, images that suggest both death and love, we hear a series of incantatory exchanges in a kind of operatic duet. The female voice recounts everything she has seen in Hiroshima, giving as her examples – which the camera follows with fast-moving shots – museum exhibits of human remains, newsreel images of hospital patients, victims with mutilated bodies, deserted animals and abandoned children, and other official evidence of the atomic destruction. The male voice, on the other hand, insists that the woman has seen nothing.

These conflicting, indeed antagonistic, exchanges between the two
protagonists set the aesthetic and moral tone of the film by way
of *a negation of vision*. In accordance with the anti-documentary
conceptualization of the film, the suggestion is that what can
be displayed and seen, and by implication what can be scientifi-
cally enumerated and recorded, amounts to a non-truth. What is
questioned by the male voice is the positivism of what appears
self-evident through (de)monstration, a positivism that the 'made-
to-order documentary' exemplifies, or so Duras seems to suggest.
By contrast, *Hiroshima mon amour*'s avant-gardism lies rather in
its reflexive displacement of such positivism.[9]

Interestingly enough, this scepticism towards a sheer display
of empirical evidence is also expressed by Bill Nichols, who, in
defining documentary, reiterates that imagistic indexicality and
evidentiariness are insufficient criteria. 'A documentary not only
documents events,' he writes, 'but conveys a distinct perspective
on or proposal about them' (2010: 126). Remarkably, Nichols
names this kind of distinct perspective a documentary's 'voice'
(2010: 125).[10] By voice, what Nichols means is an essential, albeit
invisible, something that holds the work together, that makes it
cohere as a story. Nichols's use of this little word to pinpoint an
indispensable *inner* connection even in the context of documentary seems symptomatic of the long-standing Western metaphysics
of presence that, as Jacques Derrida shows in his early work on
Edmund Husserl, tends to attach itself to the voice.[11] Following
Derrida, it is incumbent on us to ask: How does the voice come
to be (imagined as) this inner thing? If and when not inner in
this metaphysical fashion, is a voice still a voice? If not, what
is it?

A sounding board

In *Hiroshima mon amour*, noticeably, the negation of the visually
positivistic is provided by the voice of the Japanese architect. As
Duras emphasizes, this negative voice helps to amplify the question of what is or can be remembered:

> Elle lui dit qu'elle a tout vu à Hiroshima. On voit ce qu'elle a vu. C'est
> horrible. Cependent que sa voix à lui, négatrice, taxera les images de
> mensongères et qu'il répétera, impersonnel, insupportable, qu'elle n'a
> rien vu à Hiroshima. (Resnais 1960: 10)

She tells him that she has seen everything in Hiroshima. We see what she has seen. It's horrible. And meanwhile his voice, a negative voice, denies the deceitful pictures, and in an impersonal, unbearable way, he repeats that she has seen nothing at Hiroshima. (Duras 1961: 8)

The architect's voice, we might say, performs a similar function to Nichols's slash mark. It is the 'No' that punctuates the image, enabling the image to take on meaning through differentiation, through being crossed out. By giving the male voice the structural force of negation, a force that constitutes the anti-documentary momentum, the film demands that we probe the status of this voice. Where does this voice come from?

Within the diegesis, it comes from the Japanese architect, the man who pursues the French actress, looks for her on the film set after the film on peace is completed and asks her to stay with him in Hiroshima. It is his pursuit that makes it possible for the actress to slowly and steadily recollect what happened in Nevers during and after the war. The first important part played by the Japanese architect's voice is thus, literally, that of a *sounding board*. Just as he negates all the positive claims she makes about having seen everything in Hiroshima, so too does he, in the capacity of an interested listener, respondent and therapist, extract from her the missing pieces that together make up the narrative of her past traumatic experience. The mediation of the sounding board allows the audience access to the woman's compelling story of being in love with an enemy, of having to see him die a drawn-out death, of being treated as a disgrace by her community, of descending into madness and, finally, of regaining her reason and leaving her hometown. Most important, the sounding board assumes the voice of the dead German, making it possible for the woman to talk again to her former lover in an intimate, second-person address: 'When you are in the cellar, am I dead?' 'You are dead . . .' (Duras 1961: 54). This role-playing, whereby the Japanese architect momentarily becomes the German soldier in a simulated dialogue, positions the architect in an interesting *void* in relation to the actress. Because he is nothing, he can be the stage and the director as well as the audience of her recollections; he can even be the stand-in for the deceased German. The architect's insistence that his partner has seen 'nothing' in Hiroshima therefore reverberates with a subtle kind of irony: she has seen nothing because what she has 'seen' is him, the sounding board, the nothing-by-himself.

Duras's instructions about what the architect should look like are noteworthy at this juncture. To avoid the trap of exoticism (the possible notion that the actress is attracted to a man with pronounced Japanese features), Duras writes, the actor should have a 'fairly "Western" face' and 'it is preferable to minimize the difference between the two protagonists' (Duras 1961: 109). 'In short,' she concludes, 'he is an "international" type' and what makes him attractive should be immediately apparent to everyone (Duras 1961: 109). In the wake of the Nazis' racist atrocities, Duras's character specifications are understandably in step with the mandate to embrace cultural difference, a mandate that has been adopted by progressive European intellectual groups since before the post-war years. She writes that the point of the story is something universal about human experience and that national or cultural particulars such as 'French' and 'Japanese' should be forgotten: 'This Franco-Japanese film should *never* seem *Franco-Japanese*, but *anti-Franco-Japanese*' (Duras 1961: 109). Be that as it may, this authorial intention runs into a basic impediment: even if the Japanese architect does look like an international type, how is he to speak? How is he to sound like an international type?

Acousmatic Complications

Reportedly, the actor Eiji Okada, who played the architect who is fluent in French, did not speak a word of French himself and learned his dialogue phonetically by memorizing the sounds of the lines he recited.[12] Because of this little piece of information, the question raised earlier begins to unravel in unexpected dimensions: where does the negating male voice really come from?

At the level of conventional acting, of course, we can say that what Okada offers is a performance – specifically, a kind of ventriloquism, the grammatical meaning of which is incomprehensible to him. Such ventriloquism can be interpreted as a kind of Brechtian alienation (or estrangement) effect, making it all the more necessary to reflect on the implications of the sonic 'origins' at stake.

A convenient way of conceptualizing the issues at hand is found in the well-known notion, associated with a Pythagorean sect, of the acousmatic, which refers to a pedagogical situation in which the teacher remains hidden from the student, who can hear (and only hear) his voice. In sound and cinema studies, the acousmatic has been generalized by theorists such as Pierre Schaeffer and Michel Chion to indicate the condition of discontinuity of sound from its source, a condition that can be manipulated to produce phantom effects of mystery, estrangement and horror (see Chion 1994: 71–3, 128–31; 1999). With the emphasis on the separation of sound from a clearly identifiable cause, the acousmatic also facilitates an innovative way of thinking about the voice, with implications that extend well beyond the technicalities of cinema. Rather than being traceable to and integrated with a body (or the image of a body), its traditionally assumed anchor, the voice is now unleashed, so to speak, and becomes akin to an artifact, a part object. As a disembodied and unsynchronized occurrence, the voice is no longer securely anthropomorphic and instead (re-) emerges as ambiguous and enigmatic sound.

What if we were to approach *Hiroshima mon amour* by way of the acousmatic? Within the diegesis, as the Japanese architect plays different roles to help lead the French actress back towards her buried past, a number of artifactual sounds, including that of the voice of the dead German soldier, are, as mentioned, already in play. But the acousmatic is perhaps at its most suggestive in the non-correspondence between the actor Okada's vocal emissions and the meanings of the words he is pronouncing on screen. While speaking French in such a manner as to transmit the grammatical sense as intended by the filmmakers, Okada – or is it the Japanese architect? How do we draw the line? – acts, literally, in the capacity of *a foreign body* to the words he is delivering, in a basic disconnect that, even though not audible/known to the audience, renders him ontologically at once inside and outside the diegesis. Okada's performance is, accordingly, one in which the physical *sounds* from his vocal cords, the *voice* of the character he is playing and the dramatic *roles* this character assumes opposite the French actress (as her current lover, listener, respondent, therapist and former lover) each take on a singularity that is simultaneously an irreducible plurality. In the disjunctions and conjunctions among these various sonic bits and pieces – with possibilities generated by phonetic mimeticism, dramatic dialogue and audiovisual hermeneutics both within the story and extradiegetically – the Japanese actor's voice has become, we might say, an acousmatic assemblage.

A voice that is its own phantom

Once our consideration is informed by the acousmatic, a new kind of question arises with regard to the aesthetic and political avant-gardism of the film's design. That avant-gardism, we remember, is premised on the force of negation as structuration, so that the insistence 'You have seen nothing' resonates both with the anti-documentary (at the level of aesthetic form) and with anti-particularism (at the level of cultural politics), as specified by Duras. However, negation is difficult to accomplish on screen not only because of the positivity of images but also because the acousmatic concealment of the origin of the voice, a concealment that is negative in force, takes, in this context, the visible form of a character, the architect, who thus becomes a positive bearer of negation. At the same time, emanating from an actor who is 'faking' his speech, Okada's voice also undercuts its own seeming fullness of presence with an otherness, an otherness that is, however, not simply a foreign accent (say, of a Japanese person who actually speaks and understands French). If Okada's contribution to the role is, as Cathy Caruth writes, 'the unique concreteness of his voice' (1996: 51), this concreteness is, paradoxically, abstract: it is a voice that is at once itself and not itself.

To put it somewhat differently, the acousmatic is played out here not in the simple structuration or alternation between a voice and its withholding from visibility. Rather, it involves the complex occurrence of a voice that, while speaking/voicing, also withholds itself, so that its sonic transmission/audibility (as French) is indistinguishable from a sonic blockage/inaudibility (of Japanese). Although the Japanese architect seems to be a case of what Chion calls 'visualized sound' (that is, sound that is 'accompanied by the sight of its source or cause' [1994: 72]), therefore, he in fact offers something far more interesting, as what appears to be visualized sound is, in his case, not really the index of a direct or natural causal relation. If the acousmatic in Chion's formulations is potentially traumatic because of the uncertainty of sonic origins, in the case of the Japanese architect the voice is both certain and uncertain, both heard and unheard. Despite having a face, despite being visualized, this voice is, strictly speaking, its own *acousmêtre*, its own 'talking and acting shadow'.[13] Even as it holds forth in speech, this voice is also silent, un-voiced.[14]

And this is how the made-to-order documentary, dismissed by

Duras from the outset, returns in the form of a spectre, but *a spectre at the level of sound*. For shouldn't the fluent, idiomatic French spoken by the Japanese architect/actor be understood finally as a special sound effect? And doesn't this sound effect belong in none other than the category of a 'made-to-order documentary'? That is to say, much as he is (we now know) faking it, isn't the Japanese actor required to produce sounds that sound exactly like French, as though he were nothing but a perfect recording?

Thus, although the Japanese architect's voice is, from the beginning, given the important function of disputing positivistic documentary vision, the artifactual (or mechanical) manner in which the actor Okada mimics French words complicates things quite a bit, making it necessary for a more nuanced evaluation of the filmmakers' anti-documentary aspirations. Indeed, if sound were simply pitched against vision in a simple binary opposition, the male voice could probably be treated, *tout court*, as the conventional embodiment of the function of negation; the actress's assumptions about knowledge (based on what can be seen) would, in that instance, be contradicted and subverted by her partner's voice insisting on her having seen nothing. Once we put vision aside, however, and concentrate instead on the workings of sound, a different order of inquiry begins to unfold, as sound is not exactly containable or localizable even when it is seemingly embodied; as the sonic, to put it differently, is always already acousmatic, always already its own phantom. Mladen Dolar puts it this way:

> There is something acousmatic in every sound, not merely in the sense that more often than not one doesn't see its spatial source and merely makes assumptions about it (to say nothing about acousmatic media, that is, all modern media, which are premised on the impossibility of seeing the sound source). But every sound is also acousmatic in a more emphatic sense: even when one does see the source and location, the discrepancy between this source and its sound effect still persists: there is always more in the sound than meets the eye. (Dolar 2011: 131)

The Japanese architect's French-speaking voice is simply a pronounced instance of such acousmatic complications in the event of speaking in general. For even when one is speaking one's native language, isn't one's voice always already a cover – in the sense of a material medium that, while it communicates or conveys information, also hides, separates and displaces what it is communicating because of the fugitive way sound works? This is how the acousmatic rejoins Derrida's well-known deconstruction of the voice's presumed self-presence. In the cinematic apparatus, the age-old metaphysics of the voice, which Derrida exposes through his reading of Husserl's phenomenology, has found an accessible material presentation.[15]

Sonic nailing (vissage)

Given the intervention introduced by the acousmatic – namely, that any homogeneity or continuity between voice and body (or the image of a body) on the screen may (or should) now be reconceptualized as artifactual – two other, minor scenes of the film involving sound merit our attention. As the two protagonists walk aimlessly in the city before sunrise, they find themselves first at a train station and then at the night club Casablanca. At the train station, we encounter an old Japanese woman, who looks quite the opposite of the 'international type' and speaks to the architect in Japanese. At the night club, where the protagonists are seated in different corners, a Japanese man comes up to the actress and accosts her in English. Both sets of dialogues are simple and straightforward, as though the lines had been taken from linguistic primers. In Japanese: 'Who is she?' 'A French woman.' 'What's the matter?' 'She's leaving Japan in a little while. We're sad at having to leave each other' (Duras 1961: 80). In English: 'Are you alone? Do you mind talking with me a little? It is very late to be lonely. May I sit down? Are you just visiting Hiroshima? Do you like Japan? Do you live in Paris?' (Duras 1961: 81). While the exchange between the old woman and the architect is presented in the form of two natives in dialogue, their sounds inaccessible to most audiences except those in Japan, the exchange at the night club comes across as a solicitation by a local who is eager to practise his elementary English. The insertion of these two scenes seems marginal to the drifting plot line until we approach them from the perspective of sound.

Working by way of the acousmatic (that is, the separation or discontinuity between sound and its origination), it is possible, perhaps necessary, to raise a fundamental issue about the voices in these two scenes: where do they come from? How is it that they sound the (estranged) way they do? On the screen, the voices seem unproblematically attached to conspicuously Japanese bodies: shouldn't it therefore be assumed that these bodies *are* the sources of the voices? Notably, Duras herself had been critical of such facile embodiment, so much so that, according to Chion, she 'coined the idea that the contemporary cinema stringently requires voices to be *nailed down* to bodies . . . [T]his nailing . . . is for her a form of cheating . . .* "Nailing down" nicely captures the rigidity and constraint in the conventions that have evolved for making film voices appear to come from bodies' (Chion 1999: 130; first emphasis Chion's, second emphasis mine).[16]

Nailing, like the well-known concept of suture in psychoanalytic (film) theory, rightly pinpoints the artifactuality of the process at stake: needles, threads, screws and nails are needed. However, for the screws and nails to do their work in this context, something more is needed: the idea (or ideology?) of a local type. This idea nails down the Japanese sounds as 'native speak' in one case, and the English sounds as 'beginner speak' in the other. In both cases, the voices sound the way they do because they have been played and heard as types. As local types (as opposed to the international type that is the architect), the old woman and the man at the night club become sonic rejoinders to the images of the museum and the hospital, and of the victims captured on newsreel footage that are placed at the beginning of the film. Like those images, and despite sound's ephemerality, the Japanese and English sounds become in these scenes a kind of crude reality, as readily recognizable as the wounded faces and mutilated bodies. Whether or not we actually comprehend their meanings, there is an indexical quality to these sounds. Something obvious has been (pre-)assigned to them.

But what does it mean when such deictic nailing and homogenization between voices and bodies are retained in a film that explicitly brackets (or crosses out) documentary realism in its aesthetics and politics? What does it mean when documentary, as the practice that is put under erasure, seems nonetheless instrumental in bringing about a certain 'distribution of the sensible' *across cultural difference?* Positivistic evidentiariness (the something-ness of classical verisimilitude), derogated and rejected at the level of images, is nonetheless *offloaded* on to sound – and not just any sound but specifically the voices of non-Western people. Like a type of labour unwanted by the more sophisticated citizens of Europe, the documentary effect (of a crude kind of realism) has been outsourced to Europe's offshore surrogates, who are now stuck in an awkward, because a priori expunged and disparaged, time-space.

Accordingly, even though the distinctly Japanese voices (the architect, the old woman, the man at the night club) present a sonic range, from phonetic recitation to conversation between natives in the mother tongue and foreign language practice with a tourist, in Duras's and Resnais's handling they do not add up to any significant human story. If we were to close our eyes and simply listen to these characters' voices, their contrast to the French actress's voice would be striking. Unlike the latter's supple reminiscing tones, the Japanese characters come across sonically as types, local or international; they sound either like resistant exteriors when they are speaking Japanese, impenetrable to most audiences, or like skilled or unskilled mimics when they are speaking French or English. Their voices have none of the lyrical, narrative and memorial resonance that distinguishes the French actress's voice, a resonance which – exactly like Nichols's notion of voice in documentary – holds the film together *from within* with a distinct perspective. In the poignant, because affectively infinite, dimensions opened by the French actress's storytelling, the most crucial – one might say sacred – sound effect is in fact the absolute silence of the German soldier,[17] whose death authorizes her narrative. By contrast, the Japanese figures remain exoticized in their one-dimensionality. As I have been trying to demonstrate, this exoticization can in large part be traced to an aesthetic distribution of sounds. Paradoxically (and optimistically), this also means that the sounds with the status of part objects are perhaps the ones offering the greatest potential for further imaginative work, as for instance when documentary morphs into experimental filmmaking, when documentary becomes a documentary of the process of (sonic) production, displacing questions of the real altogether from content on to form.

Coda

In retrospect, *Hiroshima mon amour*, perhaps because it is so determinedly anti-documentary in conception, has much to teach us about the problematics of recording, representational realism and political progressiveness that usually accompany the conceptualization of documentary. These problematics acquire urgency when a documentary is situated between cultures, demanding that we observe it with a kind of anthropological/ethnographic alert by asking a type of question that is outside the purview of classical aesthetics: Who seem to be the insiders and who the outsiders? In this love story set in Hiroshima, where a subject matter that is tabooed, barred or deemed unrepresentable in post-war Europe (desire for a member of the German military) has found a way to reanimate itself in post-war Asia (in the form of desire for a Japanese), who seem (or sound) familiar and who seem (or sound) strange? How is *this* (anthropologically/ethnographically) structural relation handled?

In contrast to other films about the Far East from the Cold War period such as Michelangelo Antonioni's *Chung Kuo/Cina* (1972), in which the economy of aesthetic distribution follows documentary convention, Resnais and Duras eschew documentary positivism at the level of vision only to recuperate it at the level of 'native' or nativized sound. Whereas the natives in Antonioni's film are mostly seen but not heard (and when they can be heard, the volume of their voices is often lowered so they become more or less background noise), in *Hiroshima mon amour* the natives are literally given auditions in different languages. Whereas in Antonioni's film the muted sounds among the Chinese (who are always shown to be talking among themselves) constitute an auditory boundary line we can apprehend but not cross,[18] in *Hiroshima mon amour* the Japanese are given multiple sonic parts to play. Despite such differences, however, what the two films have in common is a somewhat outmoded cosmopolitanism, which remains centred in the interiority – the madness, memory, reason or curiosity – of the European traveller-cum-storyteller, fictional or non-fictional. We can now add that this interiority, this centredness, is at least as much the result of sonic as it is of visual designs. Against this cosmopolitanism's (inner) voice, the non-West – in uncanny echoes of Rancière's notion of mute speech and the silent witnesses of history – can only be heard in the form of an indistinct mass or as types (see Rancière 2011b).

Returning to the generic question of documentary, one might go so far as to argue that the claim to realism, a claim on which documentary bases its rationale, tends to become particularly contentious when cultural difference enters the picture. If, as Nichols writes on a different occasion, 'The visual is no longer a means of verifying the certainty of facts pertaining to an objective, external world ... The visual now constitutes the terrain of subjective experience as the locus of knowledge, and power' (Nichols 2000: 42), should not the same be said about the sonic and its flight from verification? Perhaps this is why sound, even in the mundane form of oral conversation, can reveal so much about the ambitious, yet ambiguous, workings of a film such as *Hiroshima mon amour*. Keeping in mind the lesson of acousmatics, in which any presumed fit or coherence between sound and reality can be taken apart (that is, can be deconstructed as the effect of some procedure of nailing together), it would seem fair to conclude that documentary as such can no longer be taken for granted as a straightforwardly realist practice. Rather, just as its boundaries are increasingly stretchable and indistinct from fiction, so is its status increasingly conceptual rather than simply practical. And it is as a fuzzy concept that documentary avails itself for various possibilities of experimentation – as documentaries, false documentaries, anti-documentaries or 'mockumentaries'.

Notes

1. The notion of distribution is borrowed from Jacques Rancière; see especially *The Politics of Aesthetics: The Distribution of the Sensible* (Rancière 2004b). The French word as used by Rancière, *partage*, having to do with sharing and distribution, and by implication with division, participation, the part, the partialized, the particular and so forth, is of great relevance here.

2. See, for instance, the interesting titles on documentary films published in the book series 'Visible Evidence', ed. Michael Renov, Faye Ginsburg and Jane Gaines, University of Minnesota Press. Notably, many of the titles reflect that documentary work tends to focus on populations bearing signs of social alterity or disadvantage. For related interest, see also the titles published in the journal *Studies in Documentary Film*. For a classic work on realism in film, including questions raised by documentary as a genre, see Kracauer (1997).

3. To borrow from a study of documentary writing, see Stott's *Documentary Expression and Thirties America*: 'the heart of documentary is not form or style or medium, but always content' (Stott 1986: 14).

4. For a related discussion, see Jean-Luc Nancy on the occurrence of music: 'music (or even sound in general) is not exactly a phenomenon; that is to say, it does not stem from a logic of manifestation. It stems from a different logic, which would have to be called evoca-

tion, but in this precise sense: while manifestation brings presence to light, evocation summons (convokes, invokes) presence to itself' (Nancy 2007: 20).

5. For an informative discussion of how overwhelmingly documentary has been adopted for purposes of didacticism, see Nichols (n.d.).

6. See Monaco (1978: 34–52); an elaborate account of how the film came about can also be heard in the recorded interview with Resnais in the Criterion Collection edition of *Hiroshima mon amour*. For the screenplay, see Resnais (1960); Duras (1961).

7. Perhaps the most famous example of such debates is Theodor Adorno's statement, made in 1949, that to write poetry after Auschwitz is barbaric (Adorno 1967: 34). Rancière, for his part, is critical of the view that certain things are deemed unrepresentable (see Rancière 2007a: 109–38). Rancière's point is that such a view about unrepresentability is at odds with the transformations in the conception of art and non-art that have been taking place in modernity, and that have fundamentally redefined the relation between form and content. For a discussion that explores Rancière's perspective, see Chow and Rohrhuber (2011: 44–72).

8. Rancière is critical of Deleuze's use of the chronological timeline, that is, an organizational logic extrinsic to cinematic images, as a way to theorize differences within the images themselves (which are, accordingly to Rancière, consistently about capture and restitution); see his discussion in 'From One Image to Another? Deleuze and the Ages of Cinema' (Rancière 2006a: 107–23). Because my focus is on sound in the present essay, a more extended discussion of Rancière's criticism of Deleuze is deferred.

9. For a sensitive and informative reading of the film and screenplay, and the rich corpus of scholarship they have generated, see Caruth (1996: 25–56, 121–30).

10. Elsewhere, in a chapter called 'The Fact of Realism and the Fiction of Objectivity', he has written in a similar fashion: 'The "vision" of the documentarist is more likely a question of voice: how a personal point of view about the historical world manifests itself' (Nichols 1991: 165).

11. For a brief example, see, for instance, the chapter 'The Voice That Keeps Silent' (Derrida 2011: 60–74).

12. See the discussion in Caruth (1996: 49–52). Caruth's source is the interview with Emmanuelle Riva, who played the French actress, in Roob (1986). Riva also mentioned this in the 2003 interview that can be found in the Criterion Collection edition of the film.

13. This is one of the many descriptions Chion gives of the term *acousmêtre* (see Chion 1999: 21).
14. This is perhaps one reason Caruth, for instance, reads the situation of language in the film utopically as the beginning of a new story, one that is yet to be told (see Caruth 1996: 43–6, 49–56).
15. See Derrida (2011: 60–74). If one is to follow a linguistic (as opposed to sonic) logic, this juncture of the acousmatic and Derridean deconstruction of logocentrism would be the place for a possible elaboration of the concept of 'enunciation' as theorized by Émile Benveniste, Michel Foucault and others.
16. The translator, Claudia Gorbman, adds that Duras's and Chion's term for nailing down is *vissage*, literally screwing down or screwing in.
17. I am indebted to Jerome Silbergeld for helping me see this important point.
18. For a more detailed discussion of Antonioni's film, see my essay 'China as Documentary: Some Basic Questions (Inspired by Michelangelo Antonioni and Jia Zhangke)' forthcoming in *Journal of European Cultural Studies*.

4

The Spectator without Qualities
Abraham Geil

Jacques Rancière's book *The Emancipated Spectator* marks his first sustained discussion of spectatorship (Rancière 2008b; 2009a).[1] This might seem a surprisingly late addition to Rancière's project of rethinking the conjunction of art and politics. From the disciplinary perspective of Anglo-American film studies, it is a belated intervention indeed. For the question of the spectator is the terrain upon which many of the most significant disciplinary battles over the politics of film theory have been waged over the past three decades. In that time, critical approaches to spectators have proliferated: feminist revisions of psychoanalysis; cultural studies models of differentially 'decoding' viewers; empirical audience reception studies; cognitivist accounts of (contingently) universal perception; historicist reconstructions of early cinema's public spheres; and phenomenological theories of embodied spectatorship – to name only the most prominent.[2] For all their differences and even antagonisms, these approaches share at least one point of consensus: whatever else spectators are taken to be, they must in the first instance be understood as *active* agents in their own spectatorship. If this position can appear as a point of commonality amid such diversity, it is because these approaches share a common foil – the Althusserian/Lacanian conception of spectatorship as 'subject positioning' that is said to have dominated '1970s film theory'.[3] The broadly shared critique of that conception alleges an excessive formalism by which the spectator is reduced to a purely passive and unitary product of the cinematic *dispositif*. Opposing that model meant above all constructing theories of spectatorship that would challenge passive universality in the name of active particularity.

Many of Rancière's remarks in *The Emancipated Spectator* appear to follow this line of critique and to echo the general

53

affirmation of an 'active' spectator. His polemic, for example, against the Neoplatonic diagnosis of spectatorship as the separation 'from both the capacity to know and the power to act' could easily be applied to Jean-Louis Baudry's classic essays on apparatus theory. Against this diagnosis of incapacity, Rancière asserts that '[t]he spectator also acts, like the pupil or scholar. She observes, selects, compares, interprets' (Rancière 2009a: 13). On the face of it, this assertion is not especially contentious. Nor is Rancière's call to 'challenge the opposition between viewing and acting', which is now a virtual platitude in film studies (2009a: 13). But given how inassimilable so much of Rancière's thought appears to that field's disciplinary coordinates, his seeming lack of originality with respect to the question of the spectator might be greeted with a certain relief, not to say condescension. Here at least, it could be said, is one point where this important thinker who launched his intellectual trajectory some forty years ago by breaking from his famous teacher has finally come around to confirming film studies in its own (somewhat more recent) rejection of 'Althusser's lesson'.

But what this point of proximity really enables us to perceive – and, I hope, to productively unfold – is in fact the radical break Rancière's conception of the 'emancipated spectator' represents from the usual function that theories of spectatorship perform within film studies (in the approaches I note above as well as the 'unreconstructed' Althusserianism they aim to correct). Put simply, this usual function is to mediate a relation between cinema and politics, the coherence of which turns largely upon the opposition of passivity and activity and a logic of effects that follows from it. To suggest the pertinacity of this function in the history of film theory and practice, we need only recall that one of the earliest and most influential theorizations of political cinema – Sergei Eisenstein's 'montage of attractions' – posits the spectator as the 'basic material' out of which a film's political effects are constructed.[4] If 1970s' film theory (or 'Screen theory') 'conceives of the spectator as passive, an unwitting victim of a system built to exercise hegemonic control' (in the words of a typical gloss [Plantinga 2008: 252]), it does so in the name of a politics aimed at blocking these hegemonic effects. The myriad critical alternatives that have emerged in the intervening years have also by and large been carried out in the name of a politics, one grounded in the active agency of differentiated spectators. At the obvious risk of flattening out the diversity and subtlety of these various methods and the political projects they forward, what I wish to stress with these (admittedly gross) generalizations is simply how the passive/active dualism operates as a *generic* structure within the 'network of presuppositions', as Rancière puts it, 'that place the question of the spectator at the heart of the discussion of the relation between art and politics' (Rancière 2009a: 2). Even an ostensibly 'apolitical' approach such as the neo-formalist method of David Bordwell's 'middle-level research' secures its preferred relation between art and politics – in this case, a relation in which politics is made extrinsic (or, at best, secondary) to those aspects of film that can be described empirically – by positing the cognitivist model of an 'active viewer' (Bordwell 1989: 11–40).

Rancière's great intervention is to conceive of the spectator's activity as a suspension of the very opposition between passivity and activity. The polemical question he insists upon is not whether a given theoretical paradigm somehow *sides* with a passive or an active spectator, but, rather, what presuppositions underlie the dualism of passivity/activity in the first place. It is entirely possible to invert the valuation of the terms (assigning passivity a 'good' value and activity a 'bad' one, or vice versa) while leaving untouched the structure that counterposes them.[5] For Rancière, this structure is not a matter of 'logical oppositions between clearly defined terms' but in fact enables passivity and activity to function as 'embodied allegories of inequality' within a *partage* (sharing and dividing) of the sensible, 'an *a priori* distribution of the positions and capacities and incapacities attached to these positions' (Rancière 2009a: 12). Suspending the dualism of passivity/activity means disrupting the alignment between positions and capacities. It is an example of what Rancière has described elsewhere as the conversion of oppositions into *intervals* for subjectivization (Rancière 1992). Emancipated spectatorship is fundamentally an act of dis-identification that produces an instance of what Rancière calls *dissensus*: 'a rupture in the relationship between sense and sense, between what is seen and what is felt. What comes to pass is a rupture in the specific configuration that allows us to stay in "our" assigned places in a given state of things' (2010: 143). That rupture severs the logic of cause and effect that would mark out a path from the viewing of a film to a given awareness about the world and from that awareness to political action. For Rancière, the political efficacy of art lies paradoxically in this very rupture in the logic of cause and effect, in what he calls the 'efficacy of *dissensus*', an immanent break in common sense that 'can happen anywhere and at any time' but for that very reason 'can never be calculated' (143).

If the generic function of the spectator in film theory (and in critical thought about art generally) is to secure a coherent relation between art and politics, this means that these two terms are assumed to designate, if not ontologically distinct entities, at least analytically separable domains that need to be put into the right relation. Arguments over theories of spectatorship then become as much about the proper relation between art and politics as about what model of the spectator will best articulate that relation. By contrast, Rancière's idea of 'the emancipated spectator' entails a scenario in which art and politics are already inextricably entangled – caught up in a 'relation of non-relation' in which they can neither be separated nor made to coincide – by virtue of what he calls the 'aesthetic regime'. He concisely states both the nature of that entanglement and its consequences for thinking political art: 'The very same thing that makes the aesthetic "political" stands in the way of all strategies for "politicizing art"' (Rancière 2009a: 74). In what follows, I will trace the logic of this apparently paradoxical situation from the vantage point of Rancière's figure of the 'emancipated spectator'.

As I hope to make clear, Rancière's conception of spectatorship as a form of emancipation is far from a late addendum to his thought. Whether or not it is named as such, 'the emancipated spectator' is there all along in his preoccupation with the aesthetic dimension of equality that runs through all of his work. It can be found not only in his study of Jacotot's lessons in intellectual emancipation in *The Ignorant Schoolmaster* (1991), to which it is explicitly linked in *The Emancipated Spectator*, but embedded also in his first great archival work, *Proletarian Nights* (1981), and the discovery he transmits there of the 'perverted proletarians' who dis-identify from their allotted place by reading and writing Romantic literature. Even before Rancière's encounter and fateful break with Althusser, before *Reading Capital* (Althusser et al. 1971) and *Althusser's Lesson* (1974), 'the emancipated spectator' is verified in practice if not quite in writing by the film-going habits of his youth. It should come as no surprise that Rancière would take the prologue to his most recent book on film, *Les Écarts du cinéma* (2011), as an occasion to reflect upon his early cinephile days and to draw a direct line from that experience to his current thinking of cinema and its *dissensual* efficacy as an 'aesthetic art'. In the final section of this essay, I will attempt to elucidate this latter link by considering how Rancière's idea of the cinephile stands as a specific name for his figure of 'the emancipated spectator'. In order to arrive at that link, however, it will be necessary to trace some of the more serpentine turns in Rancière's rethinking of aesthetics, beginning with his conceptualization of 'aesthetic experience' as an 'activity that is equal to inactivity' – the neutralization of the dualism of passivity/activity out of which the figure of 'the emancipated spectator' emerges (Rancière 2009b: 30).

Staging the 'Play' of Aesthetic Experience

Aesthetic art promises a political accomplishment that it cannot satisfy, and thrives on that ambiguity. (Rancière 2010: 133)

To see precisely how aesthetic experience suspends the dualism of passivity and activity in the spectator, we must begin at the beginning (as Rancière is fond of saying) with what he calls the 'original scene' of aesthetics (2010: 118). This scene is staged in Friedrich Schiller's *Letters on the Aesthetic Education of Man* (1795) at the end of Letter Fifteen, the text that Rancière refers to as the 'first manifesto' of the aesthetic regime and its 'unsurpassable reference point' (Rancière 2004b: 23–4). Here Schiller constructs a fictional scenario of spectatorship by placing the reader and himself in front of the colossal statue of a Greek goddess's bodiless head known as the *Juno Ludovisi*. This statue embodies the qualities of 'free appearance' befitting a divinity; it 'reposes and dwells within itself', Schiller writes, as 'a completely closed creation . . . without yielding, without resistance' (Schiller 2004: 81). This 'free appearance' produces a corresponding experience of 'free play' in the spectator who is at once pulled in and held back, caught up 'in a condition of utter rest and extreme movement' (2004: 81). And thus the spectator's experience of 'free play' before the *Juno Ludovisi* achieves the paradoxical coexistence of passivity and activity. If emancipation begins by suspending this dualism, as Rancière suggests, then we can say that the figure of 'the emancipated spectator' coincides with the appearance of art itself in this 'Schillerian primitive scene' of the aesthetic regime (Rancière 2009b: 100).

Schiller stages this scene between statue and spectator in order to dramatize his idea of the 'play-drive' (*Spieltrieb*), which he posits earlier in the letter as the mediation between the 'form-drive' (*Formtrieb*) and the 'material-drive' (*Stofftrieb*). By virtue of its mediating role, the play-drive suspends the dominance of one of these two drives over the other, preventing an absolutization that would result either in the abstraction of lifeless form or the chaos of shapeless life. For Schiller, that state of mediation is the ideal that defines at once the nature of beauty and the promise of humanity.[6] Thus, in Rancière's reading, the play-drive is assigned the double task of reconstructing *both* 'the edifice of art and the edifice of life' (Rancière 2010: 116). It ties the knot of art and politics in such a way that they can neither be severed nor fused. Invoking the long history of debates over autonomous versus committed art, Rancière remarks that '[m]atters would be easy if we could merely say – naïvely – that the beauties of art must be subtracted from any politicization, or – knowingly – that the alleged autonomy of art disguises its dependence upon domination' (2010: 116). But such stances are all attempts to cover over or annul the basic paradox contained in the formulation of art as 'an autonomous form of life', which lies at the heart of the 'aesthetic revolution' (2010: 118). That is precisely the paradox Rancière finds staged by Schiller in the spectator's encounter with the *Juno Ludovisi*:

> The goddess and the spectator, the free appearance and the free play, are caught up together in a specific sensorium, cancelling the oppositions of activity and passivity, will and resistance. The 'autonomy of art' and the 'promise of politics' are not counterposed. The autonomy is the autonomy of the experience, not of the work of art. In other words, the artwork participates in the sensorium of autonomy inasmuch as it is not a work of art. (2010: 117)

In what does this 'sensorium of autonomy' consist? And how is it linked to the spectator's emancipation? To begin with, it is necessary to clarify that the contradictory status of an artwork *that is not one* is a specific consequence of overthrowing the identification of art that obtained in what Rancière calls the 'representative regime'. Without rehearsing the whole complex set of operations involved, we can touch upon the key aspects of this overthrow exemplified by Schiller's staging of the *Juno Ludovisi*.[7] Within the representative regime, the *Juno Ludovisi* is identifiable as the product of a specific practice of the arts labelled sculpture, with its own canon of representational techniques deemed appropriate to its subjects. This set of norms for identifying and judging the products of sculpture has its proper place within the overall hierarchy of the arts, which, in turn, has its place within the hierarchical distribution of political and social occupations. The arts as a whole are autonomous insofar as they are identified by a specific set of techniques that is distinct from other ways of doing and making. At the same time, their autonomy is linked to the hierarchy of the general social order through 'a relationship of global analogy' (Rancière 2004b: 22). In Schiller's account, the *Juno Ludovisi* is severed from this entire regime of identification. Its status as art no longer derives from its conformity to the canon of representational techniques specific to sculpture but rather from a 'specific form of sensory apprehension' (Rancière 2009b: 29). This sensorium assumes its autonomy by virtue of the experience of 'free play' it induces in the spectator, a state of being that is distinct from ordinary sensory experience. At the same time, the *Juno Ludovisi*'s indifference towards its use and classification unhinges it from any determinate social destination. Its 'free appearance' addresses no one and therefore *anyone*. The autonomous experience it induces in the spectator belongs to an anonymous subject, *a spectator without qualities*. In order to see how this experience vouchsafes a promise of emancipation (for Rancière as well as for Schiller), we need to trace the idea of 'free play' back a little further.

As Rancière points out, Schiller's concept of the play-drive is a modification of Kant's systematic application of the general idea of play (as an activity that constitutes its own end) to his account of the reflective judgement of taste in his *Critique of Judgement*. For Kant, judgements of taste involve a suspension of the way objects are ordinarily apprehended by the faculties of understanding and sensibility. The object of such a judgement appears to awareness through a double subtraction: 'without concepts' by which the understanding would normally categorize an object and determine its proper use; and 'without interest' by which sensibility would normally make of it an object of desire (Kant 2001: 89–97). The corollary experience for the judging subject is the 'free play' of the faculties, which, as Rancière puts it, is 'not only an activity without goal; it is an activity that is equal to inactivity' (Rancière 2009b: 30). Rancière translates this state of equalization directly into the terms of emancipation, which is to say into an effect of *equality*. By stressing the way free play 'neutralizes' the hierarchy of the faculties, he links the 'disinterestedness' of aesthetic experience directly to the disruption of social hierarchy.

This political interpretation, already latent in Kant, is made explicit by Schiller's conversion of mental faculties into drives in the context of the French Revolution.[8] In suspending the opposition between form and matter, aesthetic experience neutralizes the dualism of thought and action that subtends the partition between those who think and those who work in Plato's homology between the order of the soul and the order of the city. The play of aesthetic experience is a 'supplementation of this partition – a third term that cannot be described as a part but as an activity of redistribution, an activity that takes the form of a neutralization' (Rancière 2009f: 2–3). Rancière's word for that neutralization is *dissensus*. Minimally defined, *dissensus* is a disruption of the normal relation between a sensory given and the sense that is made out of it (between 'sense and sense', the split homonym Rancière locates in the single Greek word *aisthesis*). 'Consensus' is Rancière's term for the normal relation between these two orders of sense, a relation of concordance that constitutes the given of a situation. Simply put, consensus defines what goes by 'common sense'. The *dissensus* of aesthetic experience ('play') reconfigures common sense at the same fundamental level and according to the same supplemental operation as politics. As with the concept of 'dis-agreement' (*la mésentente*) in Rancière's political thought, aesthetic *dissensus* is not a conflict in the usual sense of an antagonism between two already constituted entities. It is, rather, the 'staging of an excess ... that brings about a more radical way of seeing the conflict' (2009f: 3). Not a situation *of* conflict but the situation put into conflict with itself.

The implications of translating Kant's and Schiller's ideas of aesthetic experience into the terms of *dissensus* become clearer in light of the line Rancière draws to another fictional scene of spectatorship – the scenario he never tires of retelling that the French joiner Gabriel Gauny put into writing some fifty years after Schiller's *Letters*. Published in a workers' revolutionary newspaper during the French Revolution of 1848, this fictional diary entry depicts a joiner interrupting his work of laying a floor to gaze out at the vista framed by the room's window: 'he stops his arms and glides in imagination toward the spacious view to enjoy it better than the possessors of the neighboring residences' (Gauny 1983: 91; quoted in Rancière 2009a: 71). What Gauny's scene shares with Schiller's *Juno Ludovisi* lies in its neutralization of the hierarchical arrangement of the senses proper to a given social occupation. Gauny dissociates the relation between the hand and eye, active labour and idle gaze, which defines the ethos of the artisan. With this little verbal description, he constructs an immanent break within a situation of inequality by showing how 'the perspective gaze, that has long been associated with mastery and majesty, can be assumed and verified as a power of equality' (Rancière 2009g: 280). Understood as the verification of equality, Gauny's idleness and the interruption of his work is not passivity at all but the same activity of neutralization Rancière finds in Kant's and Schiller's accounts of aesthetic experience. With Gauny, however, the neutralization also works upon the crucial dimension of time. From at least *Proletarian Nights* onward, time has been central to Rancière's understanding of emancipation. According to the Platonic distribution of occupations and capacities, to be a worker is to occupy a social location in which work 'does not wait, which amounts to locking up workers in the space of their absence of time' (Rancière 2009g: 282). By taking the time 'he does not have' to stop work and gaze out of the window, Gauny cracks his situation open from the inside by staging a scene of untimely *dissensus* that locates 'another time in that time, another space in that space' (Rancière 2009g: 282).

This *dissensus*, however, is not yet 'politics' in the strict sense but something like its precondition. The scene's verification of equality 'contributes . . . to the framing of a new fabric of common experience or a new common sense, upon which new forms of political subjectivization can be implemented' (Rancière 2009g: 280). These forms of political subjectivization *can* be constructed out of Gauny's reframing of experience but not as its necessary effect. Politics stands in the same relation to Gauny's writing as it does to all other artistic practices. Rancière puts that relation in the following way:

> It is up to the various forms of politics to appropriate, for their own proper use, the modes of presentation or the means of establishing explanatory sequences produced by artistic practices rather than the other way around. (Rancière 2004b: 65)

The publication of Gauny's seemingly apolitical writing in the militant context of a workers' newspaper, *Le Tocsin des travailleurs*, is thus entirely apt at the same time that its effects are indeterminate.

Gauny's scene of *dissensual* spectatorship is no doubt familiar to most readers of Rancière. It is safe to say that no single example (or piece of writing) has appeared more often and across such a long and diverse span of his works, beginning with his doctoral thesis that became his second book, *Proletarian Nights* (1981), and extending through *The Philosopher and his Poor* (1983) to his most recent discussions of aesthetics in numerous articles and books, including *The Emancipated Spectator* (2009). Within the context of Rancière's writing on aesthetics 'as such' (Rancière 2005: 18),[9] Gauny's staging of an emancipated spectator participates in the larger historical configuration of the aesthetic regime and so has its conditions of possibility in an idea of art that emerged around the end of the eighteenth century. In this respect, it can be said that Gauny's writing belongs to a sequence that begins with certain privileged philosophical articulations (by Kant and Schiller, among others) along with the invention of new artistic institutions and forms (the museum and the novel, most notably).[10]

But if Gauny's writing comes 'after' the invention of aesthetics according to a certain historical logic of influence, its place within the itinerary of Rancière's thought is absolutely primary. Rather than reading Gauny as a kind of working-class heir to Kant's and Schiller's ideas of aesthetic experience, we might better say that Rancière puts those ideas to the test of Gauny's writing, to the untimely test of the *dissensual* force he discovered during his years in the workers' archives. This 'test' (if that is the right word) recalls Rancière's claim in the Preface to *The Philosopher and his Poor* that 'the power of thinking has to do above all with its capacity to be displaced' (Rancière 2004a: xxviii). The displacement that the Gauny example introduces into the philosophical discourse of aesthetics effectively extracts the very scenes of *dissensus* we have been considering from their 'emplotment' within that discourse. It produces a gap between these instances of *dissensual* 'play' and their resolution into new forms of consensus.[11]

In a number of his more recent texts, Rancière has traced in great detail these various consensual 'emplotments of the aesthetic promise' that stretch from Kant and Schiller to Adorno and

Lyotard (Rancière 2009g: 285).[12] Without entering into the complexity of that discussion, it is enough to note that he places them under three basic scenarios, each of which constitute one-sided interpretations of the paradoxical formula that defines aesthetic art as 'an autonomous form of life': 1) art can become life; 2) life can become art; 3) art and life can exchange their properties. For our purposes, what should be stressed is that these scenarios – each of which would close down the *dissensual* play that Rancière calls the 'very kernel of the aesthetic regime' – are not imposed from the outside but are in fact internal developments of the aesthetic regime itself (Rancière 2002b: 140). In Schiller's *Letters*, for example, the scene staged with the *Juno Ludovisi* in Letter Fifteen is but one moment within the larger unfolding of its plot. The promise of a new world that is simultaneously embodied and withheld by a form that the spectator 'cannot possess in any way' becomes, in the subsequent letters, the very means (through aesthetic education) of actualizing that promise and possessing that world – 'art becomes life'. Rancière's key intervention in the philosophical discourse of aesthetics lies in arresting the progression of that story at its most indeterminate moment – at the scene of *dissensual* play – so as to extract that scene and set it up in opposition to the very plot in which it was embedded.

As we'll see in the next section of this essay, that operation of extraction and re-combination is precisely what characterizes Rancière's conception of 'the emancipated spectator' in cinema. If Rancière's intervention into the discourse of aesthetics is intimately linked to his discovery and perpetual return to the example of Gauny's writing, this link has everything to do with the fact that Gauny is staging a scene of spectatorship. By placing that scene in a montage with the heterogeneous discourse of Kant and Schiller, Rancière is already staging a kind of *dissensual* excess. Before it could be placed in this montage, Gauny's writing had to undergo its own extraction from the Marxist plot Rancière initially brought with him to the workers' archives.[13] Much later, in the context of his writing on aesthetics, Rancière describes that plot as the 'ethical' interpretation of *dissensus*. As opposed to the 'aesthetic' interpretation, which understands the joiner's fictional possession of a vista he does not possess as the placing of two worlds in one world, the 'ethical' interpretation (perfected in Bourdieu's sociological critique of aesthetic 'disinterestedness') severs the world of appearance from the world of reality. It thereby consigns Gauny's aesthetic experience to the realm of illusion and error – *mere* appearance – reading it as a symptom of his alienation from the real conditions of his ethos as a worker (Rancière 2009f: 3–5).[14] Extracted from this plot, Gauny's scene becomes an untimely 'example' on two levels: its tableau figures spectatorship as an experience of *dissensual* emancipation by placing 'another time' in a space (the worker's ethos) defined by the absence of time for anything but work; as a piece of writing, its free circulation allows it to be put in unlikely montages (next to Kant and Schiller, for example) that disturb the partitions of philosophical and historiographical discourses alike.[15] The polemical lesson this scene bears is that there is no absolute distinction between being a spectator and being a writer, just as there is no distinction between the intelligence of floor-layers and the intelligence of aesthetic philosophers.[16] Gauny's joiner is a spectator who presupposes his equality by composing a fictional scene of emancipated spectatorship. In so doing, he employs 'the capacity of anyone whatsoever', the impersonal 'quality of human beings without qualities', and, by employing, verifies it (Rancière 2009a: 49).

The Emancipated Spectator of Cinema

Rancière has called cinema 'an art of the spectator' (Rancière 2011d: 297). As he hastens to point out, however, this is not an idea of the spectator that was born with cinema but one that had already been radically transformed within the aesthetic regime – in the ways we've just seen – well before the invention of film. For Rancière, cinema inherits this transformed idea of the spectator along with the aesthetic idea of art itself. Cinema must nevertheless use the specific means at its disposal to invent its own way of being an art of the spectator just as it must invent its own intelligibility as art in the context of the aesthetic regime. In his Prologue to *Film Fables*, Rancière dubs this situation of an inheritance that demands its reinvention film's 'thwarted fable'. To briefly rehearse this well-known story: by dint of its technical nature alone cinema appears to achieve the identity of active and passive that fulfils the idea of art in the aesthetic regime; but this dream is foiled at the very moment of its fulfilment when the representative regime returns with a vengeance to make film serve the ends of classical mimesis. Having thus conceptualized the art of cinema as constituted by this tension between the aesthetic and representative regimes, Rancière then reads individual films and filmmakers for the particular twist they must perform upon this tension in order to (re-)achieve the aesthetic idea of art, each new twist being yet another enactment of the aesthetic regime's fundamental law to always 'come afterwards' (Rancière 2006a: 10).

This is well-trodden territory in Rancière's writing on film. The question which has been less explicitly worked out (in either Rancière's own work or the growing body of secondary literature on it) is how to think the status of aesthetic experience and the spectator's potential for *dissensual* 'play' within his conceptualization of cinema as a 'thwarted fable' of the aesthetic regime. That is the question we will now take up in the attempt to draw a line from Rancière's reading of Kant, Schiller and Gauny to the figure of 'the emancipated spectator' of cinema. This is a spectator who does not simply judge or take pleasure and pain in a work of art but is 'summoned into the reinvention of the work' and, as Rancière puts it, 'comes to collaborate in the work as he looks at it' (Rancière 2011d: 297).

It is no accident that Rancière should stage his dramaturgy of film's thwarted fable with a breathless paraphrase of the young Jean Epstein. As is true of much of the writing by his fellow *photogénie* theorists, Epstein's luminous early essays are at once theoretical determinations of cinema's specificity and ecstatic reports of a spectator engaged in the poetic translation of his sensible experience of films.[17] As it turns out, for Rancière (and arguably for Epstein too), the answer to the question of specificity consists in nothing other than that latter activity of translation – the poetic decomposition and recomposition of films – which Rancière variously calls 'extraction' (*prélèvement*), 'de-figuration' or simply 'montage'. This operation effectively 'composes one film with the elements of another' (Rancière 2006a: 5). According to Rancière, it is the 'constitutive fact of the cinema as experience, art, and idea of art' and thus the activity that unites the three main figures that cinema has produced – directors, the audience and critics/cinephiles (2006a: 5). Like Godard, Epstein performed all three of these roles at various times in his life. However exceptional in itself, this biographical fact can also serve to allegorize the status of all cinematic spectators for Rancière. Such exchangeability between the positions of production and reception is what is entailed, finally, by Rancière's principle of the axiomatic equality of intelligence. In this respect, the consequences of equality for his

thinking of cinema are strictly analogous to his contention elsewhere that writing is the 'other side' of reading (Rancière 2009g:
278). The same intelligence is at work in the redistribution of the
sensible involved in reading or viewing as that which is involved in
writing or in composing images.[18]

Of course, the material heterogeneity of different mediums does
not simply dissolve before the equality of intelligence. But in order
to clarify the precise status of that heterogeneity for Rancière –
and therefore the specificity of *cinema's* emancipated spectator
– we need to first make a fundamental distinction between two
modes or orders of equality in his thought. Put simply, this is the
distinction between the axiomatic equality of intelligence, on the
one hand, and art's sensible embodiment of equality on the other.
The first order of equality is made explicit for Rancière in his
study of Jacotot's method of universal education in *The Ignorant
Schoolmaster*, but it is at the core of nearly all of Rancière's work.
This equality, as he says, paraphrasing Jacotot, is 'not an end to
attain, but a point of departure, a *supposition* to maintain in every
circumstance' (Rancière 1991: 138). Because '[e]quality is a presupposition, an initial axiom – or it is nothing' (Rancière 2004a:
223), it exists only by virtue of its verification and 'at the price
of being verified always and everywhere' (Rancière 1991: 138).
The second order of equality emerges historically in the aesthetic
regime as a principle of indifference that assumes 'anything and
everything in the world is available to art' (Rancière 2006a: 9).
Just as Rancière insists that aesthetics has its own politics, art has
its own equality.[19] And art's equality can coexist with the most
inegalitarian political messages.[20]

The purpose of positing this distinction between two orders of
equality is not to mark an unbridgeable ontological difference. On
the contrary, as Rancière has said regarding his use of distinctions
in general, it allows 'for an intelligibility of their entanglements'
(Rancière 2009g: 287). Thinking through the precise nature of
those entanglements is one of the most difficult dimensions of
Rancière's thought, for it goes to the heart of the relation (of non-
relation) between politics and aesthetics. 'The emancipated spectator', I want to argue, is a privileged site of this entanglement. But
here we must preempt a potential misunderstanding. The question
of the relation between the axiomatic equality of intelligence and
art's sensible embodiment of equality is not exactly the same as
that between spectator and artwork, at least not in the manner

of a subject and an object. Schiller's staging of 'free play' in the aesthetic experience of the spectator standing before the *Juno Ludovisi* neutralizes the dualism of subjectivity and objectivity as surely as it does the dualisms of activity/passivity, form/matter and intelligence/sensibility. Following Schiller, Rancière does not posit a 'model' of a spectator who can then be placed in relation to various different artworks. The spectator is already entwined in the knot of autonomy and heteronomy which defines aesthetic experience as 'a novel mode of experience that bears within it a new form of "sensible" universality and equality', a form which exists only on the condition that the spectator can never directly possess it (Rancière 2009b: 99).

To take up the question of the cinematic spectator first from the side of film's equality, let's return to Rancière's description of Epstein's film fable and the necessity of its (self-)thwarting: 'Even though the basic technical equipment of the cinema secures the identity of active and passive that is the principle of [the aesthetic] revolution, the fact remains that cinema can only be faithful to it if it gives another turn of the screw to its secular dialectics' (Rancière 2006a: 11). Exactly what sort of fidelity is this that is condemned to forever overturn every actual fulfilment of its own ideal? The answer, I would suggest, is the fidelity to *dissensual* 'play'.[21] As we've seen, the dialectical contradiction of aesthetics cannot be reconciled or sublated at some higher level, but it can be frozen in one-sided plots that arise from the aesthetic revolution itself. Although Rancière does not make this claim as such in *Film Fables*, the Romantic idea of art for which Epstein (in Rancière's reading) takes cinema to be the perfect embodiment – the identity of conscious and unconscious contemplated by Schelling and Hegel – is *already* one of the possible emplotments of the 'Schillerian primitive scene' of the aesthetic regime (Rancière 2009b: 100).[22] To recall our discussion from the previous section, this plot interprets the paradoxical formula of art as 'an autonomous form of life' by valorizing life (matter) over form (thought) and pursuing the scenario of 'art becoming life' (Rancière 2002b: 119). Thus, it achieves the unity of active and passive not by intensifying their play of contradiction but by subordinating the former to the latter. When Rancière declares at the end of the prologue to *Film Fables* that 'the art and thought of images have always been nourished by all that thwarts them', he gives thwarting (*contrarier*) the function of returning film to the 'contradiction that is originary and unceasingly at work' at the heart of the aesthetic regime (Rancière 2009b: 36). To thwart here means to put contradictions back into play.

If the aesthetic regime in general is characterized by the blurring of the boundaries that previously separated the arts, cinema assumes this vocation with a special voracity as the 'name of an art whose meaning cuts across the borders between arts' (Rancière 2006a: 4).[23] For Rancière, cinema's boundary-crossing does not finally result in some higher synthesis such as Ricciotto Canudo's idea of a 'seventh art' (Canudo 1993: 291–302). Rather, this equality of indifference must maintain a certain heteronomy between mediums through a play of contraries. In *Les Écarts du cinéma*, Rancière develops this claim via the theme of 'gaps' between cinema and other arts (literature and theatre, in particular). '[B]y drawing cinema outside of itself' these gaps 'reveal its inner heterogeneity' (2011i: 196–7).[24] In *Film Fables*, he describes that dynamic in terms of the need for literature and film to 'thwart' their native strengths as language and image, respectively. This requires an exchange of contraries: literature subtracts the active sense of language by assuming the 'great passivity of the visible'; conversely, film hollows out 'the visible with the word' (Rancière 2006a: 14). It is only through these 'games of exchange and inversion' with the other arts that cinema can 'make the games it *plays with its own means* intelligible to itself' (2006a: 15; emphasis added).

It follows that the surest way to close down film's auto-ludic potential is to make its artistic ideal about the purification of medium-specificity.[25] Rancière's insistence in *Film Fables* and elsewhere that there 'is no straight line running from cinema's technical nature to its artistic vocation' is therefore not a historical or a theoretical claim so much as a polemical slogan (Rancière 2006a: 11). Virtually from the beginning it has been not only possible but nearly irresistible for many filmmakers as well as critics to deduce cinema's artistic fate from a techno-ontological determination of the medium. A long and venerable tradition of modernist filmmaking within the 'fortress of experimental cinema' testifies to this fact, as Rancière well knows (2006a: 3). What is at stake for him in polemicizing against this tendency is not, however, the desire to settle once and for all the true ontology of cinema as an art. Rather, his aim is to trace the consequences that follow from positing *any* ontology as an art's a priori condition of possibility.

Posing the question in this way already opens up a moment of *dissensus* in the very terms of the debate over medium ontology. For we do not have to push this line very far before the normal order of causality reverses itself and the ontology in question is revealed as nothing other than the retrospective product of its own consequences. In other words, instead of pitting one ontological claim against another, Rancière performs a signature move of de-substantializing ontology altogether by placing it under the logic of verification.

Although Rancière usually reserves the term verification for the *dissensual* effects of equality, he is clear that consensus too depends upon a logic of verification, albeit one that effaces its dependence. He describes the political version of consensual verification as the 'the circle of the *arkhè*' (Rancière 2009f: 9). In this operation, a certain attribute (gender, race, bloodline, intelligence, wealth, education, etc.) is presupposed as the qualification for ruling over others and that presupposition is then verified after the fact by the exercise of power it legitimates. An ontology of art based on medium-specificity performs an analogous operation and traces its own closed circle of verification.[26] For Rancière's conception of politics, the *an*-archic supplement that breaks open this consensual circle is the democratic paradox, the principle that 'those who rule do so on the grounds that there is no reason why some persons should rule over others except for that fact that there is no reason' (Rancière 2009f: 10). For cinema, as for the aesthetic idea of art as such, the *dissensual* supplement resides in the paradoxical formulation we encountered in Rancière's reading of Schiller, that there is no basis for the distinction between art and non-art except that there is no distinction.

It should be stressed in all of this that Rancière's opposition to medium ontology does not mean he is inattentive to the historical and material specificities of film as a technology. On the contrary, it is precisely by refusing to make those specificities into a ground (or *arkhè*) for closing the circle of artistic invention that Rancière can posit a more radically open potential for film's technical capacities. Put most broadly, this means taking up those capacities as the means with which to 'explore', as he puts it elsewhere, 'the possibility of maintaining spaces of play' (Rancière 2006a: 3). As we've seen from his reading of Kant and Schiller, aesthetic 'play' is intimately linked for Rancière to the *dissensual* effects of equality. And it is entirely possible within his framework to posit a presupposition of equality as working in relation to a specific aspect of the medium's technicity, so long as that relation remains indeterminate rather than causal. In fact, despite his often critical and even dismissive statements about Walter Benjamin, Rancière offers his own argument about the transformation of art in the age of its technical reproducibility:

> A lot has been said about reproducibility but I don't think this is the most interesting aspect of Benjamin's thesis. What is important, I think, about the mechanical arts is precisely this change of balance in art between the skill of the artist and the look which anybody can direct at the work. . . . And I think this is something very, very, important about cinema and about photography: this kind of displacement in that now the artist is not so much the person who has a specific skill but the person who has a specific sensitivity to what is happening in the scenery of the perceptible. (Rancière 2011d: 294–304)

At first glance, this statement seems a rather uncritical variation upon Epstein's fable of the technical nature of cinema automatically realizing the aesthetic regime's idea of art: by making art into the province of the look rather than the specific skills proper to each of classically delineated arts, the 'mechanical arts' overthrow in a single stroke the entire basis for the classical taxonomy of the representative regime. Moreover, by virtue of its stress upon the anonymous look of the spectator – 'the look *anybody* can direct at the work' – the statement also seems to make photography and cinema agents for the dissociation of art from any particular social destination. Nevertheless, as Rancière makes clear elsewhere, these effects of equality are not the means by which the 'mechanical arts' carried out a revolution in the idea of art but, rather, they are what made photography and cinema *intelligible* as art according the terms of the aesthetic regime that pre-existed it. The task of theory, as we've seen above, is to trace the ways cinema reinvents that intelligibility with its own means. With respect to the equality between 'the look' of the filmmaker and 'the look' of the spectator invoked in the passage above, those means directly concern the way that the spectator herself is 'summoned into the reinvention' of the film.

Included in these means are the historically contingent aspects of cinema's spaces of exhibition. Like museums during the nineteenth century, cinemas have at certain historical junctures been egalitarian public spaces in the strong sense. That is, not just places where anyone can go to look at art but places where the art is addressed to anyone. These are places where, as Rancière puts it, 'works of art or performances of art are no longer restrained to a specific audience or a specific function' (Arnall et al. 2012: 292). The role of such spaces of exhibition points to one of the basic asymmetries between Rancière's respective conceptions of politics and art. Whereas politics by definition can happen anywhere and at any time because it has no proper domain, the very fact that the aesthetic idea of art abolishes the criteria by which the internal properties of a work of art could serve to distinguish it from non-art means that art requires the delimitation of some spatial setting (the cinema, the monument, the museum) that serves to identify it as such (Rancière 2009c). The cinema (at least prior to the partition of audiences entailed by the 'art house' versus the 'multiplex') is an especially ambiguous instance of such spaces insofar as it does not guarantee the clear distinction between art and non-art.

In his recent discussions of cinephilia, Rancière links the anonymous capacity of the film spectator directly to cinema's historical disruption of the hierarchical partitions of art. If there is such a thing as a 'community' of cinephiles, he remarks, it is 'an open community and we don't know who belongs to it. Anybody can join precisely because it is a community based on the breaking of the borders between cultural legitimacy and mere popular entertainment' (Rancière 2011d: 295). Rancière's idea of the cinephile concretizes the more general figure of 'the emancipated spectator' within a specific set of conditions for the exhibition and reception of cinema as an aesthetic art. There is a certain historical specificity to these conditions that is to be found in the phenomenon of Parisian cinephilia that took hold in the 1950s and 60s. At the same time, there is an aspect of Rancière's idea of cinephilia that exceeds this context and bears directly upon the way film as a mechanical art enables the 'equality of the look' he invokes in the passage above. That aspect lies in the 'nature of cinema' (a surprising phrase for Rancière) as a 'specific sensorium': 'I think it is very important that a film is never given as a whole. So the film is a sensation, the sensation of an apparition, of shadows, and it lives in our memories' (2011d: 295).[27] In the next and final section of this essay, we will consider how 'memory' – defined by Rancière as 'the work [oeuvre] of fiction' – becomes the privileged operation of the cinephile as an emancipated spectator (Rancière 2006a: 158).

The Cinephile without Qualities

The exception is always ordinary. (Rancière 2010: 213)

I want to approach Rancière's idea of the cinephile by departing from his writing for a moment and turning to Jean-Louis
Schefer's *L'Homme ordinaire du cinema* (1980), specifically to
the veritable cinephile's manifesto with which that singular book
opens. Although to my knowledge Rancière does not remark on
this text, Schefer's autobiographical enunciation of the 'ordinary
man of cinema' has some astonishing affinities with his conception
of 'the emancipated spectator'.[28] It is worth quoting at length for
Schefer's effortless if unwitting distillation of the ideas I've rather
laboriously tried to unfold above:

> The ordinary man of the cinema makes a preliminary and redundant
> announcement: the cinema isn't my profession. I go to the cinema for
> entertainment, but by chance I also learn something there apart from
> what a film will tell me (a film won't teach me that I'm mortal – it will,
> perhaps, teach me a trick of time, about the expansion of bodies in
> time, and about the improbability of it all. In fact, I'm always less the
> film's reader and more like its totally submissive servant and also its
> judge.) What I learn there is the astonishment of being able to live in
> two worlds at once.
>   So it's a being without qualities that's speaking now. I want to say
> just this: I don't have the necessary qualities to speak about cinema
> except insofar as I'm in the habit of going quite often. This habit
> should probably have taught me something? – naturally. But what?
> – about films, about myself, about our whole species, about memory.
> (Schefer 1995: 110–11)

All the key elements of 'the emancipated spectator' are here: the
coexistence of servitude and judgement that recalls the neutralized
dualism of passivity and activity staged in Schiller's *Juno Ludovisi*;
the putting of two worlds in one world that constructs a scene
of *dissensus* in art as well as politics; the amateur's disavowal of
specialized knowledge about the cinema in the name of the sole
qualification of being without qualities; and, finally, the linking of
this anonymous capacity to a lesson of singular universality in the
series that leaps without justification from 'myself' to 'our whole
species'. Like Rancière's idea of the part of those with no part who

polemically occupy the empty place of the whole, Schefer's 'ordinary man' is the cinephile as militant, a figure who announces: I am nothing, in the cinema let me be all.

Without attempting a more sustained comparison with the rest of Schefer's *L'Homme ordinaire du cinema*, it is enough for our purposes to linger on this opening declaration. Its implicit link between the cinephile's disavowal of official qualifications for speaking about the cinema ('the cinema is not my profession') and the condition of 'being without qualities' comes very close to the link in Rancière's thought between what he calls the 'politics of the amateur' and the activity of 'neutralization' (or dis-identification) that defines his conception of aesthetic experience (Rancière 2011c: 14). By tracing the logic of this shared link, we can shed light on how the cinephile can stand as one name for 'the emancipated spectator'.

To begin with, Schefer's idea of the 'ordinary man' should not be mistaken for a turn to empirical, everyday or embodied viewers whose flesh and blood reality can be opposed to the abstraction of theoretical formalizations. Its autobiographical mode notwithstanding, Schefer's 'ordinary man' is as much an impersonal and theoretical construction as Rancière's 'emancipated spectator'. At the same time, these constructions should not be taken as a return to the Althusserian/Lacanian formalization of the spectator as a 'subject position'. Positing a 'spectator without qualities' effectively neutralizes what is perhaps the most basic methodological assumption governing the disciplinary self-revision of film studies with respect to spectatorship: that, in the wake of Screen theory's formalist excesses, any model of spectatorship must necessarily perform a 'negotiation' between hypothetical (or formal) and actual (or real) spectators.[29] One of the key lessons of Jacotot's method of 'universal education' for Rancière is that equality 'is neither formal nor real' (Rancière 2004a: 223). And if the 'emancipated spectator' is a universal figure, it is as an *effect* of equality, or what Rancière refers to as 'the form of a *positive* neither/nor' (Rancière 2009f: 2). Both Schefer's and Rancière's figures are 'spectators without qualities'[30] inasmuch as they participate in what Schiller defines as the only generically human activity – 'free play' ('Man is only fully a human being when he plays') – which, as we've seen, is the dimension of aesthetic experience that neutralizes the hierarchy of faculties and, by extension, the partition that aligns capacities with occupations or identities (Schiller 1967: 107; quoted in Rancière 2009b: 28).

There is also an aesthetic dimension to Rancière's thinking itself, which displaces the boundaries between academic disciplines much in the way that he contends the aesthetic regime displaces the classical partition of the arts. His idea of a 'politics of the amateur' is entirely in line with this 'adisciplinary' vocation of all his work.[31] In fact, Rancière introduces this idea in the Prologue to *Les Écarts du cinéma* by way of disclosing (with evident pride) that he has never formally taught film aesthetics or theory and thus, like Schefer, his only qualifications for writing about cinema lie in his long-standing habits as a cinephile (Rancière 2011c: 14). This egalitarian affirmation of a 'politics of the amateur' is directed as fully against the partition of academic disciplines that would apportion a set place for the study of film as it is against the hierarchical partition of taste that would put a Bergman film, say, in the category of 'high art' and a Western by Anthony Mann in that of 'popular art'. But this confusion of boundaries is what film itself already does as an aesthetic art.[32] The question for us is how to understand the role of the spectator in this operation. How does the 'cinephile gap', as Rancière says of cinema's other gaps, draw 'cinema outside of itself' to 'reveal its inner heterogeneity' (Rancière n.d.: 200, 197)? And how is this operation linked to Rancière's more general conceptions of aesthetic 'play' and *dissensus* that define the emancipated spectator?

Here Schefer's enunciation of cinema's 'ordinary man' offers a final clue. As we recall, his opening declaration concludes with a statement of the cinephile's autodidactic lesson: 'This habit should probably have taught me something? – naturally. But what? – about films, about myself, about our whole species, about *memory*' (Schefer 1995: 110–11; emphasis mine). Memory has been a central preoccupation in the recent wave of interest on the part of film scholars in rethinking cinephilia, both as an historical phenomenon and as an ongoing practice of spectatorship and criticism.[33] According to this scholarship, the basic cinephilic operation involves the isolation of 'image moments' stripped from their embeddedness within a film's narrative coordinates and the fetishistic collection of these moments in the cinephile's memory (Keathley 2006: 128). In *The Remembered Film* (2004), for example, Victor Burgin describes the way the 'binding effect of the narrative is loosened' as the isolated 'fragments' of a film 'go adrift and enter into new combinations . . . in the eddies of memory' (2004: 67–8; quoted in Fowler 2012: 40). This understanding of the cinephilic operation of extraction and recombination is quite close to Rancière's idea of *prélèvement* (or de-figuration), which he describes at work in Epstein and Deleuze's film theory, as well in that cinephile *par excellence* Jean-Luc Godard's monumental work *Histoire(s) du cinéma*.

What matters, finally, for Rancière is the way memory as an operation of *prélèvement* can perpetuate the *dissensual* 'play' of aesthetic experience rather than being put in the service of a new plot that would close it down. In *Film Fables*, Rancière calls memory the 'the work [*oeuvre*] of fiction' (Rancière 2006a: 158). In doing so, he puts memory at the service of a fundamentally *dissensual* capacity:

> 'Fiction', as re-framed by the aesthetic regime of art, means far more than the constructing of an imaginary world . . . It is not a term that designates the imaginary as opposed to the real; it involves the re-framing of the 'real', or the framing of a dissensus. Fiction is a way of changing existing modes of sensory presentations and forms of enunciation . . . of building new relationships between reality and appearance. (Rancière 2010: 141)

This conception of fiction returns us to Rancière's distinction between the 'ethical' and 'aesthetic' interpretations of Gauny's scene of emancipated spectatorship (which I touched upon in the first section of this essay). The 'ethical' interpretation, to recall, understands the joiner's fiction as mere illusion and a sign of alienation from his 'true' *ethos* as a worker. This interpretation dismisses *dissensus* as the absolute disjunction between appearance and reality, between the fantasy of the joiner's free gaze and the reality of his subordinated position. It denies the primacy of fiction by seeking to 'draw a clear-cut line between what belongs to the field of appearances, representations, opinions and utopias' (Rancière 2010: 149). The 'aesthetic' interpretation presupposes that appearance and reality are always knotted together in a contingent relation and that the task of fiction is to construct a different relation between them. As Rancière writes, the original meaning of *fingere* is not 'to feign' but 'to forge' (Rancière 2006a: 158). This is only possible insofar as there is no univocal relation between appearance and reality. That is the significance of what Rancière calls the 'aesthetic cut', the gap between artistic inventions and political effects that 'precludes any direct path towards an "other side" of words and images' (Rancière 2009a: 82).

The 'aesthetic cut' can never be 'healed', and yet, like the original contradiction of aesthetics, it is constantly covered over by the very plots it gives rise to. We might say that Rancière's figure of 'the emancipated spectator' inhabits or even maintains this 'aesthetic cut', but not as some obscure zone or black box that scrambles the intentions of art on their way to producing political effects. In *Disagreement* (1995), his great treatise on politics, Rancière calls emancipation 'the modern term for the effect of equality', and, as we've seen, the emancipated spectator's dissociation of cause and effect is the result of no deeper mystery than the verification of equality (Rancière 1999a: 35). But this only becomes discernible at the level of theory when the principle of equality is assumed as an axiom, a presupposition that is never achieved as a settled matter but exists purely as the spur for its perpetual verification. 'Never would equality exist,' as Rancière says in *The Ignorant Schoolmaster*, 'except in its verification and at the price of being verified always and everywhere' (Rancière 1991: 138). The 'price' of maintaining equality as an axiom for thinking the question of the spectator and a politics of cinema is encapsulated within Rancière's formulation of the paradoxical efficacy of *dissensus* with which we began: 'The very same thing that makes the aesthetic "political" stands in the way of all strategies for "politicizing art"' (Rancière 2009a: 74).

This does not mean that the effects of a film or any other artwork on the spectator can never be calculated. It simply means that calculable effects are neither 'aesthetic' nor 'political' in Rancière's sense of staging a *dissensus*. They are precisely 'consensual' insofar as the logic of cause and effect in art as well as politics presumes an accord between an experience and the interpretation of that experience, between a 'sense given' and the 'sense made of it'. This accord must be secured by some previous emplotment of the spectator as a destination within a distribution of social occupations (or identities) and their 'proper' capacities. In an interview discussing the politics of art, Rancière puts the matter plainly: 'The main enemy of artistic creativity as well as political creativity is consensus – that is, the inscription within roles, possibilities, and competences' (Rancière 2007e: 263). In attempting to pose anew the question of spectatorship and its continuing centrality to the discipline of film studies, we would do well to include the creativity of theory here among the enemies of consensual emplotment.

Notes

1. The talk that became the title essay of this book was originally delivered in August 2004, in English, at the opening of the Fifth International Summer Academy of Arts in Frankfurt, and was subsequently published in *Artforum* (Rancière 2007b).

2. The standard book on spectatorship in post-68 film studies remains Judith Mayne, *Cinema and Spectatorship* (1993). For more recent book-length studies that approach the question of spectatorship from a variety of disciplinary perspectives, see Buckland (1995), Staiger (2000), Jancovich et al. (2003), Campbell (2005), Aaron (2007), Cartwright (2008) and Plantinga (2009).

3. Or 'Screen theory', as it is often referred to after the British journal by the same name. For a useful overview of this critical formation see Rosen (2008: 264–97).

4. In his 1924 manifesto 'The Montage of Film Attractions', Eisenstein declares that theatre is 'linked to cinema by a common (identical) *basic* material – *the audience* – and by a common purpose – *influencing this audience in the desired direction* through a series of calculated pressures on its psyche' (Eisenstein 1988: 148).

5. As Rancière writes, the 'spectator is discredited because she does nothing, whereas actors on the stage or workers outside put their bodies in action. But the opposition of seeing and doing returns as soon as we oppose to the blindness of manual workers and empirical practitioners, mired in immediacy and routine, the broad perspective of those who contemplate ideas, predict the future or take a comprehensive view of our world. In the past, property owners who lived off their private income were referred to as *active* citizens, capable of electing and being elected, while those who worked for a living were *passive* citizens, unworthy of these duties' (2009a: 12–13).

6. '[I]t is only the union of reality with form, of contingency with necessity, of passivity with freedom, that fulfills the conception of humanity' (Schiller 2004: 77).

7. What matters for Rancière in this example is not the *Juno Ludovisi* sculpture itself but the use Schiller makes of it. One of Rancière's more effective methods for elucidating the distinctions between the three regimes of art is to take a single object from classical antiquity and describe the mutations it undergoes as it passes through the field of intelligibility proper to each regime. It should also be said, however, that these trajectories are typically designed to culminate in privileged couplings – Vico's *Homer*, Freud's *Oedipus*, Schiller's

Juno Ludovisi – that exemplify the logic of the aesthetic regime in particular. For an example of just such an exercise with the *Juno Ludovisi*, see Rancière (2009b: 29–30).

8. As Rancière elaborates: 'In the Kantian analysis, free play and free appearance suspend the power of form over matter, of intelligence over sensibility. Schiller, in the context of the French Revolution, translates these Kantian philosophical propositions into anthropological and political propositions. The power of "form" over "matter" is the power of the class of intelligence over the class of sensation, of men of culture over men of nature. If aesthetic "play" and "appearance" found a new community, then this is because they stand for the refutation, within the sensible, of this opposition between intelligent form and sensible matter which, properly speaking, is a difference between two humanities' (2009b: 31).

9. It is worth noting that Rancière began to write about aesthetics 'as such' relatively late (just after he began to write about politics 'as such'). And his formulation of the three 'regimes of the arts' first appeared only in 2000 with *Le partage du sensible* (2000; translated into English in *The Politics of Aesthetics* [2004]) as the formalization of ideas he'd worked out in a different idiom in *La parole muette* (1998). This does not mean, however, that the overall trajectory of Rancière's thought can be characterized in terms of a 'turn' to aesthetics and away from politics. The article cited above is aimed at correcting that misunderstanding by recalling how his early historical work revealed politics as an aesthetic matter from the beginning.

10. Indeed, the time that Gauny and his fellow 'perverted proletarians' steal from the 'nights' that are supposed to be spent resting and replenishing their labour power for the next day's work is devoted not to the study of militant tracts but to reading and writing the Romantic literature that was not destined for them (Rancière 2012: 15).

11. In Kant's *Critique of Judgement*, that resolution takes the form of a common sense (*sensus communus*) that would mediate the social division between 'the elite's sense of refinement' and the 'ordinary people's natural simplicity' (Rancière 2009b: 98). Schiller's unfolding of the 'aesthetic state' in the final letters of his text on aesthetic education is more radical insofar as it would overcome this division altogether by actualizing the new humanity promised in *Juno Ludovisi*. But Schiller's plot also resolves the play of contraries by subordinating matter to form in the total aestheticization of everyday life.

12. For his detailed discussion of these emplotments, see Rancière (2002b; 2009b).

13. In his Preface to *The Philosopher and his Poor*, Rancière succinctly describes the essential shift in his thinking that this displacement effected: 'Behind the "positivist" question – what could a person think at such a moment in the history of discourses and in such a position within the order of society? – I had to recognize the more fundamental question: how can those whose business is not thinking assume the authority to think and thereby constitute themselves as thinking subjects?' (Rancière 2004a: xxvi).

14. Although an antagonism towards sociology runs through nearly all of Rancière's thought, his most direct critique of Bourdieu can be found in the chapter entitled 'The Sociologist King' in *The Philosopher and his Poor*: (2004a: 165–202).

15. In its aspect as a freely circulating 'orphan letter', Gauny's writing functions according to Rancière's idea of 'literarity' (*littérarité*), which he first developed in his intervention into the discipline of French historiography, *The Names of History* (1994).

16. As Rancière puts it in *The Emancipated Spectator*, his experience in the workers' archives taught him that '[t]here was no gap to be filled between intellectuals and workers, any more than there was between actors and spectators' (2009a: 20).

17. For critical discussions of Epstein and a generous selection of his writings in English translation, see Keller and Paul (2012). On the *photogénie* theorists generally and a selection of their essays in English translation, see Abel (1993).

18. Compare, for example, these two statements about readers and spectators, respectively: 'Reading is not only an activity bringing about knowledge or pleasure. It is the achievement of a redistribution of the sensible that is involved in writing' (2009g: 278), and 'The spectator is not only the individual who feels pleasure and pain or the judge who says this is good or not good. The spectator is also summoned into the reinvention of the work . . .' (Rancière 2011d: 297).

19. Rancière's conceptual scheme allows no simple reversibility between 'the aesthetics of politics' and 'the politics of aesthetics'. When the terms reverse positions their meanings shift. 'Aesthetics' in this latter couplet no longer refers broadly to the sensory fabric of everyday experience and the organization of seeing, saying and doing captured in Rancière's phrase the '*partage* (dividing and sharing) of the sensible'. Aesthetics now refers more narrowly to the historical regime in which art is identified in the singular. That identification, as we've

seen in Kant and Schiller, is no longer based on any properties of the artwork itself but solely on an experience that is autonomous from the rest of sensory experience. For its part, the term 'politics' in the 'politics of aesthetics' is no longer the name for the polemical verification of equality but is now to be understood as a 'metapolitics'. This second shift is the more potentially confusing because metapolitics is Rancière's term for one of the three approaches (along with archipolitics and parapolitics) by which political philosophy has sought to annul politics (*la politique*) in his strong sense of the term. It is not simply a matter of the indifference of the forms of artistic practice to the properly political uses to which they may or may not be put. Construed as a metapolitics, the 'politics of aesthetics' in fact 'opposes its own forms to those constructed by the *dissensual* interventions of political subjects' (2009b: 33).

20. The paradigmatic literary example of this coexistence for Rancière is Flaubert's *Madame Bovary*. See Rancière (2008c).

21. I learned to see the centrality of Schiller's concept of the 'play-drive' in Rancière's thought from Sudeep Dasgupta. See especially his Introduction to the Dutch combined translation of *Le Partage du sensible* and *L'Inconscient esthétique* entitled *Het esthetische denken* (Rancière 2007c).

22. It should be pointed out that while Schiller is a central figure in Rancière's later discussion of the aesthetic regime, he has a relatively marginal status in *Film Fables*. My claim here therefore depends on a certain retrospective reading of the Prologue to *Film Fables* from the position of Rancière's later writing on aesthetics, specifically the 'emplotments of aesthetic experience' which I address in the first section of this essay.

23. Although at times Rancière seems to suggest that cinema maximizes this border-crossing activity, he puts painting and literature on a par with film in this regard.

24. It is worth noting in passing the remarkable similarity of Rancière's description here of cinema's games of inversion and exchange to Theodor Adorno definition of 'montage' in *Aesthetic Theory*: 'Art wants to admit its powerlessness vis-à-vis late-capitalist totality and to initiate its abrogation. Montage is the inner-aesthetic capitulation of art to what stands heterogeneously opposed to it. The negation of synthesis becomes a principle of form' (Adorno 1998: 155). The crucial difference, of course, is that Adorno places this operation entirely under the sign of art's 'powerlessness' and 'capitulation' to capitalism. By contrast, the dialectical twist by which Rancière

gives montage its positive valence is condensed in his claim that 'to thwart its servitude, cinema must first thwart its mastery' (2006a: 11).

25. The paradigmatic instance of this operation is Clement Greenberg's normative definition of modernist painting as an exploration of 'flatness'.

26. 'The arts, in practice, verify the ontology that renders them possible. But that ontology has no other consistency than that which is constructed by these verifications' (Rancière 2010: 211).

27. Rancière also links the importance of memory for the experience of cinephilia in the 1950s and 1960s to one of the ironies of the mechanically reproducible art of film, namely that cinema 'was for a long time an art form whose works were not accessible to methods of reproduction. You never knew if you would see a film again, and it changed in your memory, and in the texts that discussed it' (Rancière 2011i: 202).

28. Like Rancière's work, Schefer's writing on film has been relatively neglected within Anglo-American film studies. As an indirect sign of their affinity, it is perhaps not coincidental that some of the most prominent (and earliest) exceptions to that neglect have come from the same US-based scholar – Tom Conley. See, for example, Conley (1985; 2005; 2010).

29. In her comprehensive study of spectatorship in film studies, Judith Mayne argues that 'the study of spectatorship in film theory has always involved some complicated negotiations of "subjects" and "viewers", despite claims that the two are incompatible terms' (1993: 9). For similar claims in more recent overviews of spectatorship studies, see Aaron (2007) and Plantinga (2008).

30. Although with this phrase Rancière is clearly alluding to the title of Robert Musil's novel *The Man Without Qualities* (1932–40), only Schefer makes explicit reference to Musil.

31. As he puts it in an *Artforum* interview: 'I don't speak for the members of a particular body or discipline. I write to shatter the boundaries that separate specialists – of philosophy, art, social sciences, etc. I write for those who are also trying to tear down the walls between specialists and competences' (Rancière 2007e: 257).

32. One of the 'gaps' Rancière explores in *Les Écarts du cinéma* is that between art and entertainment, the productive contradiction of which is expressed in MGM's lion's head logo with its incorporation of the motto *Ars gratis artis* (art for art's sake) into the heart of Hollywood's commercial enterprise. See Rancière (2011c: 78).

33. See Hagener and de Valck (2005), Keathley (2006), 'Project: New Cinephilia' (n.d.). For a useful discussion of recent scholarly interest in cinephilia in relation to gallery art see Fowler (2012).

5

Memories of Modernism:
Jacques Rancière, Chris Marker
and the Image of Modernism

Bram Ieven

One of the recurring tropes within modernist theories of images, and filmic images in particular, is their tendency to play out the tensions between the seeming immediacy of the visual, its epiphany-like and revelatory force that suggests a truth beyond arguing on the one hand, and a focus on the technological conditions of the image on the other. Within modernist theory these two aspects of the image can be arranged in different ways. Some modernist critics, such as André Bazin, have argued that the technological underpinnings of photographic and filmic images ascertain their historical accuracy, or at the very least satisfy our desire for the illusion of historical accuracy. In that case the technical nature of images leads to the intensification of historical representation. Others, such as Clement Greenberg, have argued that the medium-specific qualities lead away from figuration and ultimately to abstraction in painting as a way of affirming the two-dimensional nature of the canvas. In this case the awareness of the medium of an image leads to an affirmation of its sensuous and visual nature. Either way, modernism's approach to the image seems to be determined by finding a way to play out the dynamic interplay between the technical or medium-specific qualities of the image and the sensuous nature of the image. The combination of both these interests can be found in the work of modernist critics such as Walter Benjamin, Clement Greenberg and André Bazin alike. The tension between these two sets out the dialectical dynamic between the filmic image as the conveyer of both immediate historical truth (the filmic image as a historical referent) and immediate sensuous experience (the filmic image as obscuring every referent and turning to abstraction). The modernist image oscillates between transparency and abstraction, between illusion and disillusion. But this dynamic tension is there from the very start, inscribed in

83

the image and providing it with a dynamic. In short, the modernist image is engaged in a process of remediation from the very outset, all the while maintaining the hint of immediacy.

One version of this modernist theory of the image can be found in Walter Benjamin's dialectical image. According to Benjamin, the dialectical image is first of all 'an occurrence of ball lightning that runs across the whole horizon of the past' (Benjamin 2003: 403). The dialectical image brings together within it the entirety of history, folding it into one single lightning bolt, into one single image. Benjamin explains:

> Articulating the past historically means recognizing those elements of the past which come together in the constellation of a single moment. Historical knowledge is possible only within the historical moment. But knowledge *within* the historical moment is always knowledge *of* a moment. In drawing itself together in the moment – in the dialectical image – the past becomes part of humanity's involuntary memory. (Benjamin 2003: 403)

The dialectical nature of what Benjamin describes here lies in the fact that the image brings together the presence and immediacy of a 'now' with the awareness of a historical past. The insistence on time, and the clash of different time-modes – bringing together the startling but effervescent immediacy of the present with the stable but hard to grasp historical past, and the astute awareness that media form and deform time and our experience of it – all of this is decidedly modern. Importantly, the dialectical image in Benjamin's work is not concerned with the image as such; the image is here seen as a metaphor for articulating a concept of history. And yet the fact that Benjamin chooses the images to explain his views on history is telling. Whereas some modernist critics argue that the visual ends in 'mindless fascination' (Jameson 1992: 1), Benjamin contends that this immediacy and fascination also harbour a certain insight. The combination of these two (fascination for the visual and historical insight) is what makes up the dialectic of the image that is so typical of modernist criticism.

This modernist take on the image is what Jacques Rancière is up against when he embarks on a reading of modernist and contemporary art and film within a different framework. Instead of dividing the history of twentieth-century art and aesthetics into two periods, modernist and postmodernist, he brings them together under a single regime, which he calls the aesthetic regime and which reaches as far back as the aesthetic revolution of the late eighteenth century. To do this, he must show that the characteristics normally attributed to modernist art are actually part of a larger, more encompassing aesthetic regime. His criticism of the modernist image, therefore, will first of all have to consist of an alternative theory of the image, one that is not dependent on the technological underpinnings of the image that are so crucial for a modernist understanding of the image. 'One of modernism's main theses', Rancière thus suggests in *The Politics of Aesthetics*, is that 'the difference between the arts is linked to the difference between their technological conditions or their specific medium or material' (2004b: 31). In order to move away from this thesis, Rancière will substitute a technological understanding of the image for an understanding that explains how the image is itself not determined by any technological transformations but rather by a regime of relations between what can be said and what can be seen. It is within this regime, which Rancière identifies as the aesthetic regime, that images as we know them will occur. Within this regime we can also find the interest in the technical and sensuous conditions of the image. These two are then no longer the two poles of a separate modernist theory of the image but become part of a wider framework of how images work, determined by the aesthetic regime.

The Image: Naked, Ostensive and Metaphorical

Rancière's theory of the image starts by separating the aesthetic qualities of an image from its technical qualities. These technical or medial qualities in no way determine or shape the aesthetic features of the image, he argues. A different way of reading the aesthetic qualities of the image must therefore be found. By positing that the image itself is always marked by a certain alterity, that is to say by a strangeness and heterogeneity built into the composition of the image itself, Rancière develops an alternative reading of the image. This way of reading will not be guided by a fascination for the technical or medial qualities of the image but by the aesthetic regime within which an image becomes interpretable.

The alterity of the image that Rancière talks about must first of all be distinguished from the alterity that we sometimes find in modernist or postmodernist theories. Unlike these theories, the alterity he finds in the image does not stem from its material properties or from the strangeness of the cinematic medium. Rather it 'enters into the very composition of the images' (2007a: 3) Each image consists of and is subject to 'a whole regime of "imageness" – that is, a regime of relations between elements and between functions' (2007a: 4). This regime of relations is in fact a regime of contrasts and contradictions between the various elements that make up the image. These make the image readable, decipherable, but also enigmatic. The fact that the image is made up of contrasting elements first of all presupposes that each and every element of the image is of potential interest to the viewer; or in other words, that there is a radical equality between everything that is shown in the image, regardless of what the meaning and intentions of its author may have been. The point is that the image is in itself already the result of a certain regime, namely the aesthetic regime. After all, in Rancière's theory it is the aesthetic regime that imbues all things with a heterogeneous and enigmatic force. Whereas in the previous two regimes the orchestration of the visual, of the readable and of the sayable is done in such a way that everything is in its right place and only certain things can be said, seen or heard, within the aesthetic regime everything becomes of potential interest and can therefore be said, heard or shown.

In the case of the image, everything that is depicted in the image is now of interest and should be brought into the interpretation of the image. This equality within the composition of the image inevitably leads to tensions within the image itself, which is precisely what Rancière sees as essential for an image. In that sense the image itself is the result of the aesthetic regime. Unlike in the previous two regimes, the image does not demonstrate an ethical truth nor does it adhere to a specific moral code; instead it becomes the surface in which different, heterogeneous elements are brought together and must be interpreted together. The different elements will often be too far apart to enable a reading of the image that can unify all of its elements. By showing how the image itself is in fact not a unity but a heterogeneous compound of different elements, each of which is at a continual risk of clashing with the other, Rancière is able to circumvent the emphasis on the strictly sensuous or strictly technological nature of the image. The heterogeneity of the image, by way of the heterogeneity of the aesthetic regime, is also what guarantees the possibility of taking a critical distance from it – which in itself is once again a characteristic of the aesthetic regime itself.

The modernist approach to the image tends to equate the image with the visual; the visual can then be taken over by images, revolving entirely around themselves, or around their own visual properties. Rancière, on the other hand, distinguishes between the image and the visual, arguing that not all images are visual and that some even consist solely of words. Whereas modernism tends to equate the visual and the image, at least in the sense that the image itself derives its appeal from the visual force it exerts on the viewer (often by playing on its material, sensuous qualities), Rancière's philosophy of the image seems to call for a separation between the image and the visible. For this reason he begins his analysis of the image by highlighting the compositional features. This does not mean that the image itself is suddenly separated from the visible. The visible can now be reintroduced within the image as a legible element that takes part in its composition. Rancière's tendency to avoid the visual as something that makes up the core of the image is due to the fact that the very idea of the visual relates back to the modernist idea of the visual as a sensuous presence that numbs and, as a result, cannot be divided into different heterogeneous parts and is no longer legible.

In fact, in his work Rancière identifies three sorts of images: the naked image, the ostensive image and the metaphorical image. The naked image poses the immediate presence of a (historical) referent. This sort of image cannot become art, Rancière explains, 'because what it shows us excludes the prestige of dissemblance and the rhetoric of exegeses' (2007a: 22). Examples are photographs of atrocities, genocides and so on. In principle, however, these images can be concerned with any historical or political momentum as long as the viewer has the feeling she is being confronted with history in an immediate way. Second, there is the ostensive image. The ostensive image also draws attention to its presence, but this time the presence of the image is not related to its historical referent but to its materiality. The ostensive image draws attention to its immediate and sensuous materiality as an image. In that sense it moves away from the presence of the historical reference to the advantage of asserting itself as an image in the here and now. This sort of image is often connected to art. Finally, there is the metaphorical image. In a way this image can best be understood as a critique of the previous two categories of images, in the sense that it argues that the 'images of art possess no peculiar nature of their own that separates them in stable fashion from the negotiation of resemblances and discursiveness of symptoms' (2007a: 24). Instead of celebrating the presence of the image – either of its historical reference or of its sensuous materiality – the metaphorical image highlights the production, circulation and discursive context of images. In doing so it comes closest to connecting the image directly to the aesthetic regime in which it functions. The metaphorical image demonstrates that every image is a composition in which different discourses, visual elements and referents both clash and unite.

When we look at the three categories of the image that Rancière has laid out, it seems clear that the first two categories are remarkably close to a modernist conception of the image. In the first case, the naked image, there is the idea that the image represents a historical truth, or at least satisfies our desire for historical truth. The modernist film critic André Bazin has identified this as what makes the filmic image so special. Bazin argued that the purpose of images was to capture the spirit of humanity. Clearly, he argued, this must forever remain an illusion. But even so the desire to capture something of the human spirit in images has influenced our view of the image both culturally and religiously. Because of this the painterly image always remained torn between two contradictory ambitions: 'one, primarily aesthetic, namely the expression of spiritual reality wherein the symbol transcended its model; the other, purely psychological, namely the duplication of the world outside' (Bazin 2005: 11). According to a critic such as Bazin, the photographic and filmic image can only be understood when we take into account the aesthetic and psychological ambition of painting. Photography and film, after all, are able to satisfy the psychological desire that goes with our idea of the image. Early photography and cinema are certainly not technically superior to painting, but their technological underpinning does satisfy our psychological desire for a true image of reality. The photographic image, the argument goes, gives us an 'objectified' slice of reality. In Bazin's words:

> [T]he essential factor in the transition from baroque to photography is not the perfecting of a physical process (photography will long remain the inferior of painting in the reproduction of color); rather does it lie in a psychological fact, to wit, in completely satisfying our appetite for illusion by a mechanical reproduction in the making of which man

plays no part. The solution is not to be found in the result but in the way of achieving it. (2005: 12)

This psychological element also forms the core of the naked image. Although Rancière does not discus the technological aspect of the naked image it is telling that his examples for this category of images are all photographic. The technical background is used as a motivation for understanding the image as the direct or objectified representation of a historical referent.[1]

The interest in the technical nature of images is something that is typical of modernist approaches to the issue. It is also one of the aspects of modernist theory that Rancière strongly disagrees with. As Rancière explains, the modernist paradigm holds that 'the mechanical arts, qua *mechanical* arts, would result in a change of artistic paradigm and a new relationship between art and its subject matter' (2004b: 31). Whereas Bazin advocates this view with regard to the relation between technical images and reality, the reverse argument is also made within modernist theory, arguing that the advent of the mechanical arts highlighted the specificity of a medium and its materiality. This then comes close to the idea of the ostensive image, in which the sensual character of the image is emphasized. In actual fact, the metaphorical image seems to be the only category that is not immediately amenable to the modernist paradigm of the image. Playing out the naked and the ostensive image against one another, and revealing the context in which they are situated, the metaphorical image creates a composition in which different elements clash and come together.

Rancière is not arguing that the technical characteristics of images induce them to take the shape of naked or ostensive images. If that were the case he would still adhere to a modernist theory of the image. Instead, he develops a theory that is able to explain modernist theories of the image by recuperating it as a (confused) part of the aesthetic regime. This means that the ostensive and the naked image must themselves be the result of a broader regime in which pure historicity (the naked image) or pure visuality (the ostensive image) must be able to exist. They are no longer the pure essence of history or of the image, but rather the result of certain operations that can be undertaken within the aesthetic regime. The problem with modernity, Rancière argues, is that it 'tries to make clear-cut distinctions in the complex configuration of the aesthetic regime' (2004b: 25). The naked and the ostensive image both try to filter out one element that is actually part of a larger aesthetic regime: pure history in the case of the naked image and pure visuality in the case of the ostensive image. Rather than denying the existence of such a purity altogether – a postmodern move if ever there was one – Rancière endeavours to show that the purity for which modernism strives can exist, but only as the result of a much more elaborate visual and narrative construction that is made possible within the aesthetic regime. The aesthetic regime itself, on the other hand, relies on a 'constitutive contradiction', and shows how this contradiction works instead of trying to filter out one of the contradictory elements. The purity of a visual image can still exist. However, 'these "pure" situations are not the rediscovered essence of the image: they are the result of those operations whereby the cinematic art thwarts its own powers' (Rancière 2006a: 12). In his own theory of the image, as in his aesthetic theory in general, Rancière will try to provide an alternative account. He develops a wider framework in which the image itself is always a heterogeneous construct in which different elements come together, regardless of their technical nature.

Rancière is at his best in explaining this view of the image when he is dealing with film. In many of his writings about film he is concerned with explaining the purity of the image by which filmmakers and theorists such as Epstein, Bazin, Godard and Deleuze were all intrigued. This purity of the image, he argues, is the result of the image being first created within the broader context of a film fable that is then thwarted. More specifically, this process of distilling pure images is always the result of a borrowing of elements from the three different categories of images, of distilling them and reworking them. In Jean-Luc Godard's *Histoire(s) du cinéma*, for example, Rancière finds such an example of a mix between the ostensive and the metaphorical image. Recuperating fragments from old movies, Godard interrupts their narratives by arresting the images of the film, bringing them to a standstill and elevating them to the status of a visible presence that draws attention only to its own visuality – a typically modernist move. Yet at the same time, Rancière explains, there is a second principle at work in *Histoire(s) du cinéma* 'that makes these visible presences elements which, like the signs of language, possess a value only by dint of the combinations they authorize: combinations with different visual and sonorous elements, but also sentences and words, spoken by voices or written on the screen' (Rancière 2007a: 33).

For Rancière it is only when these heterogeneous combinations between different elements within one and the same composition take place that we can truly speak of an image. The metaphorical image, with its interest in combining different images and highlighting the often conflicting discourses that surround them, and with its disregard for the medial boundaries of technical versus non-technical images, is an excellent choice. The necessity of borrowing, in the case of the naked and ostensive image, means that the force of the presence that it hopes to achieve (the presence of history or the presence of the materiality of the image itself) is undone. This undoing of presence is not what the naked or ostensive image is after. Only the metaphorical image seems genuinely concerned with this undoing of a force.

Through the process of borrowing and interdependency the force of the naked image (which supposedly is nothing but the historical referent, but as it turns out is always more than just that) and of the ostensive image (which supposedly is nothing but its own presence but depends for this sheer presence on the interruption of a narrative or context) becomes undone, or at least is morphed into something that is now very close to Rancière's own conviction that an image is always the result of a heterogeneous composition. Modernism has thus been recuperated within the aesthetic regime. In a way one could say that Rancière distinguishes between three categories of images only to show that they fold into each other, build on each other and form part of the same procedure: the film fable, the narrative possibilities within the aesthetic regime.

Chris Marker's *Le Tombeau d'Alexandre*

How this process works exactly becomes most clear in the case of film. It is not a coincidence that Rancière often uses film to explain his idea of the image and his criticism of the modernist approach to the image (and, in a way, of modernism in general). Rather than denying the existence of what fascinates modernism about the image (the sheer historical referent, the pure visuality that some images exert), Rancière reveals these to be momentary and isolated instances of a narrative or fable that is constructed and then thwarted. The regime in which it becomes possible to build up a fable only to arrest it or thwart it is the aesthetic regime. I now want to take a closer look at the characteristics Rancière attributes to the filmic image within the aesthetic regime. To do so, I will focus on his analysis of Chris Marker's *Le Tombeau d'Alexandre* (1992). At first sight this documentary appears to possess all the features that a documentary film made within the aesthetic regime is required to have; yet its insistence on the technological conditions of film, and more specifically on the relationship between memory and technical images, would suggest that this documentary can also be read in a way that differs significantly from Rancière's approach, in a way that is reminiscent of the modernist approach to the technical image.

Le Tombeau d'Alexandre tells the story of Alexander Medvedkin, a Russian communist, soldier of the revolutionary army, experimental filmmaker and long-time friend of Chris Marker. Medvedkin's life spans almost the entire twentieth century. Born in 1900, he joined the Russian Red Army shortly after the revolution in 1917 and fought in the civil war for the next few years. During the early 1920s, once the civil war had come to an end, Medvedkin took up a position within the department of propaganda in the army. It was there that his troubled career as a filmmaker began. In the late 1920s he developed the idea of the film train. This was a train fitted with a fully equipped film studio, an editing room, and space for sleeping and eating. The idea was to travel through Russia and shoot footage of the *kolkhozes* that were emerging everywhere in the country as a result of Stalin's collectivization plans. The project had some success during the 1930s and Medvedkin travelled the USSR with his mobile film studio, shooting, developing and editing films and then showing them to the villagers. In 1935 Medvedkin directed his first feature film, *Happiness*. It would turn out to be deeply controversial. As one of the interviewees in *Le Tombeau d'Alexandre* explains, after having seen the film as a student 'when we came out the film we were Medvedkin's enthusiasts. And we were convinced of two things: that he was a genius and that he was shot after this film.' It turned out, however, that Medvedkin had survived.

More than just a documentary on the enigmatic figure of Medvedkin as a filmmaker, *Le Tombeau d'Alexandre* provides an incisive reflection on the nature of cinematic image and memory, friendship and politics, and history. The documentary is divided into two parts. Each part is structured around a series of letters written by Marker to his late friend Medvedkin. The documentary alternates between these letters and interviews with acquaintances of Medvedkin, film scholars and filmmakers. What interests

Rancière in Marker's documentary is the relation it has to truth and the truthful representation of history. Central to his analysis is the problem of historicity: the possibility of rendering history through film, and more specifically the fact that this very question itself is the result of the fact that history is something that becomes pertinent within the aesthetic regime. Bringing together truth and history through fiction is not only typical for the aesthetic regime, but also for modernism. Most important for Rancière is that *Le Tombeau d'Alexandre* is a documentary that explicitly and implicitly plays with the fine line between fact and fiction, between truth and falsity. Throughout the film we view in-depth interviews, quick snapshots of people, faces, scenes, found footage from historical events, and shots and images taken from other films, documentaries and archives as well as digitally modulated images. In short, *Le Tombeau d'Alexandre* 'plays off the combination of different types of traces (interviews, significant faces, archival documents, extracts from documentary and fictional films, etc.) in order to suggest possibilities for thinking this story or history' (Rancière 2004b: 38). Chris Marker's letters to Medvedkin, which are after all letters to a deceased friend, are perhaps the best example of the complex relation between fiction and history that is at stake in *Le Tombeau d'Alexandre*.

Rancière makes a more detailed analysis of *Le Tombeau d'Alexandre* in *Film Fables*. His attention now goes to the genre of the documentary as a means of conveying history through film. The documentary genre maintains a privileged relation to history. At face value it seems as if the documentary is able to lay claim to speaking truthfully about its subject matter, particularly when the subject matter is of a historical nature. In this sense the documentary genre seems to be the opposite of the feature film, in which fiction is the essence. As it turns out, the documentary genre is precisely concerned with fiction and not just with historical truth. As Rancière writes: 'The real must be fictionalized in order to be thought' (2004b: 38). Central to the documentary genre is therefore not its claim to represent history but its use of fiction to enable history to be thought, to come alive, and thus to question the very idea of history in representing it.

One finds in documentaries certain 'moments of suspension' in which the unfolding narrative is brought to a standstill and opens up new elements and turns in the film (Rancière 2006a: 17). These moments of suspension are as important to documentary films as they are to feature films. But while the feature film must evoke in its viewers the effect of reality, the documentary film has no obligation to produce the effect of reality. Instead, the documentary film endeavours to understand reality. In Rancière's words: 'The privilege of the so-called documentary film is that it is not obliged to create the *feeling* of the real, and this allows it to treat the real as a problem and to experiment more freely with the variable games of action and life, significance and insignificance' (2006a: 17–18). In order to understand reality the documentary must draw on the same sources and methods as the feature film. Marker's *Le Tombeau d'Alexandre* relies upon the 'the polyvalence of images and signs, the potential difference between values and expressions . . . that make up, in contrast to the episodes of before, the new forms of fiction of the aesthetic age' (2006a: 18). The interesting thing here is the fundamental ambiguity and plurality of meaning of (filmic) images. Within the aesthetic regime, as we have seen, images and signs are always more and less than simple representations of a pre-existing reality; they are more because they harbour the unfulfilled promise of a deeper meaning and they are less because they forever hide this meaning from us, remaining mute. Like all films – documentary or otherwise – *Le Tombeau d'Alexandre* derives its aesthetic force from its use of fabulation. The fable, as understood by Rancière, is a specific way of organizing and reorganizing reality, or representing it and presenting it.

Rancière argues that fabulation is common to all films. The fable, however, consists not simply of the creation of a narrative; more importantly it consists of the creation of a gap within this narrative that ensures that the narrative becomes unhinged, opens up for multiple meaning. 'Even the most classical of cinematographic forms, the ones most faithful to the representative tradition of carefully arranged accidents, clearly defined characters, and neatly composed images, are affected by this gap, evidence enough that the film fable belongs to the aesthetic regime of art' (2006a: 15). The fable consists of a series of discrepancies: discrepancies between what is said and what is seen, between what is seen and what can be seen. Modernism in film is merely an extreme, purified form of this procedure of fabulation. More precisely, modernism is a radicalized version of what is even more interesting in its more balanced form: the deregulated and deregulating fable of film. It tries to isolate one aspect of the fable while obfuscating or filtering out the other aspects.

The fable, Rancière explains, is concerned with the '*mise-en-scène* of a *mise-en-scène*', and with a 'counter-movement that affects the arrangement of incidents and shots, automatism separating the image from movement, voice hollowing out the visible' (2006a: 15). Still, the documentary differs in its use of fabulation in that it is not bound to producing a reality effect by presenting its viewers with recognizable stereotypes and predictable plotlines. Because it does not have to convince people that its story is real, the documentary has the unique opportunity not just to make its viewer feel that it is dealing with history, but to question history, rework it, and ask how history becomes what it is for us. This is the value of *Le Tombeau d'Alexandre* for Rancière. The documentary not only presents the life and work of Alexander Medvedkin, it presents the essence of the film fable and its relation to history. In accordance with a modernist logic, Marker isolates images in order to give them a specific discursive force: they become pure historical referents or pure spectacle. We can see this principle at work in his use of found footage of the tsars, the Russian Revolution and so on. And yet these images are no longer used as immediate historical referents. Instead they are used to question the very idea of images as historical referents. Medvedkin and his time thus become an enigma. The documentary's function is not simply to represent Medvedkin in his time but also to question the enigmatic history of the twentieth century and the role of images in it. This is what the film fable is all about in the case of documentary.

And yet Marker's own approach to film in general and documentary in particular may be somewhat different from Rancière's reading of it. While Rancière's analysis brings out beautifully the intricate relation between history and fiction that indeed fascinates Marker, he also downplays his interest in the technical aspect of the image in its relation to both history and fiction – in other words, the modernist legacy of the image that Marker is grappling with. In the course of his career Marker's interest in the filmic and photographic image has changed from fascination with the apparent veracity and immediacy of the image to an astute awareness of its contrived and manipulative nature (Alter 2006: 97–8). A recurrent theme in Marker's filmic work from the 1990s, then, is the misleading and manipulative nature of film, or better yet the misleading nature of history caught on tape. For Marker the manipulative nature of film consists in the combination of sound and image. More precisely, Marker's work is interested in what happens when a filmic image is brought together with a sound tape that seems to belong to it while in fact it diverges from the image in slight but significant ways. The mix of different media and their respective qualities is what guides Marker throughout this documentary.

In *Le Tombeau d'Alexandre* this fascination can be found in Marker's ingenious use of voice-over, the layering of different voices (the documentary opens with Alexander Medvedkin speaking in Russian with a voice-over by Marker talking about the life and times of Medvedkin, and yet based on the gestural language of Medvedkin the two seem to be saying roughly the same), and the suggestive ways in which he combines images with answers given by his interviewees. While these voice-overs seem like a perfect match for the images that they accompany, they are in fact more misleading than appears at first sight. An example can be found during the interview with the wife of Isaac Babel. In this interview we get at least three different layers that seem to go well together but on closer inspection make up a very problematic constellation. First, the motivation for interviewing Babel's wife is that Babel was a member of the Red Army during the civil war in the early 1920s, like Medvedkin. But this woman was not Babel's wife while he was fighting in the Red Army. The instances she tells Marker about, however, are never actually about Babel's time with the Red Army but rather of the time after that. She tells of Babel's own memories of his experience, she explains to us how this marked him for the rest of his life and how she experienced that – but she never tells us anything about Medvedkin. And while she tells us about a former member of the Red Army confessing to torturing a monk in order to find out where they had hidden jewellery and money, this disclosure is accompanied by images from a monastery that is almost certainly not the monastery she is talking about. The beauty of this scene, however, is that it is convincing. It is a strong scene, making a forceful point. The viewer understands that it cannot be historically accurate, that it is even misleading in a way. This paradox of having the feeling that we are getting an insight into history through images while we also know that these images are misleading – this is the paradox that fascinated modernist filmmakers who tried to create images that at one and the same time captured history immediately and focused on the strictly sensuous qualities of a technical image.

Conclusion

As Rancière rightly points out, the essence of modernism seems to be its tendency to isolate one moment of a more complex cinematographic and aesthetic experience. However, this does not speak against modernism per se. One could argue that this makes modernism into a well-defined aesthetic programme that has as its main goal to cut out certain elements of cinema and of the image in order to intensify them and turn them into the focal point around which all other cinematic gestures must revolve. To be sure, there is a certain radicalism to this programme in that it attempts to filter out one aspect of the image in favour of another. But this does not yet mean that modernism is oblivious to what exactly it is doing. On the contrary, the dialectical nature of the modernist image consists precisely in its deliberate oscillation between the representation of historical truth and immediate sensuous input; and in its attempt to achieve both these effects within cinema it consciously searches for ways to create this effect.

In his essay on Marker, Rancière is perhaps a little too quick to move from an analysis of the documentary to a more general reflection on the laws of documentary and fiction in the aesthetic regime, thus missing out on the opportunity to address some of the more remarkable aspects of Marker's work, some of which seem to run against Rancière's own take on the documentary. It is possible to interpret Marker's *Le Tombeau d'Alexandre* not just as a brilliant example of Rancière's film fable and aesthetic regime, but as a comment on and criticism of the dialectical image. This brings the documentary closer to a reflection on the modernist approach to the image. This interpretation is all the more relevant if we take into account the evolution of Marker's own ideas on the cinematic image. In his early career, Marker was close to Bazin, whose view on technical images was discussed earlier on in this essay. In a documentary like *Le Tombeau d'Alexandre*, however, Marker questions the idea of a direct access to history. By presenting the viewer with a disturbingly strange combination of images and auditory material, he unsettles the idea of the truth of images that is typical of certain strands of modernism. But despite the fact that images are not entirely trustworthy, they still provide this flash of insight that the modernist image is concerned with. It is this that is the real enigma of *Le Tombeau d'Alexandre*.

Note

1. Talking from a different but still markedly modernist point of view,
   Clement Greenberg once argued that he was against abstract photography because the photographer merely 'fools' himself, suggesting
   that for Greenberg the medium specificity of photography lies in its
   referential quality (1997: 153).

6

Aesthetic Irruptions:
Politics of Perception in
Alex de la Iglesia's *La Comunidad*

Mónica López Lerma

> What 'dissensus' means is an organization of the sensible where
> there is neither a reality concealed behind appearances nor a single
> regime of presentation and interpretation of the given imposing its
> obviousness on all. It means that every situation can be cracked open
> from the inside, reconfigured in a different regime of perception and
> signification ... [T]his is what a process of political subjectivation
> consists in. (Rancière 2009a: 48–9)

Combining black humour, thriller and horror film, Alex de la
Iglesia's *La Comunidad* (*Common Wealth* 2000) tells the story of
a gruesome community of neighbours who have signed a contract
to share the money that another of their neighbours has won in
the *quiniela* (football pools) after his death. However, their plans
are frustrated when a new arrival, the estate agent Julia, finds
the dead man's money and decides to keep it for herself. From
then on, the community will do anything (including murder) to
retrieve the money, resulting in its own destruction. When asked
about this bleak portrayal of society, de la Iglesia affirmed that
the violence and horror of the film are nothing compared to the
cruelty of everyday reality as described in the mass media (de la
Iglesia in Hermosa, n.d.). Inspired by this, the greedy and selfish
community of neighbours is intended as a magnifying mirror in
which viewers can see their 'own defects grotesquely distorted' (de
la Iglesia 2001: 53). To create this grotesque mirror effect, de la
Iglesia uses a series of narrative and aesthetic strategies: the style of
satire, caricature and *esperpento*, exaggerated theatrical performances, extreme close-ups, intertextuality, and a casting of veteran
actors from Spanish cinema, television and theatre, characterized
in an ugly and hideous way so as to make them both comic and
frightening, hilarious and disgusting.

Former analyses of *La Comunidad* have connected these strategies to the film's critical aims. For example, in the film's constant
references to Spanish black comedies of the 1950s Burkhard Pohl
finds a 'realist' sensibility that goes beyond the parodic and the
comic to denounce, from a detached perspective, an 'inhumanely
materialist society' (2007: 136, 126). Likewise for Buse, Triana-
Toribio and Willis, the casting of well-established Spanish actors
along with the use of the techniques and aesthetics (for example,
choral structure) of Spanish black comedies of the 1950s and
1960s reveal 'the nagging persistence of the [conservative] past in
the present' and sceptically interrogate Spain's modernizing present
(Buse et al. 2007: 125, 136). In turn, Mercedes Maroto focuses on
the character of Julia to emphasize the film's stance on gender relations. In her view, the film uses social caricature to denounce the
sexism that pervades contemporary Spanish society and suggests
ways for social and individual change (Maroto Camino 2005).
Shifting the focus to the old man's dead body, Cristina Moreiras-
Menor argues that de la Iglesia's use of the anamorphic look of
the camera – the look that grotesquely distorts reality and compels
viewers to look awry and not straight – aims not only to reveal
the hidden violence behind the Francoist national-communitarian
spirit that still persists in modern Spain, but also to do justice to
the forgotten, but not departed, victims of Franco's dictatorship
(Moreiras-Menor 2011). Regardless of differences in outlook
and focus, critics concur that the film's critical potential lies in its
ability to render visible the sordid reality concealed behind Spain's
democratic and European façade.

Taking as starting points Jean Baudrillard's vision of the 'consumer society' and Jacques Rancière's account of the current
'politics of consensus', this chapter suggests that *La Comunidad*
launches a powerful critique of the ideological presuppositions
and *policing* practices that condition the 'regimes of visibility' of
Western liberal democracies. However, departing from previous
analysis, I argue that the real strength of the film lies not in its
ability to render visible this order of domination or the manner in
which it chooses to represent it, but rather in its ability to create
an aesthetics of *dissensus* in Rancière's sense. This aesthetics sets
up possibilities for new forms of political subjectivation not just
within the fictional world of the characters, but within the sensory
world of the viewer. For these purposes, my analysis turns to a
marginal and often neglected character called Charlie, presented

throughout most of the film as a 'retard' (as the neighbours call him) and sex pervert who likes to dress up in Darth Vader apparel, spy on Julia with his binoculars, and masturbate while repeating the words 'The Force . . . the force' (*La fuerza . . . la fuerza*). At a given point in the film, Charlie is able to stage a *wrong* into what the film presents as the given relationship between the sensible and its meaning, facts and their interpretation, the mode of representation and its affects. Charlie's political act of subjectivation and aesthetic irruption into the viewer's field of perception disrupts and reconfigures the regime of visibility that the film imposes and simultaneously invites viewers to challenge. In this way, the film demonstrates not just the aesthetic dimension of politics, but the political character of aesthetics.

The Regime of the All-Visible

From the beginning of the title sequence, an omniscient camera-eye positions viewers as godlike figures able to see everything and everyone within the story. The sequence opens with a camera movement reminiscent of the flight of a bird that shows a majestic building with a cat in one of its windows. The camera then follows the cat into the interior of a dark room with piles of rubbish, filthy water and a decomposing corpse that the cat starts nibbling. The sequence closes with an image of the cat dissolving into a spiral, at the centre of which appears an eye belonging to the actress and the film's protagonist Carmen Maura. The camera isolates her terrified face at the left of the frame and reveals the cause of her fear: fifteen people arranged in a way reminiscent of a police line-up. As the title of the film points out, these are the members of *La Comunidad*. The title sequence marks the centrality of the building, sets a general mood of suspicion and surveillance emphasized by ominous music (Moreiras-Menor 2011: 160), and most importantly, establishes a 'regime of the all-visible', a world of total visibility in which everything (public and private, exterior and interior, appearance and reality) seems to be on show for the viewer. From this position, the film invites viewers to critically examine two different but interconnected regimes of visibility that at one and the same time distribute bodies, images and places and determine what can be seen, said and thought: first, there is the regime of 'sensory commodity' proper to the consumer society symbolized by Julia; and second, the regime of the 'saturated community' proper to the society of consensus symbolized by the neighbours.

Julia and the consumer society

The film opens with an image of the estate agent Julia on her cell phone talking with her husband in front of the building shown in the title sequence. As she approaches the building to meet her clients, she finds a joker playing card on top of a sewer with the name Madrid written on it. The image of the sewer symbolizes Julia's entry into the building: it is as if she were opening the entrails of Madrid, as Moreiras-Menor points out (2011: 160). Julia opens the door to find a dirty foyer with filthy walls, damp stains and a rubbish bin with the name of the street on it: 'Carrera de San Jerónimo 14' – the street of the *Congreso de los Diputados* (Spanish Parliament). Notwithstanding the decaying condition of the building's interior, Julia focuses on the 'superb advantages' of its location when trying to sell the apartment to her clients: 'You can go anywhere from here', she tells them. From that moment, the film transforms the building (a metaphor for Madrid and hence for Spain) into a theatre of deceptive appearances, wherein individuals find themselves ascribed to specific forms of sensory commodity within a global market economy.

As Jean Baudrillard argues in *The Consumer Society*, consumption is a whole system of values that has become naturalized, not by fulfilling individuals' desires for comfort, satisfaction and social status, but rather 'by *training them in the unconscious discipline of a code*, and competitive cooperation at the level of that code' (Baudrillard 1998: 94, 192; emphasis in original). Through TV, advertising and the mass media, 'the logic of consumption' confers on commodities not merely a use-value and economic exchange-value, but most significantly a sign-value: a sign of status differentiation (Baudrillard 1998: 61). By acquiring and displaying material goods, by their way of consuming, individuals attempt to differentiate themselves from others, that is, to gain prestige, status and identity. The consumer experiences this process of differentiation as one of freedom and choice, rather than as '*one of being forced to be different*, of obeying a code' (Baudrillard 1998: 61; emphasis in original). The first part of the film illustrates this double process of differentiation and homogenization: the way in which the sign-value dimension of the commodity simultaneously establishes the mode of perception and signification so that consumers can no longer distinguish between the real and its representation.

The first compelling example of this comes from Julia and her husband Ricardo, who has recently started to work as a bouncer in a disco. The couple's problems begin when Julia finds the apartment she is trying to sell so luxurious that she decides to spend a romantic night there with her husband. The apartment, with its TV, leather sofa, king-sized waterbed and even a jacuzzi and a Finnish sauna, symbolizes everything she lacks and wants to possess. Its fancy decoration and material comforts, its central location and the perfection it radiates hold the promise of bridging the distance between what Julia is and the fantasy of what she aspires to become, where all its objects are 'thinly disguised narcissistic delusions transferred onto the idealized commodity' (Gabriel and Lang 1995: 95).

Julia's self-delusions are interrupted by the arrival of Ricardo, who feels frustrated after finding out that his friend Antonio Pesadas – a former colleague in the insurance company that made them redundant years earlier – is driving a Mercedes taxi, while he is a mere bouncer in a disco. In a society where people compete to reaffirm their social status, Ricardo defines himself by comparing his lifestyle with that of Pesadas. Having drawn the shorter straw, the comparison makes him feel inferior and envious. His self-esteem and pride hurt, Ricardo is unable to share Julia's excitement about the apartment. Their romantic night is utterly ruined when they begin to use the waterbed and cockroaches start falling from a crack in the ceiling above. The apparent perfection of the apartment is as false as the promises that Julia sells her clients. In addition, a cutaway shot from the bedroom to the outside shows someone dressed in a Darth Vader costume and breathing heavily spying on them with binoculars, revealing that the apartment does not even guarantee the privacy it promised the couple.

The film is no less negative about the inhabitants of the building. The first time the neighbours appear on screen is when the fire department enters the building, alerted about the water leak from the apartment above Julia's. *Mise-en-scène* and cinematography link the neighbours' first appearance on screen to a series of TV images that Ricardo and Julia are watching after their experience with the cockroaches. The TV programme shows a couple of vultures in close-up, looking for prey from a tree while a voice-over comments on the images: 'The vulture, nature's gravedigger, devours the dead. When one vulture finds a carcass, twenty more appear to share it. A voracious jackal joins them. The sombre party continues until nothing's left.' From a low-angle shot that echoes the image of the two vultures looking for prey from a tree, the camera shows Encarna and Paquita wearing dark housecoats and standing in the old stairwell of the building. A zoom-in brings them closer to the viewers so that the couple's excitement can be seen when they look towards the old man's apartment, since they have been watching him for years, as the film will later reveal. Eager to confirm the old man's death, the rest of the neighbours gather round in front of his apartment like vultures before a carcass: Charlie (who turns out to be the heavy-breathing character dressed in Darth Vader apparel), his controlling mother, Dolores (who slaps him in the face for 'dressing like a drag queen!'), Ramona (who also slaps Charlie in the face), Julián and Hortensia. When a fireman mistakes Julia for the community's administrator, the neighbours turn their attention to her, positioning her as the intruder, the jackal who does not belong to the community: 'Who's she? Who are you? We don't know her.' The rapacious nature of both neighbours (vultures) and Julia (jackal) is made apparent shortly after the discovery of the old man's corpse. Domínguez, another neighbour, is seen digging through the old man's rubbish, while singing a pirate song: 'Fifteen men on a dead man's chest . . .' Moments later, Julia sings the same pirate song when she finds 300 million pesetas stashed under the floor of the old man's apartment.

The first part of the film ends with a mirror-like repetition of the earlier sequence at the luxurious apartment: while Julia dreams about the possibilities that the money could bring her, Ricardo's arrival interrupts these dreams. He says that he has quit the disco because the owner has beaten and humiliated him. Julia tries to tell him about her stroke of luck, but Ricardo shuts her up, arguing that he prefers not to imagine anything. At this precise moment a TV advertisement with the catchphrase, 'The strongest drug isn't speed. It's MONEY', displays a series of images of expensive cars and beautiful women, forcing him to imagine precisely the things he cannot afford. The TV advertising produces a contradictory effect on the couple. On the one hand, it increases Ricardo's frustration and resignation ('In this life, we'll never put our asses in one of those, unless we catch Pesadas' taxi', he tells Julia). On the other, it increases Julia's materialistic desires. The moment she has all the money for herself, her individualism runs amok: she gets rid of everyone standing between her and her desires, including her husband, whom she has no qualms about 'eliminating' through a heart attack when Oswaldo, a Latin lover and dance instructor, offers her a night of passion. This double effect reveals that '[t]he very process of production of aspirations is inegalitarian, since resignation at the bottom end of the social scale and freer aspirations at the top compound the inequality of objective possibilities of satisfaction' (Baudrillard 1998: 63).

In a society where money is the 'strongest drug', individuals such as Julia become 'addicts', 'unable to live without self-delusions, mediated by material goods, which ultimately aggravate [their] condition' (Gabriel and Lang 1995: 98). Those who on the other hand cannot see themselves as consumers are made invisible; like Ricardo, they are erased from the given regime of visibility. By keeping everyone in his or her place, the logic of the market ensures that individuals do not question their role as consumers: '[m]otives, desires, encounters, stimuli, the endless judgments of others . . . [and] the appeals of advertising . . . make up a kind of abstract destiny of collective participation, set against a real background of generalized competition' (Baudrillard 1998: 65). This is the double strategy of the market society: an ideological logic based on social homogenization and a concrete social logic based on structural differentiation (Baudrillard 1998: 66, 50).

The community of neighbours: the politics of consensus

The second part of the film opens with the fake welcome party that the community of neighbours organizes for Julia so as to inquire about her knowledge of the money. While they all wait for Julia's entrance, the scene visually positions the community's administrator, Emilio, as a commanding figure. At the moment Oswaldo announces Julia's arrival everybody is seen looking at Emilio, who orders everyone to get ready and, as the music begins, directs their moves like the conductor of an orchestra. Following Emilio's cue, the neighbours put on a show of an ideal community to entice Julia and prevent her escape. The significance of this farcical performance, I argue, consists less in confirming the viewers' suspicions about the rapacity and hypocrisy of the community than in the possibility of critically examining the regime of visibility that organizes the neighbours as a community and assigns each their respective places, powers and functions. By showing the performance of the neighbours while simultaneously revealing what is going on behind the scenes, the film discloses the gap between what the neighbours present as the 'common' of the community and the underlying divisions that define it (Rancière 2004b: 12).

The neighbours' performance takes place in three acts, each act reconfiguring the regime of intelligibility and the sense of community (Rancière 2009c: 31). Act one starts off with the fake party. Julia asks if all the people at the party are neighbours. Oswaldo responds that they are a 'very tight community'. Emilio adds that all the neighbours share a common interest in the building, as most of them have lived there all their lives. As an aside, Paquita and Encarna reveal that the only neighbour who did not share an interest in the common good was the old man, who went crazy after winning the *quiniela* and never wanted to leave his apartment – apparently because he was too afraid of them, they say, laughing hysterically. As if wanting to dispel any doubts, Oswaldo repeats that they are all like a family and that he feels lucky to live in the building. The scene closes with an image of the community pretending cheerfully to sing and dance together around Oswaldo and Julia.

The second act opens in the lift, when Julia tries to escape with the money in a suitcase after discovering the true intentions of the community. While in the first act the neighbours introduce themselves as a community bound together by a shared sense of belonging and identity, in this act they portray themselves as a contractual (that is, legal) community based on an agreement that allegedly entitles them to equal shares in the old man's money. First, Domínguez, who warns Julia that the neighbours are trying to kill him, explains that the neighbours agreed to watch the old man day and night to prevent him from escaping with the money, and then to share it after his death. He also explains that the engineer, the former resident of the luxurious apartment, did not accept the rules of the community and suddenly 'disappeared'. As the two try to exit the lift, Domínguez's body gets stuck between floors and is brutally cut in half. At this moment, Hortensia tries to get the money but Julia subdues her. Under threat, she tries to convince Julia of the 'good faith' of the community: the old man didn't enjoy his money, and the neighbours, wishing solely that it should not revert to the tax administration after his death, decided to sign an agreement to distribute it in equal shares. The rest of the neighbours join them on the staircase and try to persuade Julia to share their community of interest: 'There's enough money for everyone in there. You got what you needed to have. You won your share.'

Act three opens when Emilio violently forces Julia to enter the luxurious apartment. In a sort of monologue, Emilio places Julia as an outsider who is threatening to destroy what is presented as the ethical bond of the community. Even though they gave her the chance to 'be one of them' and 'share the luck' of living in the building, she has chosen instead to pursue her own pleasures and interests. The selfishness of which Emilio accuses her clashes with the values of solidarity, respect and sacrifice which the community predicates about itself: 'I feel sorry for your kind . . . You people think only of yourselves . . . You people don't want responsibilities . . . Well, we are different here. This is a community.' As evidence Emilio lists each member's particular needs ('García . . . needs a little car to get around town. Paquita . . . needs to get her teeth fixed'), aiming to position the community on higher ethical ground.

Whereas on stage the neighbours portray themselves as an ideal consensual community (on the basis of a shared identity, agreement and an ethical bond), behind the scenes the film unmasks an order of domination based on inequality and exclusion. This is most explicit in a conversation that takes place between Charlie and his mother at the fake party. Charlie asks his mother's permission to leave. His mother replies that he has to stay because Emilio says so. Charlie then complains that he never wanted to be part of it and that they forced him to sign the agreement ('You made me sign it'). His mother warns him that if he leaves he may end up like the engineer, which reveals that under the guise of agreement, the community is concealing the fact that there are individuals who, like Charlie, are not willing partners.

Throughout the film the community treats Charlie as an inferior being (a 'retard', as Castro calls him), dependent on his mother's care and incapable of independent will and thought. By relegating Charlie to this category, the community excludes him from the public space of collective negotiation and decision making. As Charlie is a 'retard', his unwillingness to participate cannot be recognized as 'disagreement' but as mere noise that need not be taken into account. By denying his capacity to speak and to think and act independently, the community justifies Charlie's exclusion. Paradoxically, in order to maintain the illusion of consensus, Charlie *must* sign the agreement. By his signature, Charlie is *included in the community without being part of the community*: he 'consents' to the given distribution of parts and functions without being allowed to participate in the making of that distribution. Through Charlie's 'inclusion', the community effaces any trace of false counting and exclusion, constructing a 'saturated community' in which the entirety of places, roles and identities are distributed, 'ruling out any supplement' (Rancière 2011e: 249).

By keeping everyone in their place, the logic of consensus dismisses any possible miscounting in the configuration of the 'common'. By this logic, 'the givens of any collective situation are objectified in such a way that they can no longer lend themselves to a dispute, to the polemical framing of a controversial world within the given world' (Rancière 2009c: 48). There are only two options for those who would challenge the consensus: either they are made to accept the common project, values and rules, and become members but not participants of the community (like Charlie); or, if they refuse (like the old man and the engineer), or are otherwise perceived to have violated the rules (like Domínguez), they become a threat that has to be eliminated, if necessary by force. Hence, when Julia sees through Emilio's rhetoric and accuses him of being 'a fraud and a thief, like [herself], like everybody' and of using the neighbours, Emilio stops pretending and tries to kill her. The scene ends with a confrontation to-the-death between Emilio and Julia, in which Julia finally kills him.

Dissensual Scenes: A Community of Equals

From the outset the film has established a regime of the all-visible that allows viewers to critically observe the gap between appearance and reality in both consumer and consensual societies. The film shows how the interplay of the logic of the market and the logic of consensus confines individuals to a depoliticized place: the market through its order of differentiation and competition; consensus through its order of classification and identification. These two logics transform society into a homogeneous and objectifiable *police-like* order that prescribes a specific regime of visibility that simultaneously 'passes itself off as the real' (Rancière 2010: 148), and imposes codes of conduct that determine individuals' behaviours and attitudes, discouraging them from questioning their assigned places and roles.

However, this regime of the all-visible presents a threefold dilemma: first, it establishes a hierarchical relationship between viewers and characters (viewers can see what the characters cannot); second, it establishes a position of mastery over the viewer (the film explains the 'reality' that viewers are not able to see for themselves); finally, it presents this reality as univocal and incontrovertible, 'the world as it is', which becomes altogether visible to the viewer with all its appearances and realities, inclusions and exclusions, and that the viewer has to accept as the world he or she lives in. Arguably, this topography of hierarchy, mastery and ineluctability risks reproducing the police order that the film claims to denounce. In this section, I show how Charlie, seemingly the least capable character in the film, stages a *dissensus* within the film's regime of visibility that, by exposing the contingency of the given, generates a new topography of the possible. This is precisely the point where Charlie's political act of subjectivation and the aesthetic irruption within the viewer's field of perception meet.

The last part of the film opens with Charlie unexpectedly entering the old man's apartment through a hole in the ceiling (which he planned to use with the old man) to help Julia escape. As Charlie and Julia make their way out to the rooftop, Charlie exchanges the suitcase with the money for another identical one, unbeknown to her. On the rooftop the following dialogue takes place:

> *Charlie*: This is my plan. You escape. I'll create a distraction, like in the Death Star.
> *Julia*: What Star?
> *Charlie*: Han Solo distracted the Stormtroopers while Luke and the Princess fled, remember?
> *Julia*: This isn't *Star Wars*.
> *Charlie*: The Force is with me.
> *Julia*: They could kill you.
> *Charlie*: Don't worry, nothing will happen. I'll play dumb as always. Trust me.

Julia runs off with the suitcase and Charlie, still dressed in his Darth Vader costume, confronts the neighbours with a fake plastic sword. Oswaldo and Castro wonder 'Why is this retard here?' and beat him up. His mother pronounces 'Your father was right. We should've drowned you at birth,' and they all go after Julia.

In the quoted conversation between Charlie and Julia, Charlie uses the fictional world of *Star Wars* to explain his plan of escape. When Julia warns him that he does not live in a fictional world but in one where he could actually get killed, Charlie tells her to trust him and assures her that he will 'play dumb as always', implying that nothing will happen if he continues to play the marginal role that the community assigns him. At the same time, Charlie's confession that he will play dumb 'as always' reveals his playing dumb as a deliberate strategy, which makes him smarter than he looks, demonstrating to the viewer that 'dumb' is not a category to which he belongs. Behind the role the community has assigned him – and that he has playfully adopted – is an intelligent person capable of outsmarting them. By playing 'dumb' – by making himself of no account – Charlie not only manages to distract the neighbours and facilitate Julia's escape, but also to protect himself – had the community realized his true plans, he would most likely have been killed.

Thus what appears at first as a utopian fantasy – the fantasy of a freak dressed as Darth Vader rescuing Princess Leia from the Imperial Stormtroopers – becomes the narrative framework for what is actually happening. In the end, Charlie becomes Han Solo, able to defy the Galactic Empire (the community) in order to help Princess Leia (Julia). Likewise, his words 'The Force is with me', used earlier in the context of masturbation, become representative of his real strength, forcing viewers to recast him no longer as a freak or a pervert. For the first time, Charlie dissents from the identity, role and place that he had been assigned and inscribes himself as an equal not in the field of perception of the community – which continues to hear his words as mere noise and perceive his actions as invisible – but in that of the viewer. Charlie's appearance as a political subject (not the 'illusion', but his emergence) introduces a heterogeneous element into the viewer's field of perception that at once breaks it and reconfigures it. By acting out the presupposition of equality,[1] Charlie brings a *wrong* into the open: like the rest of the neighbours, the viewers had been practising the same politics of exclusion that they thought they were criticizing.

In a central way, Charlie's aesthetic irruption is a dispute over the film's own configuration of the sensible in relation to the viewer, that is, over the frame within which the film invites viewers to observe something as given. By demonstrating that he is *other* than expected, which is not to say that he reveals a reality concealed beneath appearances, Charlie stages a *dissensus* between two sensory worlds: 1) the regime of the all-visible, which presents itself through identification and classification as incontrovertible reality; and 2) the world created by Charlie's political subjectivation, which through dis-identification and declassification breaks apart the unity of the given and exposes its contingency. The meeting point between these two worlds sketches a new *sense* of reality – a new configuration and ways of making sense of it – that subverts hierarchy and mastery and opens up a space for a 'community of equals' between Charlie and the viewer – a horizontal community with no assigned places or destinations.

This aesthetics of *dissensus* can have a political effect, following Rancière, provided that one no longer understands this as a relationship of cause and effect (Rancière 2009a: 15). The politics of the film escapes the intentions and strategies of the filmmaker, for between the idea of the filmmaker and the sensation and comprehension of the viewer there is always a 'third thing', 'the film itself', whose meaning is owned by no one, is controlled by no one, but nevertheless subsists between them (2009a: 14–15). The political strength of *La Comunidad* does not lie in the specific effects it aims to produce in the viewer or in the way it invites viewers to critically observe a certain reality. It is rather the encounter between the film (insofar as it is a 'third thing') and the viewer (insofar as emancipated from the totalizing gaze of the camera) that makes Charlie's aesthetic irruption political.

Charlie and Julia: After the Political Act of Subjectivation

Charlie's political act of subjectivation has unforeseen consequences for Julia. In the climactic scene in which Julia and Ramona confront each other under the gigantic equestrian sculptures, Ramona replicates but inverts Julia's earlier words to Emilio in order to make her admit that she is like the rest of the neighbours ('You're just like us, like everyone!'). This time, however, Julia sees her reflection in Ramona and rejects the identification – 'No. I won't be like you!' – and throws the suitcase with the money at Ramona, who, in trying to catch it, falls to her death in the courtyard of the building. A low-angle shot shows Julia looking down at Ramona's body. She lies on the floor the same way Julia (and the old man) did moments earlier in the old man's apartment, which visually suggests that Julia could be the one lying dead had she not renounced the money. Viewers learn about the community's fate from a newspaper headline shown in close-up: 'Neighbours kill each other for money that doesn't exist', referring to the fake Monopoly money that Charlie had put in the suitcase.

Several days after the incident, Julia reads the following ad in the newspaper: 'Darth Vader needs Princess for a serious relationship. Julia, I need you. The Force is with me. Those interested go to "El Oso y el Madroño".' Julia meets up with Charlie at the bar and asks him directly: 'Why didn't you tell me you switched suitcases? They almost killed me.' Charlie explains that had he told her, the neighbours would probably have guessed it and she would not have been able to escape. More importantly, Charlie admits that he also wanted to see if Julia was like his mother.

The final scene closes with an image that both replicates and distances itself from the fake party that the neighbours organize for Julia. If that scene presented a grotesque image of the community of neighbours pretending to sing and dance happily around Julia and Oswaldo so as to inquire about the money, this last scene shows a grotesque image of a 'community' of freak-look-alike clients happily dancing and singing around Julia and Charlie, while the latter shares the money with everyone. The ambiguity of this 'false' happy ending has led critics to different interpretations, which vary between understanding it as a comeback to the anachronism that the community of neighbours represents (Buse et al. 2007: 135–6), or as the creation of 'an *other* community' that transcends it (Moreiras-Menor 2011: 159). In my opinion, and by way of conclusion, such ambiguity could be interpreted as both return and departure, both as the impossibility of eliminating every order of domination that coexists and as the possibility of creating new forms of political subjectivation (new Charlies) that are able to dissent from the regime of the given.

Note

1. Equality, as Rancière understands it, is not 'a goal politics sets itself the task of attaining. It is a mere assumption that needs to be discerned within the practices implementing it' (Rancière 1999a: 33).

7

Inhuman Spectatorship

Patricia MacCormack

In *On the Shores of Politics* Rancière describes the task of politics as giving substance to the evanescent moment which regulates the multiplicity of ecstatic pleasures found in *demos*, what he calls a 'jubilant' ethics. Evanescence is found in the 'in-between'. The evanescent moment is defined as the event of 'the philosophical realisation of the art of politics' (Rancière 1995: 19). As these three trajectories of art, politics and philosophy coalesce to transform themselves as in-between discourse, they emancipate the evanescent moment from being an ideational or mythic impossible utopia, opening out the possibility of a realizable utopia. The future of the image and the flesh of expression are found through their seduction in excess of meaning as anticipation, gesture and effect. These ideas have many resonances with cinema studies. As Rancière corporealizes politics, so too film theory can take representation itself away from recognition and repetition and thus the subjectivity of spectatorship away from centralized human positions whose patterns of apprehension shatter into a dissipative multiplicity.

A democracy of spectatorship raises a series of issues which address the past political mobilization of alternate voices of aesthetic expression and spectatorial affect, leading to the difficulty of thinking a community of spectators but not spectatorship as necessarily solitary. I will lead this to a configuration of spectatorship as an artistic mode of expression – spectatorship as relation with but also unto itself as art. Through Rancière's elaborations of the art of images, played out in a theatre of material expression which replaces any adherence to the pitfalls of the idea of representation as meaning, this chapter will explore the suggestion by many philosophers, such as Lyotard (1991), Guattari (1995), Foucault (1997), Blanchot (1993; 2003) and Deleuze (Deleuze and Guattari

1994), that art belongs to and makes us inhuman and a-human, negotiating the very premise of the human, and thus by being art, spectatorship is beyond the human. A turn towards inhuman spectatorship's desire in thought potentializes an inhuman and thus ethical mode of desire for and with film. This chapter will take Rancière as part of the group of theorists of the inhuman cited above to show that not only can all modes of cinematic relation be inhuman but also that we can, optimistically, inhumanize the potentials of perception of all cinema to dissipate and make dissonant the uses, effects and perverse relations between images, theorists and subjects to open up futures.

Rancière's exploration of the philosophical encounter between art and politics shows that the effacement of a centre effaces the concept of the subject as not empirical but constitutive, and 'becoming-inhuman . . . is the very language whereby *aesthetic* fiction is opposed to *representative* fiction' (2007a: 126). Genius, according to Rancière, is 'not knowing', jubilance not being and ethics found in the unrepresentable but nonetheless encountered. The category of human as spectator which precedes the image but is required as the location of its expressivity seems a broad and ambiguous category, but at its core the human is used as a vindication for the search for affirmation of the powers inherent in those who seek their own categorization as worthy subjects who simultaneously decide who counts as human and who does not – be they creators or receivers – and more specifically spectatorship as a patterned terrain of power which these subjects occupy. The concept of the image and its limits precedes selves to coalesce multiple intensities into categories prepared for the possibility of existing as jubilant spectators, not the potentialities of existence of image or spectator. The parameters of the spectator offer liberation to their oppressed when alterity is included in the subsets of different possibilities of being spectator or when the other as image, though no less materially affective for being so, achieves acceptable levels of registers of being resonant enough with human perception. Being a human spectator can insinuate being capable of one kind of perception and perceptibility. This mode is formulated by all orders of signification and all things having to be signified so they may be ordered. Nothing escapes. Concepts of the inhuman and a-human spectator do not oppose the human. The prefix a-, a-desire, a-signification and a-human, denotes without connoting. It is before, between and beyond, most importantly without correct or possible apprehension and its amorphous isomorphic oppositions. 'A-' prefixed terms are no less concrete or material for being such, they simply demand the 'we' that perceives alter. We seek catalysts to become inhuman and a-human spectators in order to go without. The inhuman is neither human nor not human. The very category itself is no longer available, either for purposes of evaluation or existence. Spectatorship is an example where becoming inhuman requires a not-knowing and not-being, not through what Rancière critiques as nihilistic humanism, but the human becoming aesthetic, an enfleshed corporeal aestheticization of politics, not a series of empty shopping-list 'transgressive' representations, licit or illicit. Cinema as art offers us the connection with asignifiable particles that demand that we perceive beyond human comprehension, or the image (as multi-sensorial emergence including sound and other despotic elements) cannot emerge. Inhumanism does not seek additions, opposites or radical others. The inhuman shows the hypocrisy of history evaluating worthy, rational and civilized behaviour premised on the spectre of the category of 'human being' as register of the qualities of actions and knowledge, both in ways the spectator comes to the image and coalesces with imagistic intensities. Becoming a- and inhuman gifts the comfort of being a subject to possible encounters with the outside – within self and connected to other elements as a band of consistency, potentiality beyond possibility, thought beyond knowledge, perception beyond what we believe is able to be perceived (and how). The scariest part is that we continue to exist when there are no categories, inevitably where world becomes cinema and cinema world. The gift of self should be scary, because politics is about risk and art the exploitation of potentials of what can be experienced as cinema. Rancière's ethics offers techniques of regulating the risks and limits of spectatorship and the politics of aesthetics – the evanescent in-betweens of desire, seduction and spectatorship as anticipation, jubilance and gesture.

Despotic elements of alterity in familiarity with images as recognizable and ways by which apprehension of images logically collide with inhuman spectatorship add on to multiply elements of singular constitutive paradigms which elicit oppression so that the image is emphatically more than one. Discussion often limits itself to what has been (experience of possibilities of perception) and what is to come (recognition, sometimes inclusion, sometimes radicalization of modes of perception). Liberation comes in my use of Rancière and other theorists of the in- and a-human through the falling away of human spectatorship rather than the becoming-human through the comforting assurances of images confirming one world populated by representations of subjugated others which is still needed but along a different trajectory of enquiry. Lee Edelman demarcates that 'the most crucial and constitutive dramas of human life are those that can never be viewed head on, those that can never be taken in frontally, but only approached from behind' (1994: 175). Edelman claims that the 'front on' gaze of the singular plane sees nothing, which Irigaray's work would dismiss as a phallologic search premised on female sexuality/genitalia as having nothing to see or being seen as nothing only through a (particular kind of) human gaze (Irigaray 1985: 47), picked up by much post-psychoanalytic feminist film theory. By claiming that his work resists standpoint theory as based on 'human experience' as a minoritarian activist, Edelman emphasizes the problems with both the terms human and experience; however, he persists with and insists on identity, even if it is one of performance over registering. Seeking the dramas is a ruse for actualizing the human via vindicated as authentic modes of perception, constituted by the affirmation of the possibility of the human which precludes the search. Edelman urges theoretical transgression within activist discussion and vice versa. For spectatorial theory, modes of perception are activisms which dissipate the unbound spectator's openness to the outside of registering; however, it does not entirely forget the invisible, silenced or detrimentally represented subject of history. It does, rather, take inspiration from the unrepresentability at the core of the non-dominant.

Spectatorship, like all philosophical enquiries which require a loosely defined subject as a point of relation over a dividuated isolated essence, is formed of a constellation of specific territories which intersect to create their own unique terrains. Butler's connection between the difficulties of rationality as it is responsible to actual corporeal human beings can be seen in her discussion of Levinas. She states that responsibility 'cannot be tied to a conceit of a self fully transparent to itself . . . *reason's limit is the sign of our humanity*' (2005: 83; my emphasis). Art as inhuman catalyst is experienced beyond systems of logic and so can be used to navigate Butler's recognition that reason makes us human and we are human because we claim that truth is found through reason. There is no reasonable representation, or reasonable perception. The

Enlightenment thought that she criticizes as a necessary residue towards ethics is precisely what Rancière and other philosophers of the inhuman forsake. Continental philosophers often wrote as a response to remarkable, radical and historically significant real-life events, such as May 1968, the Reale Law, and for Lyotard and Rancière the Holocaust and so forth. Of the event they grappled with how to represent without reduction, and testify without singular authorization. While I suggest that their concepts seek inhuman intensities as an ethical turn, they are very much part of their own concrete political moments, the actuality of which is reduced to representation, ideational and aesthetic. The proliferation of trajectories and the strange relations they create, rather than their commensurability or incommensurability with 'authentic' representation, 'activism' and 'identity', is a manoeuvre of inhuman cinematic coalescence.

Rancière claims that equality is not democracy and justice not the management of wrong (1999a: 63). This means that any attempt to represent the wrong event or wronged neither manages nor erodes it. The traditional relation of politics and aesthetics to philosophy posits representation for and as philosophy as an analysis which comes after the political sphere, and only when a representational material philosophy replaces politics can politics be achieved. The place of *demos*, before the performance of a philosophy, that is, before representation and hoped for reception, is retarded.

> The demos is there, with its three features: The erecting of a sphere for the name of the people to appear; the unequal count of this people that is both whole and part at the same time; the paradoxical revelation of the dispute by a part of the community that identifies with the whole in the very name of the wrong that makes it the other party. (1999a: 62)

Can the spectatorial-image sphere be a liberatory demos? The place of demos describes our condition of emergence and recognition as a human one, because only humans can populate a political democracy and only by being acknowledged in this place of demos can we count as human, by virtue of these three features. These three features themselves are what define humanity and thus humanity is simply a pre-formed space of occupation which occurs when the material actuality of certain flesh is occupied by these features. A politics of inhuman spectatorship is prevented from emerging as a philosophy of ethical cinema when film theorists come into being only through the context by which spectatorship could emerge in the antecedent order of signification. The fight for recognition of the representation of the other – as wronged or made invisible – would then homogenize the other both as aesthetic figure or 'character' and as spectator, while ghettoizing it as other. The other represented, perceived and perceiving would find its political position transgressed through the elements of the antecedent order and seek to identify with the dominant order so that it may count as part of that order. This justifies the conditions of oppression because it seeks those conditions to no longer oppress the now reified community of wronged other, what Rancière points out is the 'emergence of a part identical with the whole' (1999a: 61). Many issues arise here which refer back to the very conditions of possibility by which feminist psychoanalytic film theory, as one example, emerged as a necessary and combative politics of deconstruction of objectification and project of liberatory inclusion without assimilation. The politics of female representation, beginning with the fight for different recognition and the right to self-representation, became an incremental inclusive politics of the 'add-on' – racial others, non-heteronormative sexualities, the historically violated and so forth – did identify with the oppressor as the politics first incepted the peopling of the oppressive regime with recognition of new kinds of people who had been 'wronged'. To be righted was to be made a minority with an ambition to be subsumed, but still always as a minority, into the majority. Righting the wrong atrophied the other through the system of the same and subsumation vindicated the system itself by only offering inclusion, not paradigmatic shifts in the mechanisms of emergence. Representation as inclusion cannot liberate perception as activism.

Beyond representation of the other, by the other, inhuman spectatorship both challenges the subjectivization of the spectator in relation to visualized subjects and the space of the cinematic demos. It demands encounters with desire, not, as Rancière laments of politics, a result of policing – righting the wrong, participation without interference – but of expression and multiplicity. The expression of inhuman spectatorship is a voice of reception, an activist passivity, without commonality, a community of the uncommon, not because each spectatorial participant is different but because the tenets of perception itself are neither forthcoming

nor deferential to particular conditions of possibility that ensure
the structure by which the future may emerge. When the demos
demands a response by the oppressed to the question which does
not yet exist, it performs the elliptical function of subjectivization
of which Rancière is so critical in his negotiation of Althusser. 'The
field of knowledge is thus structured as a weaving of questions and
answers that do not belong to each other but whose very disparity is an earnest of sufficiency: an enormous reserve of answers to
bad questions waiting for good questions' (Rancière 2004c: 133).
Within this elliptical logic the others of representation are allowed
political inclusion when their questions fit with pre-formed answers
awaiting them – on the side of creation of film, is it an authentic
representation, on that of spectatorship are we watching it right?
The structure of inclusion is a question to which the answer
already exists and thus political liberation through representation
or primary presentation its own new form of oppression. What,
then, does inhuman spectatorship do to this system? Rancière sees
philosophy with politics as encompassing 'phrased chaos, linkages
without syntax, whispering, music and other expressive voices'
(2007a: 58–9). A politics of inhuman spectatorship makes all
cinematic expressivity despotic, and is impossible within the logic
of representation of consistent patterns of aesthetic encounters. A
unified voice of the oppressed or non-included must be a different kind of voice, not one with different content, and it does not
belong to the represented or non-represented. All spectators must
become inhuman. It is the 'subject' of the spectator as actualizing
an expressivity in the world as speaking subject that must change,
not the image as speech (the inhumanism of which will necessarily follow). The shift from the image as communicative speech to
sonority, timbre, whispers, visual shimmers, kinetic quiverings
and other visual-vocal aberrations inclines towards an inhuman
mode of expression as one of art not politics, or politics as art.
This is what Rancière demands when he calls for a political philosophy as politics without politics, metapolitics, the politics of gaps
and the beyond. 'Anti-representative art is constitutively an art
without un-representable things. There are no longer any inherent
limits to representation, to its possibilities. This boundlessness also
means that there is no longer a language appropriate to a subject,
whatever it might be' (2007a: 137). The ethical turn occurs when
the jubilance towards possibilities and impossibilities of art simultaneously addresses what Rancière, discussing Lyotard, calls 'an

ethical logic of denunciation of the very phenomenon of representation' (2007a: 131). Rancière sees the bearing down of structures
upon the events through which they are incarnated as irreducibly
singular as planes of expression. For Rancière discourse is never
extricable from events, which is where disagreement differs from
Lyotard's 'differend' (1999a: xi).

By enhancing alternative modes of aesthetic expression without
privileging any one mode or one constitutive expressive form,
Rancière circumvents, and offers a salient warning against, the
risks of hyper-performativity or what he calls exaggeration of
elements of alterity, which are transgressive or considered inherently more artistic or unrepresentable than any other. The object
of representation is there, irrefutably, undeniably, perhaps even
devastatingly. It is not a shadowy simulacrum which revels in the
perceived lack of its own presence. However, it is unrepresentable and the event of our experience of it unthinkable (2007a:
130–1). Lyotard invokes the contradiction in the sublime where
we must bear witness to what cannot be apprehended as testament to itself but which is indeterminate. Rancière's attention to
the incommensurable notion in Lyotard's critique of a structuring
of the sublime laments the impasse in creating a relation between
unrepresentability and un-thinkability as itself establishing a dialectic of indeterminacy. What Rancière's redemption of Lyotard
offers is the idea of a submission (2007a: 136) – by the object and
presumably the event itself, a painful experience of ecstatic, irrefutably activist, passive reception because we must bear witness to
the impossible without renouncing the event. Here Rancière sees
Lyotard offering a way out of Hegel's end of art, where the beyond
insinuates 'bad infinity' (2007a: 136). Rancière both extends and
circumvents Lyotard's sublime beyond as a fidelity to an original
debt. Correspondence between representation and aesthetics is
repudiated in favour of correspondence as a paradoxical event
that encounters the event of its own system of making the desiring aesthetic moment possible, not as nomenclature but indeterminacy with accountability. Such a configuration of the event
resonates with the spectatorial event – all spectatorship is event
without precedent of expectation and possibility, and reflection
as affirmation – while being indeterminate and outside traditional
dialectics. It nonetheless accounts for its affects and shows ethical
address to its own paradoxes. The conditions of presence are
altered. Here is where the ethics of the shift from spectatorship

as identity-based politics of representation to spectatorship as a
form of art itself occurs. Beyond a politics of inclusion with the
risks of the three tenets of demos, inhuman spectatorship is absolute; it is everything as despotic expressivity capable of catalysing
inhuman affect, not an aberrant object. As inhuman spectators we
are neither the same nor disparate, neither unified nor multiple:
inhuman spectators seeking alternate revocations with perception
and relation. Rather than, as Rancière critiques, vocalizing a desire
for representation which leads to the perils of performative exaggeration, we spectators are *desirings*.

   In a political philosophy of inhuman spectatorship desire is
voluminously present but without the possibility of representation
because it is never the same as itself. It is better then to understand
desiring as a-desire, permanently present, beyond presented object,
limit or consciousness. Certain terms arise which seem antitheti-
cal to poststructuralism's repudiation of essence, but it is precisely
where these emerge that Rancière redeems the vacuity of much
postmodern thought and the image and reminds us of the material
ethics poststructuralism seeks. Political collectivity *is* apolitical,
but only insofar as it is a living paradox, with the emphasis on life
– neither metaphor nor analogy. The image thus is also apolitical
in and of itself. The grave question of how to activate politics as a
living paradox beyond these two temptations is also the question
without answer, or the answer which cannot find a suitable question. Film is politics without syntax, activism paradox through
ecstasy, the constant state of spectatorship as desiring liberated
from positive pleasure or negative repudiation, from time and location. Extricating itself from the syntaxes of desire – for the object,
its mode of representation or voice, its resonance with spectatorial
subject, emergence through recognition-representation and most
crucially for the appropriate question to which the self-object is
the 'good' *or* 'bad', 'authentic' *or* 'inauthentic' or even 'art-film'
or 'failed art' answer – inhuman spectatorial desiring is ecstasy.
Ecstasy, like art itself, like the event, is immanent. It is beyond
causality and pre-formed futurity. It is what the subject is, not
what the subject is in, like spectatorial desiring, the noun itself
becomes verb. But it has very definite, concrete affective qualities
and brings into being through the unique qualities of its ecsta-
sies new patterns of potentiality, perception and expression. It is
adamant in the relations it creates, but inhuman spectatorship as
a state of desiring cannot represent or describe, only acknowledge

and tactically reflect on the specificity of new conditions produced. Ethical address comes from the distancing of self from self to momentarily slow the space-state of ecstasy to allow the self to recede. The interval is the point of reflection but because events of ecstasy are unrepresentable ethical reflection can only ever be a fleeting relation of proximity and affectivity. This means the image is liberated from representation by being a part of an unrepresentable event. The event cannot be reflected upon as an externalized and reified strategy of address – a desiring relation between two, the material human cleaved from the synthetic image. It presents, as the necessary impossible of observing, the effects and dissipations of objects, both of which are material, through desire, without ever being able to be an observer. Like ecstasy itself, the cinematic image as politics hurts as much as it pleasures, and, like politics, is neither good nor bad, right nor wrong, but 'the double specificity of political dialogue' (Rancière 1999a: 43). Political rationality comes from a freeing from choice – good/bad, pleasure/pain, right/wrong – thus the in-between and the beyond takes as its first moment the forsaking of duality, which Rancière states serves subjectivity. Subjectivity serves also the division between logic and alogia, the division of 'man' as machine with rationality. To adhere to this division, remaining faithful to the perceived extrication of logos from the mechanical animal of Aristotle, stays with the arithmetic of the animal as plane of exchange and allocation. Inhuman spectatorship can neither be allocated nor exchanged. It also cannot serve its own subjectivity as the subject is mobilized. So the speech of asubjective politics is simultaneously animal and logical, thus must be inhuman. Rancière sees political speech 'at once argumentative and poetical' because we are no longer the '"we" nor the identity assigned to it' (1999: 59). Inhuman spectatorship manifests as politically real, as actual flesh which virtualizes new possibilities of further actualizations of constantly new flesh, but there is no 'we', neither of the image–spectator relation, nor the 'audience', and no identity. Logic comes from the inhuman non-we experience of images, but is logical as it uses language to elaborate and think, actualize and incant. The relations this logic makes are tangible and its effects are irrefutable. Inhuman logic sees no illogically pre-human/human division of sense-thought, a-representation does not follow an image/subject divide, and a-reality accepts material realities of both image and spectator without signification or reification. Desiring as and through these is how inhuman spectatorship emerges, as activist event of art, against the politics of inclusion, allocation, measurement and policing.

Rancière suggests 'the power of art [equates with] the obliteration of the boundaries between the human and the inhuman, the living and the dead, the animal and the mineral, all alike merged in the density of the sentence or the thickness of the pictorial paste' (2007a: 27). What much Continental philosophy has offered in its own negotiation of subjectivity is precisely why few have limited their theory of film as demarcated art object as extricated from 'life' philosophy. Spectatorship as a self, even if its is an expressive power of self, while encompassing the kind of activist philosophy often necessary for pragmatic alterations in, for example, representative inclusion and creation by and of alterity, is incommensurable with residual subjectivity as a dialectic logically perceiving subject. More correctly, Continental philosophy's spectatorial subject is neither subject nor spectating-subject, as we find in Rancière's work the shift from noun object to adjectival element (1999a: 72). The shift is not simply for the minority because, as stated above, the grouping of the oppressed is unsatisfactory for a turn towards evanescent demos. The extrication, however, between alterity itself and the dominant takes risks if the dominant is also not acknowledged as an expression of force – a kind of *style*, whose adaptability to offer the answer which demands the oppressed choose the correct question in order to be included knows no limits. Thus by not privileging minoritarianism as expressive force against the dominant as atrophied group Rancière makes clear the in-between space as decentring both elements and thus the opposition itself dissipates, forcing all engagements to alter their tactics and thus the nature of their group*ing*.

The phantasy of the collective insinuates a relatively straightforward wiping out of that group. Inhuman aesthetic expressivity forms with the spectator a dance. The dance of the transgressive (but never for their own sake) with the dominant is precisely that – a gestural dance where the making evanescent of the spaces of the dance – the territory or demos and the puissance of the conjugal relations of bodies as political matter – is the focus. Where all are minority none are minoritarian-ed, but all spectatorial desire, expressivity and openness to affect becomes accountable as its own affective specificity and power. Thus Rancière in his collapse of binaries names them boundaries, spaces and tempos rather than demarcated entities. The binaries which collapse do not privilege the space between spectator and image but the consistency of the qualities of relations when their categorization disappears, so even the notion of both and neither becomes unsatisfactory. The matter of elements is a question. The political ethic tries to address (but not answer) the question of the specificity of relation without breaking it into one of two, or two plus the space between as a privileged third site. So the question asks how do we shift politics from oppositional apprehension and inclusion to an activism formed of spectatorial image encounter as a dance? As dance is gestural art, it is part of two art forms Rancière focuses on – poetry and the image. Art is not different to politics but understanding politics through and as art may allow differing modes of expression of alterity imperative to all. As my interpretation of Rancière argues, the inhuman will be not opposed to the human, but will be all. This creates a resonance with the aims of spectatorial desiring–affect–alterity to demand an acknowledgement of the constant state of desire present within all subjects and relations that simultaneously demands accountability. The density and consistency matter (and materialize the matter). The question is not what but how? How, when inhuman spectatorship is art, does politics shift the *demos*?

Two elements are emphasized in the work of Rancière, neither of which are extricated from politics nor de-politicized: the image, which encompasses anything that is visually apprehended (or a-apprehended) and the word. Rancière demarcates three orders of the image. The naked image refuses any possibility of resemblance as it testifies to an absolute reality and thus does not define itself as art. The ostensive image, while acknowledging itself as art, claims a pure presence without need for a signified. If the naked image testifies to absolute reality then the ostensive testifies to pure art. The metaphorical image is defined by dissemblance and delimitation, creating localized singular consistency. The metaphorical is always a relation. But it does not oppose the norm with the not-norm, the traditional with the subversive, it is a plane of disfiguration or 'shared surface' (2007a: 105). Pure art and impure art are not two principles but differing organizations on the same plane (2007a: 105–6). The question is how can we make inhuman the organization? By way of a tactical explication of resonances how can these three organizations show the possible emergences of an inhuman spectatorship?

The first organizing principle addresses the human most directly. For this reason I will survey the naked image in that it may help negotiate the crucial, problematic and ultimately indecidable issue of 'real-life' politics and spectatorship as 'theory'. As minoritarian spectatorship and representation (as opposed to, say, the use of a politics of desire in most Continental philosophy) came from specific issues of rights of certain bodies and the irrefutable violence perpetrated upon the bodies of these minorities I think it essential to raise the issue of 'real-life violence', to which most naked images testify. This offers a way in which Rancière's work on the image can help film theory as political philosophy to go beyond the real-life/theory split, while still acknowledging the suffering of bodies. Testimony to naked reality is a difficult but perhaps necessary phantasy of relation. Witnessing an image of the absolute reality of an event requires a belief in that event without our presence. Our presence thus must be imagined as real in front of the image whose event-reality lacks in us, while the reality of the event, poverty-stricken in its lack of us at the moment of its reality, demands our belief in that reality. The subject and authenticity need to be retained to an extent. Frequently these kinds of images are testifying not to a reality – they are rarely ordinary – but to a horrific event and lamentation of erroneously termed 'inhumanity' – the suggestion that for something to be inhuman means it is nothing more than a brutish devaluation of the human. This insipidly insinuates both that everything that is not human is inhuman, thus brutal, and that the human should be valued more than anything. Most often these events are never about the image or even testament to its reality. The real is neither the event of the image nor the authenticity of the spectatorial relation. It refers to one of the few ideas which are irrefutable, namely death. It is a rare case when 'death of what' as a poststructural negotiation of subjectivity loses its force. The political territory is not one of reality/phantasy, falsity/truth or presence/lack but of the effects by which a turn to this kind of image taken as real can show the horror of the powers of a certain treatment of other emergences of 'life' upon a specific territory of relation. It is precisely because the territory is seen to be 'human' only so far as certain persons are understood as counting or not counting as human that these events of violence happen.

These images are testament to a particular configuration of the organization of elements, and this organization is precisely that which is most traditionally understood as human. The human organizes the territory and the witnessing of that image. But as Rancière points out 'one must annihilate oneself and also annihilate one's claim to be an interpreter . . .' (2004c: 85). Indeed Rancière sees the imperative to take the word (and multi-sensorial cinematic image as one kind of 'word') as real in its affects as both absurd and annihilating the very flesh of the reader, as a wound. (This argument raises many complex and impossible issues addressed by Lyotard [1988], Derrida [1992a] and Nancy [2000] among others.) What I am concerned with here is not the issue of testament of violence per se via representation but of territories which result in it. Knowledge of an event does little, exposure as testament is problematic at best, if representative without reterritorialization of mode of expression and perception. Thought incited through the encounter with an image demands a response to the conditions of the territory by which an event occurred. Some issues which could express a naked relation of inhuman spectatorship are most obviously the acts and results of the refusal of rights for alterity – irreducibly human acts.

The focus on rights creates an unsatisfactory demos of subsumation and simultaneous expulsion. Just as we may ask 'what do spectators (minoritarian or majoritarian) have in common' which demands a homogenization of an oppressed or dominant group, we also ask what benefits are gained by bearing witness to the oppression of minoritarians? A relation of art with the naked image insinuates naked qualities of the oppressed. Minority representation and readings emerged as a direct and radical repudiation of any grouping of persons based on shared perceptive identity-based standpoint politics. Like the image which doesn't necessarily name the victim of violence, spectatorship doesn't name its inherent qualities – not what we are but *that* we are. As it is difficult to understand inhuman spectatorship extricated from a binary of being opposed to another, especially only one other, term, inhuman spectatorship offers an escape route from the problems of categorization of image Rancière sees as working against a political philosophy, no matter how adamant and eventually 'recognized' minoritarian spectatorship is. If the human is the ubiquitous category which begins with a locus of dialectic communication of transcendental subject with transcendental image then counting as human necessitates a categorization (always within a hierarchy, always essentialized in order to find the appropriate space).

An inhuman art, which in this chapter posits inhuman spectatorship as an art politics, can be testimony to an event in that it neither accepts nor refuses. Rancière claims of art that it is always a slippage, and when it is given an impermeable genre or 'institutionalized' as unreal, the slippages of art-reality are denied. He says books are

> attestations to the existence of what they discuss . . . Fiction forms part of reality as a particular space-time in which socially acceptable laws (passion drives one mad) produce fantastic consequences with which one can amuse oneself without trouble, since they do not go beyond the imaginary situation. (2004c: 88–9)

We must believe in fiction, to which all film belongs as creative emergence in spite of genre, as testament to its effects rather than as describing it as reality. Fiction which alters terrains moves desire for conservative economies of knowledge towards inhuman passions of thought. If the naked image demands testament without imagination it is because the events are unimaginable. Only thinking – imagining – the conditions of potentialities which made them emerge can apprehend the territory in order to acknowledge the gravity of the event. Irreducibly separating fiction and reality institutionalizes the image as real but without any inflammation that demands we act. Fantastic consequences – ethical revolutions – can come only through realizing the image as unimaginable but no less real for being so. Making inhuman our relation with the naked image as one of art over raw testament is the only way ethical consequences can emerge. Rancière emphasizes that liberty comes only from incommensurables (1999a: 42). The naked image sees art and reality as incommensurable and thus risks turning from liberty, while the experience of the metaphorical image demands incommensurables as the very principle of opening new futures, 'a fresh sphere of visibility for further demonstrations' (1999a: 42).

The ostensive image may seem more appealing in 'confessing' itself as art. However, here I wish to take Rancière's use of art to its limit. Art, as film and spectatorship, is a practice of thought or, for Rancière, a labour (but without capital). The metaphorical image refuses art as extricated from other spheres as it functions as a playing on 'the ambiguity of resemblances and the instability of dissemblances' (2007a: 24). If inhuman spectatorship is the infinite in-between which knows not the binaries it is between, nor the nature of its own between-ness, then it can offer a form of art in that it is made of 'an articulation of two contradictory operations' (2007a: 71). The collapses which invoke art as slippage perform for Rancière a perversion. While film, painting and words express, extend and occupy different spheres, they share the nature of art as 'the abolition of allocation' (2007a: 105). Here we are reminded of the pitfalls of allocation and exchange discussed in *Disagreement*. The power of literature is the power 'of indeterminacy or metamorphosis . . . [transformation] is indeed literal and at the same time it is not so' (2004c: 153). Spectatorship as desiring, rather than exemplifying a mode of subjective practice, expresses a labour which indeed plays on the ambiguity of resemblances in that it obstinately challenges its fellow desiring schemas to insert it. If inhuman desire exploits 'incorrect' perception of represented objects then inhuman spectatorship shows a space of incorrect definition of film itself, desire as ubiquitous, as rudely subsuming yet failing to be and being beyond all other desires.

Modes of resemblance are challenges which may assist in deconstructing traditional dialectics of desire. Inhuman spectatorship doesn't resemble anything except its place within the broad category of cinematic desire, so its resemblance is always a dissemblance. For political philosophy, without genesis or destination, transformation still needs to come from some 'where' or 'thing'. The inhuman spectatorial subject, even when understood as an expressive art manifestation, the space where the inhuman fights its contestations, and the point of desire which incepts a need for inhuman political philosophy, are all necessary residues if we are to think the difficult task of inhuman spectatorship as both grave and limitless, art and no less activist for being so. Through the metaphorical image, art 'is no longer framed by an autonomous history of minority forms or a history of deeds changing the world. Thus art is led to query the radicalism of its powers, to devote its operations to more modest tasks' (Rancière 2007a: 24–5). The metaphorical image performs a double function – to cause rupture and to de-nullify the image's reduction to one of exchange, circulation and the absence of being a metaphor for anything else, which is, having no relations. After Rancière art could be the query that is a response which comes from desiring radicalization without simply becoming a radical. Inhuman spectatorship is always and nothing more than the devastating rupture of concepts of desiring subjectivity and dialectics in the face of the simplest phenomenon of film. To return to the crucial element of Rancière's understanding of art, however, images are metaphorical in that they perform actual operations but without being inherently present to themselves as art or to us as naked. They show art itself as performing resemblances and dissemblances, both with strange bedfellows (non-art, real life – the naked) and with themselves (without metaphor – ostensive). In capitalism, after Lacan, access to any concept of desire beyond lack is compelled to negotiate with desire as everything, a shift back from want to archaic need. Inhuman desire, inasmuch as it precedes the symbolic, is not a return to an infantile or atrophied state. It is a new need, an a-semiotic need, because an irresistible *must*. Desire that lacks wants a thing, a goal, an object and to be an object, objects within the cinematic frame, the object who gazes. It seeks its own allocation through the functioning of desiring operations which place the object of desire in its own correct place. Desire for equality through inclusion, for reparation, for 'counting' is the double task of being enough like and enough unlike the dominant. At best the desiring other can become a fetishized transgressive who gets a place only because they are coveted for their powers which can at any time be either replaced or slaughtered – the redundancy of the exhaustibly transgressive image. At worst the desiring and represented other is ghettoized. Slaughter and ghettoization when we finally come to count are real issues with corporeally devastating actual effects resistant to signification, yet ironically they can be lamented and resisted only when the minoritarian other is signified.

This space of apparent real-life politics is anti-politics for Rancière. But as this so called real-life political desire to count comes only via being signified, the desire and the self both belong to the space of the desire–lack, want–object systems. The inhuman will, and can never, count because it can't be counted, allocated, made equivalent. It has no opposite and thus its desiring project also has no other to covet. The inhuman is neither in opposition with nor equivalent to. This is true of both its self and its want. But it is nonetheless a deeply political philosophy, it comes about because we must still fight for a political philosophy, yet as we are compelled by Rancière to fight beyond the established system, we are fighting for and towards nothing we can apprehend or think. Like children as germinal – not pre-adult but pre-signifying – we have to have, we are sustained by . . . what? The 'what' is the

trickiest point of political philosophy. It must be material enough
to mobilize but amorphous, adaptive and most importantly incon-
clusive; an expressive, gestural political philosophy or, as already
suggested, a dance between rather than within spheres. Rancière's
modest tasks of art are modest political spheres. The inhuman
in spectatorship cannot, and does not seek to, shift the territory
of the world because this is an operation of replacement. Only
modest little tasks of creative perception and unthought openness
to affect can open spaces for new political philosophies, dissipat-
ing the territory without creating new allocations, like the oft-cited
example of a drop of water in a pond. The inhuman queries its
radicalism, it is accountable, yet it is also necessary. Its powers of
transformation are inevitable, like our inevitable need for certain
things. Indeed, the shift from need to want is the crucial moment
of being incepted as human. The need for desire means we no
longer count as human. So it goes beyond and cannot be allocated
to a certain system. Like art, the inhuman in that which encounters
art is a creative expression of what is possible in that it expresses
possibility itself – potentiality. Art makes the ordinary extraordinary, it seduces us with elements as minute as they are grand,
topics, frames, movement, particles which take our breath away.
We don't know why or how, and rarely what, but the seductions
of the cinematic image create the openings that show us, not what
is there to be seen, but that the possibilities of seeing and modes
of desiring are infinite. The tasks occur within all space as the
same, not a special artistic space. To love art is to love as art, and
inhuman spectatorship as political philosophy, but always coming
from and associated with a politics of desire, can here be seen as a
politics of art. Rancière's project of thinking a political philosophy
could, without homogenizing the specificities of each, also include
his work on art. When politics becomes art:

> The art of politics is the art of putting the democratic contradiction
> to positive use; the *demos* is the union of a centripetal force and a
> centrifugal force, the living paradox of a political collectivity formed
> from apolitical individuals. The *demos* is forever drawing away from
> itself, dispersing itself in the multiplicity of ecstatic and sporadic pleas-
> ures. The art of politics must regulate the intermittency of the *demos*
> by imposing intervals which place its strength at a distance from its
> turbulence, at a distance from itself. (1995: 15)

The inhuman is a contradiction. Not between the binaries of correct and incorrect apprehension which occur in reference to subject in relation to image-objects, nor even between dominance and alterity. The inhuman elucidates the inevitable contradiction between being human and being overwhelmed at all moments, differing only in speeds and consistencies, by being not noun but verb, not a desiring subject but nothing more than 'a' desir*ing* and a-desiring. Quiet moments of political tasks are tactical intervals.

Rancière discusses the lyrical mode of expressive speech as having potential democratic function as it speaks through the 'I' and mimetically, like the metaphorical image, without recourse to notions of authenticity, art as falsity and transparency. He raises the beautiful concept of meaning without sense but as sensory. Politics occupies 'the non-signifying, the non-representative' (1995: 13) yet it can be argued that the wonder of art is its non-representative capacity. The aesthetic revolution abolishes 'the distance between the *eidos* of the beautiful and the spectacle of the perceptible; the ability of the beautiful to make itself be appreciated without concept' (1995: 18). Poetic images, only poetic through their encounter with the spectator, are the free play of imagination. The reconciliation between nature and liberty is the moment of politics. Rancière calls the poet the 'wanderer' (2004c: 14) because freedom comes as a result of the freeing up of the allocation of concepts to perception. The poet is the perceiver as much as (if not more than) the creator. Accessing nature through imagination affords liberty. Nature is not its own sphere but simply that which must be perceived as it is in relation to us. This does not preclude or exclude self as part of nature. Crafting an inhuman self takes the self as the first point of nature which makes self an inextricable part of all territories and inhuman perception as an artistic plane. If nothing else, nature is the inhuman. Art, requiring imagination, emphasizes that the freedom to perceive comes with ethical accountability. Mimesis does not copy in relation to the perceived self but neither does it fail to acknowledge the external element as compelling a form of perception. It wanders. It encounters as 'communication of feelings and of natural associations of ideas in a state of excitement' (Rancière 1995: 19). These words, associated inevitably with desiring – beautiful, excitement, sensation and sensuality – are not objects eliciting results. They describe the experience of philosophy, not of things and their meanings or projected interpretation. Like desiring, they are states because the beautiful causes excitement without conversion, indeed *because* there is no conversion. Here liberty could be found both in political philosophy and because of the difficulty of the task of political philosophy. Rancière calls sublime art the unthinkable:

> Between what is visible and what is intelligible there is a missing link, a specific type of interest capable of ensuring as suitable relationship between the seen and the unseen, the known and the unknown, the expected and the unexpected ... Genius is an active power of nature, opposed to any norm, which is its own norm. But a genius is also someone who does not know what he is doing or how he does it ... the aesthetic revolution establishes this identity of ignorance and knowledge, acting and suffering, as the very definition of art. In it the artistic phenomenon is identified as the identity, in a physical form, of thought and non-thought, of the activity of a will that wishes to realise its idea and a non-intentionality, a radical passivity of being there. (2007a: 112–13, 119)

Inhuman desiring is often maligned for being vague, without antagonizing orienting referent, not knowing what it wants. It cannot because it doesn't know itself, only that it is a wanting self, voluminously so. There is no object to know, no concept to subsume. In film there is all of the world and what can materialize in it through the infinite tools available, primarily thought, that is wanted and to be wanted by. The inhuman risks the self it does not know and this is why it is jubilant rather than sacrificial. It gifts itself nonetheless without debt or demand, because connexions occur that no longer expose meaning through the abyss between self and other, observer and art, desiring subject and object. To lose oneself in this way is a form of grace. Grace may be encountered as the loss which is not felt as loss but as production of ecstasy. Inhuman spectatorial thought not only incarnates in a physical form but its radical passivity shows an insurgent grace, seeking liberation and political ethos as much as the ecstasy of self as cinema.

8

Cinemarxis: Rancière and Godard

Mark Robson

A grey corrugated iron fence on the corner of a street, probably London, shot from across the junction as cars pass in front of the camera. People stroll by. A young man walks up to the fence and begins to spray in large letters, one letter at a time:

CINEMARXIS

and then a bright red bus passes between the camera and the corner, and the scene is cut.

Cinephilia and Cinemarxis

Jacques Rancière writes substantially on Jean-Luc Godard in *La Fable cinématographique* (*Film Fables*) (2001), *Le Destin des images* (*The Future of the Image*) (2003) and *Les Écarts du cinéma* (2011), in the essays 'La Sainte et l'héritière: à propos des *Histoire(s) du cinéma*' (1999) and 'Godard, Hitchcock and the Cinematographic Image' (2007), and discusses him in interviews including 'L'Image fraternelle' (1976) and 'Jean-Luc Godard, la religion de l'art' (2003), now both reprinted in *Et tant pis pour les gens fatigués* (Rancière 2001a; 2006a; 2003; 2007a; 1999b; 2002a; 2007d; 2009d: 15–32, 301–12). He is also a repeated point of reference in the pieces that make up the *Chroniques des temps consensuels* (2005), written between 1996 and 2005.

The sequence that I began by describing appears in Godard's film with the Rolling Stones, *Sympathy for the Devil*, also released in the director's own cut as *One plus one* (1968/2011). What exactly is the relation between cinema and Marxism that Godard's portmanteau conjures? (Might there be a relation between portmanteau and montage, a politics of portmantage?) CINEMARXIS is only one such slogan to appear in the film, others including FREUDEMOCRACY and SOVIETCONG. These latter in particular recall the slogans either written or chanted by the students in May 1968, who famously borrowed 'CRS = SS' from striking miners in the 1940s (see Ross 2002: 107).[1] But the very incompletion of the graffitied CINEMARXIS points to a characteristic of Godard's thinking and to a certain pervasive thinking of the inheritance of May '68: there is a sense of the unfinished, but also of chances missed and opportunities lost. Such a potential for melancholy becomes unmissable by the time of Godard's *Histoire(s) du cinéma*, and it is perhaps no surprise that it is this work in particular to which Rancière will address his harshest criticisms.[2]

On the surface, there might appear to be distinct points of convergence between Godard and Rancière. Both began to think about film in the ambit of *cinéphilie* and moved in the late 1960s into an engagement with Maoism. Equally, in the late 1960s Godard could make statements such as the one to be found in the documentary film *Voices*, made at the time of the filming of *Sympathy for the Devil* by Richard Mordaunt; commenting on the relation between politics and film, Godard suggests that the point is not to make movies for the workers, but instead to find out what kind of films could come from the workers. This sounds distinctly like something that could have been said at certain points in his career by Rancière. Equally, Godard's troubling of genre, including his refusal of the usual distinctions between fiction and documentary, often made through the invocation of analogies with other kinds of text or image, might echo in some respects Rancière's 'indisciplinarity'. While there are several trajectories of this kind that might fruitfully be pursued, the purpose of this discussion is to open up some of the key differences that underpin the apparent similarities.

Hence, in bringing together Rancière and Godard, I am hoping both to open up certain questions about Rancière's thinking on cinema more widely and to address his treatment of Godard across several texts. For Rancière, one of the key aspects of this sense of cinema and indiscipline is that it means that film – like literature – constructs a world. And while such worlds might be to some extent shared, that sharing inevitably involves division as much as conjunction. Looking at the conjunction of Godard and Rancière might also allow us to pose some initial thoughts on the paths that each has taken from a specific moment, that is, May '68. This is partly why I have chosen *Sympathy for the Devil/One plus one*, an admittedly less than obvious choice, but a film that was formulated and filmed at precisely that moment (in fact, Godard got into a dispute with the film's producers because they felt he had unnecessarily increased the costs of the film due to his absence in Paris offering support for the students).[3] Rancière's repeated attention to Godard indicates the latter's importance for him, and also perhaps shows an awareness that Godard's is a position from which it is necessary to be disentangled, but it also shows his productive disagreement with someone who shared a particular moment of Parisian *cinéphilie*, and its extension in the *Cahiers du cinéma* and the *nouvelle vague*.[4] At the same time, such disagreement also indicates a sharing of something – *cinéphilie* – that he will characterize as itself a form of *dissensus*. In an interview with Oliver Davis, Rancière says: 'cinephilia was a kind of unauthorized intervention, the shattering of a certain form of cultural legitimacy' (Rancière 2011d: 295). There was a conscious belief that certain hierarchies were challenged by the tastes of the young cinephiles, and this was based on a sense of cinema's history as much as its present. Godard infamously claimed that the young French film critic-directors of the 1950s and early 1960s – those such as Bazin, Truffaut, Chabrol, Rohmer and Godard himself, associated with *cinéphilie* and the *jeune cinéma* and who would become the *nouvelle vague* – were the first to grow up with an informed knowledge of film, that is, with a strong sense of their precursors, formed at the showings at the *Cinémathèque* and the cinema clubs of Paris. However untenable this might seem as a claim, it is striking in its exemplification of Godard's belief that even the most radical forms of filmmaking are responsive to and bound up with the tradition of the art form, however agonistically. In this, Godard is not so far from the modernist poetics of the T.S. Eliot of 'Tradition and the Individual Talent' and thus from a certain Romantic inheritance given its strongest voice in a particular understanding of the modernist avant-garde.

The Politics of Cinema

One possible if tangential route into thinking the politics of cinema would be to think in terms of Rancière's analysis of the politics of literature.[5] As Rancière points out, there are three elements that are usually taken into account in addressing such a

politics: the political commitments of a writer; the depiction of
a 'situation' or issue that is itself deemed political; and what a
particular work may make happen.[6] The first of these possibilities
– associated most obviously with a Sartrean notion of *engagement*
– for Rancière, leads nowhere. Neither does the representation
of structures or institutions, however critically. What needs to be
taken into account is what has come to be known as the distribution and redistribution of the sensible or perceptible [*le partage du
sensible*]. If there is a politics of literature, this is because politics
is conceived as the possibility of the configuration of a certain
form of community in which objects are seen to be shared, which
also means that those objects can be taken as the occasion for
disagreement between those designated as subjects. There are thus
no objects, situations or institutions that are or are not essentially
political. As Rancière puts it:

> Political activity reconfigures the distribution of the perceptible. It
> introduces new objects and subjects onto the common stage [*la scène
> du commun*]. It makes visible what was invisible, it makes audible
> as speaking beings those who were previously heard only as noisy
> animals.
>
>   The expression 'politics of literature' thereby implies that literature
> intervenes as literature [*en tant que littérature*] in this carving up
> [*découpage*] of space and time, the visible and invisible, speech and
> noise. It intervenes in the relationship between practices and forms of
> visibility and modes of saying that carves up [*découpe*] one or more
> common worlds. (Rancière 2006d: 12; 2011f: 4)

The terms of Rancière's description of politics here are those made
familiar in his other work. Drawing on readings of Plato and
Aristotle, Rancière emphasizes in this passage the double forms
of visibility and invisibility. The common is that which is shared,
but the sensory dimension is key: *la scène du commun* is both a
stage on which things may appear but also therefore a staging that
invites spectatorship.

    The crucial element here is pointed up by Rancière himself:
what do we understand by this idea of 'literature . . . as literature'?
What he is not indicating here is an essence of literature, if by that
we might understand either a formal or content-based sense of lit-
erariness in itself. Rancière's thinking of literature, like his thinking of art more generally, rests on the co-implication of the work,

the modes of perception that govern how the work is perceived or fails to be perceived, and forms of ordering the world in which that artistic object and those who perceive it exist.[7] For Rancière, this suggests not only that there is a relationship between, say, literature and history which might render a literary work susceptible to a historicization, but that there is a historicity to the concept of literature itself that cannot be thought in terms of shifts in 'context' alone, that is, without also putting the concept of literature itself into play in the determination of those contexts. In *The Politics of Literature*, Rancière recognizes that there have been attempts to take this historicity into account. But they have largely been informed by a modernist conception of literature, he suggests, and thus literature was caught between the two poles of autonomy and instrumentalization. Either it was characterized as intransitive, poetic, materializing language into a thing, that is, into the thing of which it spoke, or else as communicative, the prose of the world, expressing, persuading and representing, becoming political in the alignment of the materiality of the signifier with the materiality of political action.

It is precisely this modernist paradigm of the politics of literature that Rancière will also find in thinking about cinema. The analogy between cinema and literature is one that has met with a great deal of resistance in film theory. Yet this is one of the central moves in Rancière's own approach to cinema, and it is impossible to draw out his sense of 'cinema as cinema' without making such connections.[8]

Under the Stones the Beach

Sympathy for the Devil/One plus one contains many of the elements that were in the process of becoming characteristic of Godard's filmmaking. The genre of the film is decidedly mixed. In part it is a documentary, charting the process of recording a single song as it takes shape in the studio. The band's performances are marked both by careful planning – it is clear that Mick Jagger has a version of the song in his head before they begin to record – and improvisation; there are false starts, repeated takes, overdubs, interruptions and flashes of inspiration that reflect on Godard's own process of filming. The scenes that we see are both repeatable and singular, and so the band will play the song or parts of it again hundreds of times, but each time differently. Perhaps Godard was drawn to the project by these iterations, having claimed in an early piece that 'a political cinema is always rooted in repetition' (1972: 16). The overall structure of this strand of the film clearly tends towards the linear, however, since they are moving towards the fixity of the 'definitive' version of the song familiar from the recording. To some extent, watching the film is a process of coming to see what was already known before it began, and thus process is emphasized over product. (The inclusion of the completed version of the song at the end of the film was a choice made not by Godard but by one of the film's producers and led to a violent confrontation between the two when it was screened at the London Film Festival.)

But there are also parts of the film that are clearly fiction, particularly a last scene on a beach in which the mechanics of filming (tracks, camera, the use of cranes and booms) are made apparent, all the time exploiting symbolic elements (red and black flags, for example) that make it more than a making-of film or a piece of metadrama. Interspersed in the footage of the Stones is a sequence of scenes featuring members of the Black Panther movement, including their reading of texts and manifestos, their drilling with weapons, and so on. Then again there are some quasi-parodic 'interviews', including one with a character called Eve Democracy, and scenes in which a character reads a political text in a shop selling mainly comic books, political pamphlets and pornography. Godard thus overlays the politics of race, sexual politics, leftist street slogans and obvious fiction on to the 'documentary' footage.

This is effectuated through a form of montage that has become emblematic both of Godard and of the moment in the late 1960s in France in which the technique was the subject of considerable discussion. As Philip Watts describes in an article on Rancière entitled 'Images d'égalité', those associated with cinephilia were drawn into debates around montage that included the 1969 publication of writings by Eisenstein in the *Cahiers du cinéma*, which also published a roundtable discussion on montage, and celebrated articles by Jean-Pierre Oudart and Jacques Aumont. Oudart wrote in a review of *One plus one* that Godard's film called into question the *bouclage* (tying together) of bourgeois society 'by the juxtaposition of elements that cannot be amalgamated' ['par la juxtaposition d'éléments non susceptibles d'amalgame'] (cited in Watts 2006: 361–70, 365). As Watts points out, montage has to be understood broadly, to include not only techniques of cutting and editing for the purposes of continuity but also the moment of rupture, bringing together images and sounds not tied together by the space and time of the narrative. Watts adds to this a social sense – under the name of the society of the spectacle – in which montage is also seen as the mechanism by which society constructs and represents itself. Thus, he proposes, to think about montage is to think about the distribution of the sensible (Watts 2006: 365). The question for Rancière will be: what form of redistribution?

This blending of genres is in line with Godard's Brechtianism, his alienation-effects heightened by the soundtrack and the *mise-en-scène*. In the interview with Eve Democracy, for example, at one point the sound of birdsong swamps the dialogue, and she is frequently concealed behind trees and foliage as they walk and talk. Godard is giving us an utterly familiar form, but with discomforting twists. Far from being a true dialogue, the interview is trite and unenlightening, the interviewer largely making statements rather than posing questions, with the interviewee reduced to single-word answers. Such devices recur throughout the film. Passages of dialogue are too quiet to be heard, diegetic sounds intrude loudly on the foreground. And the Black Power sequences include a series of moments that play into supposedly standard white fantasies, nakedly paranoid, in which young blonde white women, dressed in white, are brought to their junkyard HQ to be mysteriously maltreated, apparently shot and then displayed as if dead. Interpretation of the sexualized violence that the viewer might intuit but is not shown takes its cue from the pornographic texts read aloud in the bookshop. A later sequence follows a symbolic but semi-comic drill in which a row of black men pass weapons down the line and back, as if in training for the inevitable battle to come. The temptation is to link this in an instrumental way to the texts being read, from Eldridge Cleaver, LeRoi Jones and others, but the frame for this fantasy of racial threat and civil strife is at least as much the repeated invocation of the war in Vietnam.

The performative and instrumental dimensions of language itself becomes one of the film's central concerns. Characters read texts aloud, dictate them to others, record them on a tape machine, prompt the speech of others, echo the lyrics of the Stones' song, spray words on walls and windows and cars. The graffiti slogans both recall the Parisian streets and look forward to Godard's use elsewhere of text as writing-on-the-screen, most commonly in boldly capitalized, often enigmatically empty phrases, but also appearing as handwriting, typewritten sentences, facsimiles of printed text. This is not so much a use of text in place of an image, or as a kind of subtitle or caption that explains an image, but rather a use of text-as-image and image-as-text, reflecting an inseparability, a chiasmatic mutual self-definition, perhaps a quasi-hieroglyphics.[9]

Recent films such as *Éloge de l'amour* (2001) or *Film socialisme* (2010) use short part-phrases that can be combined and repeated. In *Éloge de l'amour*, Godard rotates DE L'AMOUR and DE QUELQUE CHOSE, to invite the semi-sentences 'De l'amour de quelque chose' (Of /for love of something) or 'De quelque chose de l'amour' (Of /for something of/about love).[10] In *Film socialisme* the phrases are DES CHOSES and COMME ÇA, giving '(Of / about) Things like that' and 'Things (are) like that'. This film also plays in a similar way with place names: Odessa, Hellas (rendered as HELL AS), and so on, inviting identifications at once cultural, historical, political and filmic (Odessa echoing Eisenstein's *Battleship Potemkin*, for example). But this form was already apparent in earlier films.[11] Such phrases also combine with more conventional quotation and aphorism in other films including the *Histoire(s) du cinéma*.

Embedded in *Sympathy for the Devil* there are also aphorisms that themselves seem to be both repetitions or quotations and simultaneously to be designed to be repeated, such as 'The only way to be an intellectual revolutionary is to give up being an intellectual.' The strong pedagogical imperative that underpins Godard's project is made explicit, but these slogans are destined for what are described as 'schools of deculturalization'. But since these words are given to the largely hopeless interviewer of Eve Democracy, it is not clear how seriously the viewer is meant to take this idea.

Indeed, Godard's use of quotation in such ways has always presented something of a puzzle. Godard draws on the words of others frequently without identifying sources, or else simply citing the names of authors. He sometimes accompanies these quotations with photographs of the authors, as if presenting an image of the one whose words are being heard allows for a tying of word to image, of text to source – or is it rather to accentuate the inevitable distance between them?[12] And who are these texts for? As Jonathan Dronsfield has suggested, prompted by the appearance of Alain Badiou in *Film socialisme*, lecturing to no one on Husserl, 'To quote from a text is to speak it not to someone other but to oneself, and in doing so to hear oneself as someone other' (Dronsfield 2010: 87–105).[13] Godard's use of Badiou to speak (for) Husserl, then, is a further form of alienation, and this might suggest that when similar tactics are used in the *Histoire(s) du cinéma*, for example, he is not so much appropriating others' words as placing a further space between his on-screen persona, the voice-over that might otherwise be taken as a narrator, and his position as author (or as *auteur*). Repeatedly, then, Godard disturbs the usual distinctions between documentary and fiction, but both forms are subordinated to a 'lesson', to the whole of which they are the discrete but juxtaposed fragments, even if it appears to be a lesson that Godard is trying to learn as much as to teach through the film.

Godard's Histories

The conventional distinction between documentary and fiction is also rejected by Rancière, but for other reasons and to other ends. When Rancière wants to describe documentary as documentary fiction, he is using fiction in a strongly idiomatic sense, as he suggests in a passage on Chris Marker: 'Fiction means using [*la mise en œuvre*] the means of art to construct a "system" of represented actions, assembled forms, and internally coherent signs [*signes qui se répondent*].' Fiction is thus less an imposition than the putting to work of what is already given (Rancière 2001a: 202; 2006a: 158). He continues by suggesting that in thinking about the relation of documentary and fiction film one has to be clear where the difference lies. Documentary is a genre of fiction, but nonetheless it treats the real in a manner different to that usually thought of as fiction:

> Documentary does not side with the real against fictional invention. Simply put, for documentary the real is not an effect to be produced. It is a given [*un donné*] to be understood. (Rancière 2001a: 202–3; 2006a: 158, translation modified)

This does not mean that documentary 'fiction' is somehow opposed to the 'real'. As he puts it in *The Politics of Aesthetics*: 'The real must be fictionalized [*fictionné*] in order to be thought.'

Clearly this doesn't mean subject to invention as imagination in the usual sense of the word 'fictionalized', but rather something closer to 'fictioned', that is, given a distinct form. He continues: 'Politics and art, like forms of knowledge [*comme les savoirs*], construct "fictions", that is to say, *material* rearrangements [*réagencements matériels*] of signs and images, relationships between what is seen and what is said, between what is done and what can be done' (Rancière 2000a: 61–2; 2004b: 38–9). Form is thus not simply added to a content for which it acts as a neutral container but has a materiality and thus material effects. It is precisely such a perspective that will govern Rancière's reading of Godard's later work.

The first section of Rancière's *Les Écarts du cinéma* is entitled 'Après la littérature'. The first essay in that section, 'Le Vertige cinématographique', dedicated to the work of Hitchcock and Dziga Vertov, also ends up by taking us back to Godard.[14] What Rancière proposes is that Godard's use of Hitchcock in his *Histoire(s) du cinéma* might be read as if he were treating a series of images drawn from Hitchcock's films as if they were images in or from Vertov's *Man with a Movie Camera* (Rancière 2011c: 43). Godard undoes [*défait*] Hitchcock's narratives in favour of a montage animated by the fascination of the image.[15] What motivates this, Rancière argues, is the knotting together of two arguments concerning the history of cinema. First, there is Godard's sense that Hollywood's industrialization of cinema acts to displace a certain utopian vision that, for him, characterizes the twentieth century. The second is cinema's 'treason', that is, its subordination of its machinic capacity to establish relations between phenomena to its use in the service of telling stories. This establishes the mission of the *Histoire(s)*:

> L'entreprise des *Histoires* est alors une entreprise de rédemption: la fragmentation godardienne veut délivrer le potentiel des images de sa soumission aux histoires. En inventant des relations inédites entre films, photographies, peintures, bandes d'actualité, musiques, etc., elle fait jouer rétrospectivement au cinéma le rôle de révélateur et de communicateur qu'il a trahi en s'asservissant à l'industrie des histoires.

> The undertaking of the *Histoire(s)* is thus an undertaking of redemption: Godard's fragmentation wants to free the potential of images from their submission to stories. In inventing unseen relationships

between films, photographs, paintings, newsreels, music, etc., it ret-rospectively makes cinema play the role of that which reveals and communicates, a role it has betrayed in enslaving itself to the story industry. (2011c: 43–4, my translation)

The story of film that Godard tells is thus a story of a fall, of a paradigm lost. But there is a sense that, however inventive Godard's connections between cinematic and other images may be, they may also be inventions (*inventer* is the verb used in French to say that someone is making something up). To liberate cinema is to liberate it from narrative, but freeing it from one set of bonds involves tying it otherwise.[16]

Rancière explains that this is not simply a matter of fragmen-tation of existing narratives. When Godard takes images from Hitchcock's films and turns them into icons, he also effects what Rancière calls an 'aesthetic transformation', that is, 'Images are no longer elements that you extract from one work and paste into another work. They become shadows in a theatre of memory. And the filmmaker becomes a kind of poet calling the shadows, sum-moning them from the kingdom of shadows' (Rancière 2011d: 297). But while the filmmaker-poet may be the one who 'makes' something from these fragments, that making must also involve the active participation of the spectator, a form of collaboration that rests on the equality of the look, on the shared capacity for anyone to look at anything.[17]

The liberation that Godard identifies as a task involves think-ing about the image in two contradictory ways. The image is, on the one hand, an icon on which the perceptible world imprints its traces, figuring film as a veil of Veronica. But on the other hand, the image is also a sign open to infinite combinations and recombinations with other signs. The camera sees what it sees, blindly recording without will, but it is equally the apparatus that makes possible endless acts of communication, like the telephone exchange in Vertov's film. There is the machinic recording of the lens, but also the look of the cameraman or director. Rancière thus distinguishes between the image-icon that interrupts all stories, suspending their animation, and the image-sign that puts every-thing in relation with everything else, claiming that Godard must avoid at all costs the identification of one with the other. This is not a technical but a philosophical and political problem. The dif-ficulty resides in the question of identity:

C'est le dilemme de l'identité entre l'absolu de la volonté qui boul-
everse les formes du monde sensible et l'absolue démission de la
volonté au profit des énergies d'une vie qui ne veut rien.

It is the dilemma of the identity between the absolute will which disrupts the forms of the perceptible world and the absolute resignation
of the will in aid of the energies of a life that wants nothing. (2011c:
46, my translation)

Not a triumph but a failure of the will, a *démission de la volonté.*
Or rather a further echo of the inheritance of a strand of German
Romanticism within the aesthetic regime in which the work of art
becomes the identity of a conscious process and an unconscious
process, of actions willed and unwilled that undo the privilege of
action in the Aristotelian representative schema.[18] The movement
from painting to photography is a technical development not
simply in terms of reproducibility in Benjamin's terms but also in
terms of looking. At the same moment that photography reduces
the importance of the skill of the hand of the painter, it makes
the 'art' of photography a matter of selection: photography is an
art of looking (Rancière 2011d: 297). The gap between the look
and movement is crucial, since it will become one of the central
issues in Rancière's thinking about the aesthetic regime of art in
Aisthesis.

Godard's Image

In his reading of Godard in *Film Fables*, as in his reading of the
Histoire(s) du cinéma elsewhere, what Rancière finds most problematic is Godard's approach to the image. This is exemplified
most powerfully in Godard's treatment of Hitchcock. Rancière
cites a particular moment that has drawn considerable attention in
Godard's documentary:

We've forgotten why Joan Fontaine leans over the edge of the cliff
and what exactly Joel McCrea went to do in Holland. We've forgotten what makes Montgomery Clift keep an eternal silence and why
Janet Leigh stops at the Bates Motel and why Teresa Wright is still
crazy about her Uncle Charlie. We've forgotten what it is that Henry
Fonda is not exactly guilty of and to what end the American government hired Ingrid Bergman. But we do remember a handbag. But we

remember a bus in the desert. But we remember a glass of milk, the sails of a windmill, a hairbrush. But we remember a row of bottles, a pair of glasses, a musical score, a bunch of keys, because it is with and through these that Alfred Hitchcock succeeds where Alexander, Julius Caesar, and Napoleon fail: to take control of the universe. (Godard 1998: 78–85; cited in Rancière 2001a: 218; 2006a: 172, translation modified)[19]

Godard plays here with an economy of remembering and forgetting that privileges the image as icon, the object that floats free of its anchorage in the plot of the film. In the French text that Rancière cites from Godard, what is translated here as 'But we do remember' is given as 'Mais on se souvient', and this repeated interruption acts like the cuts of Godard's montage, marking the point of the edit, the black screen that intervenes as one image is confronted by another. Philip Watts makes the intriguing suggestion that in Rancière's writings on cinema his repetitions of the word 'mais' ('but') in quick succession mark a suspension in his argument that mimics moments of suspension in the films he describes. This use of 'mais', says Watts, is the putting into writing of cinematographic montage as understood by Rancière, that is, as a suspension of movement (2006: 369). Godard's use of the same strategy, using the same word, seems more than coincidental.

As Laura Mulvey suggests, Godard here exploits the possibility for any filmed object to be fetishized.[20] Godard is right to indicate the potential that these images possess, opening the passage by which they might become iconic and thus allowing them to stand in for the films from which he extracts them, but what he neglects to mention, says Rancière, is that their affective power derives precisely from the places given to them in the films' plots. As Rancière puts it, 'Godard clearly makes his point by dissociating things that are indissociable' ['De tout évidence il dissocie des indissociables'] (Rancière 2001a: 219; 2006a: 172). But this separation from narrative is accompanied by a second operation, which is to change the nature of the images so that they may take on their role as icons of pure presence. For Rancière, the objects on which Godard focuses work in Hitchcock's films in a thoroughly Aristotelian manner. Their purpose is the 'purification of the passions', that is, they act both to evoke fear in the spectator and to purify that anxiety. Despite his claims for them, Godard's icons are wholly embedded in the representative regime. So rather

than using montage to animate images, Godard's fragmentation of
Hitchcock's films enacts a form of anti-montage, using cutting to
produce the inverse of the effect achieved by Dziga Vertov.

In common with Godard, Rancière conceives of the spectator's
relation to cinema in terms of remembering and forgetting, but for
him what results from this forgetting is not a series of fragmen-
tary images but precisely an effort to remember that engenders
new forms of telling. Rather than taking us away from narrative
towards the image as icon, our responses to cinema take us from
one fable to another, to further fictions.

Seizing Shadows

What seems to emerge most clearly from Rancière's repeated *aus-
einandersetzung* with Godard is the significance of forgetting in the
creation of a world that cinema enacts. Separating himself again
from forms of Marxist historiography that stress the necessity of
remembering the overlooked in the service of counter-history,
Rancière puts into play a historiographical disagreement, that is,
the possibility of two incompatible visions of the world and two
incompatible forms of expressing that difference. This disagreement takes place not by posing one set of facts against another but
instead by demonstrating that the meaning of the so-called facts
is not univocal or universal. As Rancière repeatedly stresses in his
work, it is a matter of dealing with what is given. What Rancière
wants to open up in Godard's documentary work in particular is
its fictive element, but this needs to be understood both in terms of
the history that Godard tells and the mode in which it is related. As
Rancière points out, at the heart of Godard's project is a paradox
that cannot be wished away: Godard wants to say that the history
of cinema is a history of lost opportunities, a history of betrayal
and of a fall from aesthetic grace that condemns cinema to being
an art without a future. CINEMARXIS in the melancholic mode
envisaged by Godard is destined to incompletion, definitively
missing its moment, in a gesture of bad utopianism that Rancière
always rejects. And yet the telling of this story, of this history in
the form of video documentary that Godard chooses, is possible
only by virtue of the images and sound that are in fact to be found
in the fictions that he condemns. As Rancière puts it: 'These "lost
opportunities", in other words, are so many seized opportunities'
['Ces « occasions perdues » sont donc autant d'occasions gagnées']

(Rancière 2001a: 236; 2006a: 186). There is no need to offer other examples, to bring hidden images to light from out of the historical shadows; if they are hidden, it is in plain sight.

For Rancière, all documentary film is documentary fiction; it is always a matter of selection, structuring and relating.[21] *Sympathy for the Devil* and *Histoire(s) du cinéma* both engage with the resources of fiction in accordance with an underlying pedagogical imperative. In Rancière's resistance to Godard's lesson, there is a counter-pedagogy as well as a countering of a certain way of telling history, even if this does not add up to a counter-history per se. Documentary, like fiction, becomes a struggle with the given that itself becomes part of the given, part of the inheritance that its viewers will need and want to interpret after their own fashions, according to their lights, but also according to their shadows.[22]

Notes

1. Another slogan not used by Godard was: 'Je suis Marxiste – tendance Groucho.'

2. For an exploration of this conjunction of the unfinished and the melancholic, see Gibson (2005: 61–76).

3. This suggestion is made in the documentary filmed during the shooting of *Sympathy for the Devil*, *Voices* (dir. Richard Mordaunt), now included on the Blu-Ray edition of the film.

4. On the extraordinary way of writing that flows from this love of film, see Rifkin (2009: 81–7). For a more general discussion of the phenomenon in France, see Baecque (2003).

5. For a fuller discussion of this aspect of Rancière's work, see Robson (2009).

6. Here I am adapting the opening sections of Rancière (2006d).

7. This is restated in the opening pages of Rancière's latest work, in which he insists that the privilege enjoyed by art stems not from intrinsic qualities but instead from its place in the distribution of social conditions. See Rancière (2011g: 9).

8. For a different unfolding of this relation between literature and film, see Robson (2011).

9. Rancière proposes that one of the roles given to the artist in Balzac's *La Peau de chagrin* is that 'He gathers the vestiges and transcribes the hieroglyphs painted in the configuration of obscure or random things' ['Il recueille les vestiges et transcrit les hiéroglyphes peints dans la configuration même des choses obscures ou quelconques']

(Rancière 2001b: 36; 2009e: 35). Note that this engenders a form of writing, that is, transcription.

10. For an analysis of Godard's use of the aphorism, see Laügt (2012).

11. This is related to Godard's use of the frame and opaque black or white surface as an indication of the legibility as well as visibility of the image, as read by Deleuze (1983: 24; 1986: 14).

12. The subtitle of the printed text for this film makes this process explicit (Godard 2010).

13. Dronsfield dubs what I have called above quasi-hieroglyphics the 'written image', and suggests that 'the image of the written word is Godard's specific contribution to the categorial images structuring the history of cinema' (2010: 93). There is not the space here for a fuller engagement with Dronsfield's sense of Rancière's reading of Godard.

14. Godard was the founder with Jean-Pierre Gorin of the Dziga Vertov Group, active from 1968 until its dissolution in 1972.

15. Behind Rancière's attention to Godard's use of Hitchcock is, of course, also the 'taxonomy' of cinema produced by Gilles Deleuze in his two books on cinema, a project also hinging at crucial moments on the interpretation of Hitchcock. See the discussion in Tanke (2011: 128–36).

16. Richard Neupert has described Godard's technique, from *À bout de souffle* onwards, in terms of 'dysnarration' (Neupert 2002: ch. 6; 1995: ch. 5).

17. This links to Rancière's insistence on the importance of spectatorship in the aesthetic regime, most obviously in the essays in 2008b/2009a.

18. For a fuller account, relating this to and differentiating it from Freudian notions of the unconscious, see the discussion in Rancière (2009e).

19. I have restored the repetition in Godard's phrasing that Battista's translation elides.

20. See the discussion in chapter 8 of Mulvey (2006).

21. See the comments on Chris Marker, for example, in Rancière (2011d: 302–3).

22. This essay was drafted before I was aware of two recent articles that I would have liked to have taken into account: J.M. Bernstein, 'Movies as the Great Democratic Art Form of the Modern World (Notes on Rancière)' (Deranty and Ross 2012: 15–42), and Lisa Trahair, 'Godard and Rancière: Automatism, Montage, Thinking' (Deranty and Ross 2012: 43–65).

9

Jacques Rancière's Animated *Vertigo*; or, How to be Specific about Medium

Richard Stamp

As early as 1957 I had begun to construct mechanical drawing machines, reasoning simply that since the motion picture phenomenon is a precise incremental stepping process, a drawing tool capable of incremental variation would be useful. It is important to explain that I was not motivated to create representational images with these machines but, instead, wanted to create abstract pattern in motion. . . . My first machine, 1957, was immediately put to use in an unexpected way when Saul Bass included a few short sequences, drawn upon hundreds of animation cells with the machine's stylus, for the title to Alfred Hitchcock's film *Vertigo*. For one with such visions as mine centred in the fine arts, (an art so 'fine', incidentally, as to be quite invisible), such applications as titles to a not very significant movie were scant reward. (Whitney 1980: 184–5)

In a 1971 article for *American Cinematographer*, the monthly publication of the American Society of Cinematographers, an experimental filmmaker explains how he started developing 'animation mechanisms' over a decade earlier. These machines are conceived as tools capable of 'drawing' with precisely controlled incremental variations that might match the 'precise incremental stepping process' that underpins the cinematographic apparatus of celluloid film and its machines (the camera, the editing table and the projector). Although he claims that he began his work with the aim of making something 'useful', he then confesses, with wry self-deprecation, to a feeling of disappointment when his first machine was unexpectedly 'put to use' for the title credits of 'a not very significant [Hollywood] movie'.[1] His aim, after all, was not to create representational images but 'abstract pattern in motion'; not simply a movie 'special effect', but a new form of kinetic art. Yet his work, when it was remembered, would become known

149

chiefly as a set of pioneering experiments in the use of computers in cinematic effects, and as a progenitor of an industry that was only just beginning to emerge in the Hollywood of the late 1960s and early 70s. His name was John Whitney – and his name for this newest of arts was 'motion graphics'.

The 'usefulness' of Whitney's inventions and this new 'art' are further demonstrated by the fact that by 1971, the time of writing his article, he had developed a sophisticated analogue computer-controlled animation machine capable of producing the 'slit-scan' effects that inspired Douglas Trumbull to create the famous 'Stargate' sequence for Stanley Kubrick's *2001: A Space Odyssey* (1968). Furthermore, he had also become one of the first artists to experiment with the new digital computers (thanks to a fellowship with IBM in 1966–8) that would come to provide the platform for the very visual effects industry from which he was already trying to distance himself. But Whitney was no enemy of Hollywood; he was embedded in a network of commercial design, television and film industries. During the 1950s Whitney was a freelance filmmaker and animator, directing cartoons, commercials, 'idents' and title sequences for television programmes, even designing and producing commercial architectural installations.[2] It was one of the latter, a series of etched glass panels for a Los Angeles restaurant, that drew his work to the attention of the graphic designer and filmmaker Saul Bass, who in 1957 had been commissioned by Alfred Hitchcock to design the title credit sequence for his latest film, *Vertigo* (1958).

This chapter in part sets out to tell something of the story of this collaboration through the optic of Jacques Rancière's insistently 'cinephilic' writing on film. It will focus on the way that Rancière's own reading of these title credits and another part-animated sequence from *Vertigo* extend and develop his counter-reading of film as a 'thwarted fable'. His account of the different relations of image and narrative in these two sequences will provide an opportunity to revisit, test and supplement the particular formulation of medium-specificity – and most importantly, its critique – that characterizes his formulation of the aesthetic regime of art. Ultimately, it will argue that Rancière's insistence on 'thwarting' the claims to medium-specificity – as a way of rethinking what 'medium' can mean – offers up interesting and productive ways of situating animated media within a series of specific historical moments.

Fables of a Thwarted Medium

> The artistic procedures of cinema have to construct dramaturgies
> that thwart its natural powers. There is no straight line running from
> cinema's technical nature to its artistic vocation. The film fable is a
> thwarted fable [*une fable contrariée*]. (Rancière 2006a: 11; 2001a: 19)

In the prologue to a recent collection of his essays on film, *Les
Écarts du cinéma* (2011), Rancière aligns his work with a certain
idea and practice of cinephilia. Cinema, he explains, 'isn't an
object that I would have studied as a philosopher or a critic. My
relation with it is a play of encounters and gaps [*écarts*]' (2011c:
8).[3] The readings of particular filmmakers, films or theoretical-
philosophical texts that he presents in this book, as in the earlier
La Fable cinématographique (2001, translated as *Film Fables* in
2006), draw on such 'encounters' and 'gaps' in order to put back
into question, or redistribute, the relations between cinema, art,
politics and theory. Rancière's avowed cinephilia is therefore
related to a number of central concerns of his work as a whole.
First, insofar as it is a relation to cinema that concerns passion
before (but not excluding) theory, cinephilia articulates part of
the 'democracy of diversions and emotions' of popular culture
that can be traced back to his archival work in *Proletarian
Nights* (1981); and second, it generates 'a positive understanding
of art's impurity, one that is in no way ironic or disillusioned',
through which he can interrogate one of the dominant categories
of modern aesthetic theory – namely the modernist paradigm of
medium-specificity and its application in policing the purity of an
'art' against the 'commercialised aestheticisation of life' identified
with 'the popular' or 'kitsch' (2011c: 9). Cinephilia, he suggests,
entails a relation to its object that goes by way of *impure pleasures*. In other words, while his description of cinephilia as an
introduction to a 'positive' understanding of the 'impurity' of art
is at least partly autobiographical, it also reintroduces the logic of
what he calls 'the aesthetic regime of art'.

The relation of cinema to the aesthetic regime of art, which
operates in Rancière's work as a counter-description of the aesthetic project of modernity, is therefore double. In *Film Fables* he
recounts that the earliest theoreticians of cinema – Jean Epstein is
his principal example – saw it as the art that would finally accomplish the task of 'undoing' or 'thwarting' the forms, genres and

plots of representational art. It would be *the* modern art form. For Epstein, he argues, cinema appeared to achieve 'the becoming-passive of writing' for which Flaubert strove, and the appropriation of not only all previously existing art and genres, but also 'anything and everything in the world' that had been previously not been available to art ('non-art'), a dual impulse that can be traced back to Romanticism (Rancière 2006a: 9). However, he immediately notes that this apparent parallel between the pure creativity of an art without rules and the mute expressivity of things themselves rests upon an obvious disparity; namely, the passivity that writers such as Flaubert had to *work* to achieve in their writing was itself already embodied in the very *automatism* of the cinematographic apparatus. For Rancière, two consequences flow from this observation: first, that by embodying the process of passive de-figuration at the heart of the aesthetic regime, 'cinema as an *artistic idea* predated the cinema as a *technical means* and distinctive art' (2006a: 6; my emphasis); and second, that insofar as it 'suppresses the active work of this becoming-passive' cinema demonstrates that it is equally suited to 'restoring' the very representational forms, genres and plots that modern painters and writers had tried to 'subvert' (2006a: 10). This final point is the decisive sense of 'thwarting' [*contrariété*] that defines the relation of the cinematic apparatus to the aesthetic regime of art:

> The cinema's continuity with the aesthetic revolution that made it possible is necessarily paradoxical. Even though its basic technical equipment yields the identity of active and passive that is the principle of this revolution, the cinema can only be faithful to it by giving one more turn to its secular dialectics. (2006a: 11; 2001a: 18–19, translation modified)

If the aesthetic regime of art is conceived as the process of undoing the forms and codes of the representational regime, cinema cannot but extend that process by turning against or 'thwarting' it. This is the form of cinema's belonging to the aesthetic regime – and why, for Rancière, there can be no straight line between the 'technical nature' of the cinematic apparatus and its 'artistic vocation'. The latter cannot be simply read off the former because the very passivity of its automatism evacuates it of any purpose or activity intrinsic to its nature. The camera sees everything, automatically, and for that reason it simultaneously relinquishes any control over the images it generates – it is equally well suited to constructing stories of romance and suspense as it is to generating images of 'pure' abstraction. It is arguably this 'one more turn', the manner of its twisting or thwarting the logic of the aesthetic regime of art, that remains specific to cinema.

In this sense, Rancière's reading of Epstein, followed by essays on Deleuze and Godard, demonstrates the self-defeating nature of any appeal to the specificity of film as a medium. All three thinkers, he claims, attempt to 'extract, after the fact, the original essence of the cinematographic art from the plots the art of cinema shares with the art of telling stories' (2006a: 6). In order to tell the 'truth' of cinema as the medium of the pure moving image, he argues, they must 'extract' those images from the stories that they tell. What all three thinkers would share, then, is a desire to *retrieve* the cinematic image from its subordination to story; a desire for *restitution* marked by the inheritance of Epstein's formula that 'cinema is to the art of telling stories what truth is to lying' (Epstein, cited Rancière 2006a: 1). It is just such a dream of retrieving the properly cinematic capacity of automatism from the strictures of narrative forms and genres that drives Deleuze's diagnosis of the 'crisis of the motor schema', the network of reactive relations that gives the movement-image its coherence, after the end of the Second World War. If Deleuze famously locates this 'crisis' in the films of Hitchcock, which exist 'at the juncture of two cinemas, the classical that he perfects and the modern that he prepares', it is because he isolates images of the 'paralysed' subject-protagonist – Jeff, photographer-turned-voyeur in *Rear Window* (1956), and Scottie, ex-policeman and acrophobic in *Vertigo* – in order to argue that each film revolves around the transformation of the active hero into a passive spectator (Deleuze 1986: x, 204–5). However, these are in no sense pure optical and sound 'images': in each case, the extracted image of the character in paralysis remains an integral device for the story. Rather than blocking the narrative action of the 'movement-image' and the causal relations of the 'sensory motor schema', the character's paralysis facilitates it. Rancière observes that '[t]he camera is not paralysed by Scottie's vertigo, but turns his vertigo into the opportunity to create the spectacular effect [*un truquage spectaculaire*] that shows James Stewart hanging from a gutter over a vertiginous abyss' (2006a: 115; 2001a: 155). In order to extract the pure medium trapped within these stories, Deleuze has to construct an idea of a classical cinema that misses the non-coincidence of the medium of cinema with itself.

By returning this cinematographic fable of the camera's becoming-passive to its Romantic origins Rancière argues that this fable is itself 'grafted onto the cinematographic machine' because it already 'belongs [*propre au*] to the aesthetic *moment* of cinema more than to the distinctiveness [*la spécificité*] of its technical means' (2006a: 6; 2001a: 13). This distinction between what *belongs* to cinema's 'aesthetic moment' and what is *specific* to its 'technical means' provides the hinge by which Rancière gains leverage on the notion of what a 'medium' can mean. It entails acknowledging the historical blurring and 'border-crossing' between arts, rejecting the narrow view of medium bound to a specific material or technical apparatus. He insists that, '[l]ike painting and literature, cinema is the name of an art whose meaning cuts across the borders between the arts' (2006a: 4; 2001a: 11, translation modified). To ask what a medium can mean is therefore to enquire into the specific configurations of sense and perception presented in a particular work or artifact. In a more recent interview, he insists that a medium is always 'a milieu or a sensorium, a configuration of space and time, of sensory forms and modes of perception' (Rancière 2008e: 185). A medium matters insofar as it always (only) mediates.

The remainder of this chapter takes up Rancière's counter-reading of *Vertigo* in which he exploits this gap in the apparent coherence of Deleuze's concepts, particularly in the mutually thwarting relation between image and narrative that Deleuze must ignore in order to redeem cinema as the medium of pure images. Consequently, the analyses that follow will argue that Rancière's film fables require us to hold simultaneously on to two apparently contrary positions: first, that recognizing cinema as an art in relation to other arts entails rejecting the modernist principle of medium-specificity; and second, that these relations themselves require us to rethink the 'medium' as always, each time, giving rise to a specific sensorium, as moments of a perpetually thwarted mediality.[4]

Cinematographic Vertigo

To think the art of moving images is first to think the relation between two movements: the visual unravelling of images proper to cinema, and the process of deploying and dispersing appearances that more

This twisting logic of a thwarted medium characterizes all of Rancière's cinematographic fables, but it appears to take on a particularly isomorphic resonance in his reading of the turbulent vortices of Hitchcock's *Vertigo*. In 'Le Vertige cinématographique: Hitchcock–Vertov et retour', Rancière stages an encounter between cinema and literature, drawing on the adaptation of the film from Pierre Boileau and Thomas Narcejac's 1952 detective novel, *D'Entre les morts*.[5] The point of returning the film to its literary source text is not so much to relate these two 'aesthetic figures' and their 'powers' to the classical matrix of literary adaptation – the relation between 'showing' and 'saying' (2011c: 18) – but to argue that thinking through the art of moving images entails thinking through the 'gap' between the 'visual progression [*déroulement*] of images proper to cinema' and the 'deploying and dispersing' of appearances more generally characteristic of 'the art of narrative plots' (2011c: 25). The different capacities of literature and cinema are neither the exclusive property nor the limit of what is possible in any one medium, but rather describe the manner in which each 'cuts across' the other.

Rancière's reading of *Vertigo*, then, focuses on the convoluted intertwining of spectacle and plot, which divides the narrative structure of the film into two distinct 'scenarios'. The first part of the film comprises a 'romantic or symbolist scenario', which leads up to the staged suicide of Elster's wife, Madeleine, and could be said to be structured around the 'capture of a look' (Scottie's fascination with the 'image' of Judy pretending to be Madeleine); and the second part effectively reverses this circuit in an 'Aristotelian scenario' whereby Scottie's projection of his 'visual fascination' on to Judy - as he forces her to transform (back) into Madeleine – leads to his discovery of the 'intellectual machination' of Elster's plot (2011c: 27). Insofar as Hitchcock's fabled 'mastery of suspense' is associated with the intricate coordination of these two movements – the flow of images and narrative of appearances that Deleuze associates 'bringing the cinema to completion' – Rancière draws attention to two episodes in which this calibration breaks down: Scottie's nightmare after the inquest into the staged suicide of the true Madeleine; and the scene in which Judy writes a letter confessing to her deception, revealed to the spectator through her voice-over. Once again, what interests Rancière is the impurity of the cinematographic medium, its non-coincidence with itself, which is revealed in a resistant 'gap' between these two orders of appearance and movement. It is in this sense that both episodes will be shown to exceed what is required for the smooth calibration of the interlocking scenarios of machination and fascination.[6]

The first of these two sequences occurs at that narrative 'hinge' between the two parts of the film, just after the death of Madeleine. Scottie is haunted by guilt, caused by his inability to climb the stairs of the tower from which he has seen Madeleine fall. Rancière describes the sequence in the following way:

> The nucleus of the dream is the ancestor Carlotta's bouquet, which Scottie had seen in her portrait at the museum and which the fake Madeleine repeatedly copied. Here the bouquet explodes into a multitude of petals before we see Scottie's head, separated from his body, zoom through space towards the cemetery where an open grave awaits and then the Mission where it is his own body that crashes into the roof. (2011c: 29)

Rancière confesses that this sequence causes the spectator 'a certain discomfort [gêne]', and he is right. In fact, when he suggests that such 'gaudy [voyant] effects' go further than *necessary* 'to make Scottie's mental vertigo perceptible', it might be added that his brief description omits to mention the most garish of them: the heady mix of throbbing colour filters that pulses in time with the accompanying pulsing habanero score (2011c: 29–30). What interests Rancière are the narrative consequences of these effects: the visual 'exacerbation of the representation of vertigo' in fact 'weaken[s]' it, effectively reducing it to 'a bad dream to be dispelled' (2011c: 29). In other words, it contributes to setting up the narrative of Scottie's 'recovery' that will unfold in the second half of the film. But we need to ask what is the *cause* of the spectator's discomfort here? Is it this 'excess' over what was required to make us 'experience' Scottie's illness, or the 'weakening' of its narrative power – and is this aesthetic 'flaw' the result of anything more than poor design and production?

Rancière suggests that Hitchcock might have had in mind the dream sequence from *Spellbound* (1945), designed by Salvador Dalí, which intimates at a *surrealist* context for Scottie's nightmare sequence. However, it is also possible that the surreal qualities of this sequence are those equally associated with the use of *animation* effects and techniques. The production design of *Vertigo* famously features innovative special effects, such as the so-called 'vertigo shot', the simultaneous pull-out/zoom-in used to convey Scottie's experience of acrophobia (this is the '*truquage spectaculaire*' to which Rancière refers in his essay on Deleuze). But other sequences, like Scottie's nightmare, draw on established filmmaking techniques, including those more associated with animated films. The title credits attribute this 'special sequence' to John Ferren, who had worked with Hitchcock on *The Trouble with Harry* (1955), and his 1957 treatment for this 'animated nightmare sequence' (Aulier 1998: 147) makes clear both the 'cartoonish' sources of its key effects as well as the 'rhythmical' conception of the whole.[7]

> The flowers come alive, grow and fade, become florescent [*sic*], change color, start whirling in a dizzy maze – like pinwheels – and enlarge rapidly to cover screen. . . . Scottie falls. Faster beat. The pit takes over the entire screen as strips of color on what would be the sides of the grave appear [around] Scottie's windblown head. These strips stream back in Disney fashion,[8] giving the illusion of terrific speed. The scream starts. The strips begin, colored deep red. At the same time there is a mustard color (dirty yellow) pulsation on Scottie's face. The receding red strips change through purple to sharp acid green yellow. (These are deliberate dissonant colors.) . . . Reverse angle showing Scottie falling as a pure, unshadowed, black, profiled mass . . . which is shown briefly in the clear yellow light. (Ferren, quoted in Aulier 1998: 148–50)

The same three elements that Rancière identifies in his description – the exploding bouquet of flowers, Scottie's separated head and his falling body – are here identified as two-dimensional *graphical* figures imbued with the illusion of movement. In other words, they are *animated*. The flowers 'come alive, grow and fade'; the 'strips' that generate the 'illusion of terrific speed' around Scottie's head are duly described in the shorthand of 'Disney fashion'; and the silhouette of Scottie that falls to the roof is rendered in two-dimensions as a 'profiled mass'. If the overall effect of this sequence is 'uncomfortable' or 'garish', then it is inextricably bound up with these animated graphical effects and their place at the centre of a screen saturated by a 'Color Throb or Pulsation', which Ferren envisaged would 'increase the hypnotic effect, center

the spectators [*sic*] attention and make the apparent reality unreal'
(quoted in Aulier 1998: 148).

The turn to production details does not contest or refute
Rancière's reading, but rather seeks to supplement it by giving
yet another twist to the thwarted fable of cinema. As Ferren's
notes suggest, the design of this sequence is expressly aimed at
creating the 'hypnotic effect' of the 'unreal' reality for the spectator. The fact that the positioning of the spectator at the centre of
this sequence is achieved through *animation* is not an argument
for reclassifying the film, but it does prompt us to reconsider the
place and meaning of 'animation' within the film as a whole, both
in terms of production techniques and the aesthetic sensorium
of effects that it generates. The mixed media of Scottie's nightmare sequence – with its transitions between 'live action' shots
of Scottie, Elster and Carlotta and the 'cartoon' figures and backgrounds such as the exploding flowers and zoom effects – suggests
further examples of exchange, however 'clumsy', between different 'aesthetic figures', supplementing the kinds of 'border crossing'
between cinematography, literarity and theatricality that Rancière
describes in his essay. This mixing of media genres is most directly
encountered in the title sequence produced by Saul Bass and John
Whitney.

Animating *Vertigo*

Scottie: What's this doohickey?
Midge: It's brand new. Revolutionary uplift. It does everything a bras-
    siere should do. (*Pause*.) Works on the principle of the cantilever
    bridge.
Scottie: It does?
Midge: An aircraft engineer down the peninsula designed it. He
    worked it out in his spare time.
Scottie: (*Admiringly*.) A kind of a hobby. A do-it-yourself type thing.

Although Midge's explanation of the 'doohickey'[9] that Scottie
tentatively prods with his walking stick doubtless contains a sly
reference to the cantilever bra that Howard Hughes (millionaire
film producer and aircraft designer) is supposed to have designed
for his 'star', Jane Russell, Scottie's admiring reply also returns
us to John Whitney, who throughout the 1950s was busy engi-
neering his 'gadgets' further down the California coast in Pacific

Pallisades, Los Angeles. Whitney's 'hobby' involved repurposing the discarded technologies of industrial design mechanisms and military targeting-control computers in order to build a 'do-it-yourself' machine-controlled animation apparatus. As Whitney himself explains, he used the first of these 'gadgets' to animate the geometrical 'Lissajous' figures that introduce *Vertigo*.[10]

We first encounter these spiralling figures in the title credits after a series of extreme close-up shots of an anonymous woman's face, eyes and mouth, which are overlaid with the names of the film's cast and its director. The title then advances from 'deep within' the eye before flying forward and up towards the top of the screen, leaving the camera to settle on an extreme close-up of the woman's eye, from out of which appears the first of a series of geometrical figures. These figures change with each title card and the shifting, suspended chords of the score. Always in the centre of the screen, their rotations appearing to spin them towards the spectator, as if in a zoom shot. As each figure advances it holds an extreme close-up position that then frames the black space in which the next figure appears. The final figure, however, reverses this orientation by moving quickly from foreground to background, dragging the preceding figure with it as it disappears into the woman's eye under a crimson red filter, and is immediately replaced by the advancing director credit.

A number of qualities are immediately striking about these abstract, rotating figures. First, they exhibit both *regularity* and *variation* in movement and pattern: with one exception they all rotate anti-clockwise, and for about ten seconds, yet sometimes extended in overlapping combinations and sometimes reduced in moments of smooth acceleration. Second, their spiralling motion generates an effect of *illusory depth* as each figure appears to advance and recede without occupying an identifiably dimensional space, although they begin and end deep within the black space of the eye (a 'spiralling' motion that is an illusion in the tradition of children's *trompe l'oeil* toys). Finally, we cannot fail to notice that the conjunction of their abstraction with the stark photography of the close-ups of the woman's face and the repeated suspended motifs of Bernard Herrman's score is a powerful demonstration of film titles' capacity for *condensation* and *prefiguration*. Indeed, for Rancière, the title sequence for *Vertigo* appears to 'encapsulate' a perfect 'coincidence' of the movement of images and the machinations of the plot:

> The deployment of the film's images at first appears to follow exactly the logic of the story. This coincidence is already encapsulated [*résumée*] in Saul Bass' titles, where a play of abstract spirals comes to connect three ovals which themselves conjure up a rather more carnal reality: a lying mouth, a panicky glance, a glamorous [*fascinant*] chignon. These titles give the visual formula of the narrative logic that will bring together three kinds of vertigo: Scottie's acrophobia, the manipulation carried out by the murderous husband in order to make his wife's suicidal impulse believable, and finally Scottie's fascination for the fake Madeleine. (2011c: 26–7)

According to Rancière, the interplay of these geometrical figures with a series of oval part-objects is 'positioned to serve' the film's narrative logic: it not only sets in motion the 'game of machination' which captures Scottie's gaze (his fascination with Madeleine), but also suggests the inverse 'revelation' of this game, after the murder, when Scottie's 'illness' becomes the vertiginous means by which he discovers his deception (2011c: 27). As the apparently 'perfect' calibration of the logics of image and story, this introductory graphical sequence contrasts with the 'gaudy effect' of Scottie's nightmare sequence. Rancière describes its operation in quasi-mechanical terms as a 'visual device', or *dispositif*, that sets in motion this 'artistic machinery' of enmeshed romantic-symbolist and Aristotelian scenarios (2011c: 26–7). In other words, these animated spiral motifs become an *animating* device whose hypnotic effect is repeated and varied throughout the film: in the tightly knotted arrangement of flowers in Carlotta's nosegay and of her hair in a chignon; the 'vertigo shot' that removes any stable visual reference point for the spectator in order to express the sensation of Scottie's acrophobia; the square spiral of stairs in the tower, designed to maximize the effect of this simulated disorientation; the twisted figures of the falling policeman, echoed in that of Madeleine/Judy, and of Scottie himself in his nightmare; the spinning 360-degree shot of Scottie and Judy's consummating embrace. Situated in relation to the film as a whole, the abstract exercise of visual colour, shape and motion generates a motivic movement that withholds harmonic resolution, visually as well as aurally, threatening to enfold Scottie and the story in a series of looping returns. In this way, Rancière partly adopts one of the central tropes of *Vertigo* commentary (see Allen 2007; Brill 1988; Pomerance 2004; Srebnick 2004), which is to read the spiral motif as a synecdoche that would generate a reading of the film as a whole.[11]

As we saw in the previous section, however, Rancière sets up this carefully calibrated cinematographic *dispositif* in order to show how it breaks down in the two 'excessive' sequences of Scottie's nightmare and Judy's confession, but at this point the deployment of images in the title sequence appears to be completely synchronized with the logic of the story. This suggestion conceals a claim about the particular configuration of media at play in this sequence, which allows us to think about how the animated effects of this *dispositif* help to compose a specific sensorium. The place to start is to note that Saul Bass's design mixes different forms of media: cinematography, typography, animated motion graphics, orchestral score.[12] Bass himself described 'what a title can do' in terms of 'set[ting] mood', 'prim[ing] the underlying core of the film's story', or 'express[ing] the story in some metaphorical way' – similar formulations to those used by Rancière – with the aim of 'conditioning the audience, so that when the film actually began, viewers would already have an emotional resonance with it' (Haskin and Bass 1996: 12–13). Whether the title credits are described as 'the prime underlying core of the film's story' (Bass) or 'the visual formula of [its] narrative logic' (Rancière), it is clear that neither one claims to extract these abstracted images from the narrative plot of deception and obsession. Instead, both designer-filmmaker and philosopher-cinephile underscore the ways in which the titles 'express' the film's story, and thereby create what we might call, borrowing Rancière's term, a *sensorium* that is dependent upon this particular mixing of media. This is how we might understand Bass's own reference to 'conditioning' the audience, which is at first glance rather more reminiscent of Hitchcock's own public statements about 'manipulating' the audience. There is something less precise, less instrumental, in the effect of these abstract figures; something that a contemporary review in *The Hollywood Reporter* recognized (while remaining ignorant of Whitney's contribution) when it stated that '[t]he animated spirals of Saul Bass's title designs create an effect of dizziness and audience participation at the very start' (cited in King 2004).

Just as Ferren's nightmare sequence recalls surrealism, there are numerous parallels between the use of these abstract graphic figures in a Hollywood film and their contemporary familiarity as examples of modern art, not least in the emphasis on abstraction and kineticism. According to Pat Kirkham, these 'startlingly modern' figures were seen at the time as examples of 'modern art in motion' (1997: 18). But Emily King (2004) goes much further, arguing that hiring Bass and Whitney to design and make the titles was 'one of Hitchcock's attempts to ally himself with the avant garde rather than the *Kitsch*' – a desire for his art to be taken 'seriously'. This latter suggestion of a disjunction between 'art' and 'cinema' initially seems to reflect Whitney's own self-deprecating comment on the 'fineness' of the former and the 'insignificance' of the latter. However, the contradictions of Whitney's own aesthetic project add a further twist to the thwarted medium of cinema – one that returns us to the relation between cinema as an art and as a technical apparatus.

From his earliest abstract films, made with his brother James in the 1940s, John Whitney saw the machine as the future of such an art. In a 1946 essay, written to accompany these films, they suggest that 'the abstract film can become the freest and the most significant art form of the cinema' because 'it will be the one most involved in machine technology, an art fundamentally related to the machine' (Whitney 1980: 144). This machine aesthetic might remind us, to borrow Rancière's suggestion about the *Vertigo* titles, of Dziga Vertov's 'camera-eye', of a time when 'cinema applied itself to deploying a vertigo of the gaze [*un vertige du regard*]' that embodied 'the explosion of energies of a new world' (2011c: 35). The machine-eye of the camera and cameraman is everywhere present in *Man with a Movie Camera* (1928), even to the point of becoming magically animated – in the manner of early trick films – in the final section of the film, as it connects and orchestrates the energies of all the activities it shows. It is in relation to this animated omnipresence of the camera that Rancière notes the blind functioning of its automatism: the camera may see everywhere and connect everything, but it can only do so by operating 'like a telephone exchange' – 'The eye only connects if it gives up lingering over what it sees, if it gives up looking' (2011c: 45). This dialectic of omnipresence and impotence that Rancière identifies in Vertov's utopia of 'cinematographic communism' (2011c: 42) finds a possibly unlikely analogue in Whitney's own machines for visualizing abstraction. Rancière does not pursue this analogy between camera and telephone exchange other than to underscore the automatism of both as mere 'transmitters' or relays for movement and information; but this crossing between communications technologies – between the telephone and the camera as mediums of exchange – recalls Friedrich Kittler's adage that '[m]edia cross one another in time, which is no longer history' (1999: 115). Indeed, this overlapping calls into question the historical purity or specificity of any medium, which recalls Whitney's description of his own 'philosophy of the gadgeteer': 'It seems to be characteristic of this time,' he says, 'that innumerable so-called blind alleys submerged by industrialization revolutions are eventually rediscovered' (1980: 159). This anachronistic media-industrial history, of which the *Vertigo* title credits are but one example, is not peculiar to Whitney, since it is characteristic of a wider history of animation and moving image media that children's toys, discarded machines and gadgets are always beeing 'rediscovered' and put to new uses. But the particular results of Whitney's 'gadgeteering' are quite consequential for the cinema.

The machine that Whitney used, according to his son, Michael, was a mechanized pantograph – a device developed for the accurate scaling and reproduction of intricate designs, such as in minting or engraving (see Whitney 1997). According to Dan Aulier, Whitney faced two interrelated problems in producing and animating the Lissajous figures for Bass's title sequence: first, to construct an animation stand that could rotate 360 degrees continuously without entangling wires; and second, to build control linkages between the movement of a rotating base and floating pendulum that drew each spiral. Aulier explain that '[t]he machine that controlled the spinning base was connected to the pendulum, which allowed for the two to move in a controlled pattern, making it possible to create the spirals' (1998: 153). It is this multi-directional synchronous control that Whitney is describing when he refers to his earliest mechanical drawing machines as 'a drawing tool capable of incremental variation'; and it is the exact measurement of movement that is innovative in Whitney's machines, which develop into increasingly complex devices for synchronizing the camera movement and exposure with the base or plate holding the material to be animated. Although still reliant upon the frame-based (analogue) medium of celluloid, these machines operate outside a strictly manual frame-by-frame technique of traditional animation, attaining a degree of fluid transformation that will later emerge with digital filmmaking. As Whitney himself ruefully reflected of these machines, some ten years after *Vertigo*: 'It was only with a kind of hindsight, a kind of delayed double-take, that I realized I was working with a machine that was really a mechanical model of the modern digital computer graphic systems' (1980: 171). Indeed, the abstract images and effects that he went on to produce with his next DIY machine – which he built using discarded war surplus analogue computers from M5 anti-aircraft gun directors (Whitney 1980: 159) – came to inaugurate the catalogue of visual effects for Hollywood movies, MTV and the visualization algorithms for iTunes and screensavers everywhere.[13] What we might be seeing in the abstract figures in *Vertigo*'s much-discussed title sequence is a kind of redistribution of elements within the cinematic image, which cuts across and rearranges the relations and meanings of the medium. It is at one and the same time one of the earliest examples of (analogue) computer graphics in the cinema and a remediated remnant of nineteenth-century scientific entertainments.

In spite of his weak protestations, then, Whitney's 'fine' art is no enemy of so-called commercial cinema or its industry. This is because, as Rancière remarks of the uncanny parallel between Mallarmé and Behrens, 'industrial production and artistic creation are [both] committed to doing something else than what they do – to create not only objects but a sensorium, a new partition of the perceptible' (2010: 122). Hence, although Whitney turns to these remnants of pre-cinematic visualization devices – pendulums, pantographs, harmonographs – as a way of creating pure abstractions and countering the representational aesthetic that Disney standardized with the multi-plane camera, the resulting 'spectacular effects' are just as easily turned back into devices for the generation of the 'emotional resonance' with the story and its characters that Saul Bass sought. Like Vertov's machinic dream of a 'cinematographic communism', Whitney's own technical innovations are destined to be recycled 'to the profit of the old art of stories' (Rancière 2011c: 45). In this context it becomes possible to situate the spinning geometric figures of *Vertigo* – unlike the 'garish effects' used in the nightmare sequence – as an early incarnation of an avowed 'anti-Disney' aesthetic, albeit one that necessarily thwarts itself. Rejecting the use of 'static fixed interrelations' between fore-, mid- and backgrounds by which Disney's 'multi-plane pans' had achieved ever greater degrees of animated verisimilitude, Whitney decreed that no single point in the pictorial plane should be fixed in relation to any other – 'It is strictly forbidden to have anything to do with two or more points having fixed spatial interrelations' (Whitney 1980: 200). Yet this rule, most clearly visible in the two rotating, spirograph-like 'rose' figures of the sequence, achieves the very contrary result of producing the highly effective dizzying perceptual field required for the *Vertigo* titles. We might offer this story of Whitney's experiments in motion graphics as another kind of thwarted fable whereby the aesthetic effect is neither reducible to nor predictable from the specific technical and material nature of the mechanism – but nor is it entirely thinkable without them.

Conclusion: The Specific Variability of the Medium

> A medium is something through which or by means of which something specific gets done or said in particular ways. It provides, one might say, particular ways to get through to someone, to make sense; in art, they are forms, like forms of speech. To discover ways of making sense is always a matter of the relation of an artist to his art, each discovering the other. (Cavell 1979: 32)

It might be objected that the preceding analysis risks overdetermining the technical-material craft of image-making at the expense of a rich description of how medium reveals itself in the spectator's experience of watching and evaluating a (or rather, *this*) particular film. This, I take it, is Stanley Cavell's point when he criticizes (academic) film analysis for 'getting technical', the only relevant technical issues being those in front of the spectator's eyes. His example is apt in the present context: 'you may not know how Hitchcock gets the stairwell to distort that particular way in *Vertigo*, but you can see that he got it' (Cavell 1979: xxii). This is a fair point. Indeed, there are useful parallels between Cavell's rethinking of medium-specificity and Rancière's 'thwarted fable'. Like Rancière, Cavell distances the concept of 'medium' from a privileged reference to its material or technical basis; like Rancière, he locates the meaning of the medium to the process of making sense of each particular film; and like Rancière, this shift reflects Cavell's privileging of spectatorship (and a certain cinephilia) as the locus of film criticism. Indeed, we might be tempted to map Cavell's statement of the always-particular (and thus variable) 'specificity' of any medium on to Rancière's redescription of the medium as 'a surface of conversion':

> A medium is not a 'proper' means or material. It is a surface of conversion: a surface of equivalence between the different arts' ways of

making; a conceptual space of articulation between these ways of making and forms of visibility and intelligibility determining the way in which they can be viewed and conceived. (2007a: 75–6)

A subtle yet decisive difference from Cavell emerges here, however, because Rancière's reading of a film – in this case, *Vertigo* – as a particular network of relays *between different arts* allows him to cleave to the matter of the medium and its 'ways of *making*' precisely insofar as he cleaves or divides it, *from* itself and *across* very different media histories and categories. To know about an art and its 'ways of making' (such as Whitney's) in this context is not to privilege technical craft at the expense of accounting for the position of spectatorship, or the relation between aesthetic and political sensibilities – that is, to retreat from theory into practice – but to refuse to continue to treat them as if they existed separately. As Rancière reiterates time and again in his writings on aesthetics, this argument distances itself from lamentations about the political and social decline of art just as much as it refuses any attempt to redeem the aesthetic as an ethical project. Consequently, Rancière's rethinking of what a medium can mean intervenes in a contemporary context characterized by alternating celebration and lamentation regarding the 'demise' (or 'rebirth') of something called 'cinema'. This cinephile's affirmation of art's disciplinary and historical 'impurity' allows him to recast 'medium' as 'a sensible milieu, a particular sensorium' capable of being redistributed anew in each moment or work – and therefore never predictable in its meaning or effect.

Notes

1. It is worth noting that Whitney's rather dismissive reference to a film now considered to be one of Hitchcock's 'classics' (if not his masterpiece) would also have reflected a not-uncommon view in the early 1970s. After some poor reviews and moderate box office returns on release in 1958, from the late 1960s onwards the film's reputation suffered further from the limited availability and variable quality of prints (see Barr 2002: 12–13; Aulier 1998: 174–8).
2. Whitney had also worked as a commercial animation director for television, directing a trio of animated shorts for UPA's *Gerald McBoing-Boing* television series in 1955.
3. Sudeep Dasgupta situates Rancière's engagement with film in terms

of his broader 'in-disciplinary' method: 'Rancière's engagement with cinema is less that of a "film theorist" than a cinephile's poetic engagement with the history of cinema' (Dasgupta 2009: 339). Rancière himself gives more direct recollections of cinema-going in a recent interview with Oliver Davis (Rancière 2011d).

4. Or as Rancière puts it more succinctly in a recent essay on photography: 'the idea of the medium's specificity is always an idea of mediality' (Rancière 2011h: 37).

5. *From Among the Dead* was for a time the working title of Hitchcock's film.

6. However, it might be objected that, of all of Hitchcock's films, perhaps *Vertigo* is less the product of a concern for narrative suspense than the themes of obsession and the uncanny associated with a surrealistic 'cinema of the fantastic' (see Conomos 2000). I thank Catherine Constable for reminding me of this point.

7. Although John Ferren's detailed sketch sticks closely to the outline drafted by Hitchcock and scriptwriter Alec Coppel (see Aulier 1998: 42–3), he seems to have been given free rein in visualizing the sequence. It was already Hitchcock's established practice to give artists considerable freedom to design and produce particular special sequences or effects (for example, Dalí and Bass).

8. The minutes of the meeting of 4 September 1957 at Hitchcock's office give 'animated' instead of 'Disney' here (see Aulier 1998: 146), a not-uncommon synonymy.

9. An unspecified object or device, *esp.* a mechanical one, *Oxford English Dictionary*.

10. These oscillating figures are named after the French mathematician Jules Antoine Lissajous (1819–68), who first produced them using a light reflected from an arrangement of vibrating mirrors (similar to the principles that produce Chladni patterns). They are also known as 'Lissajous-Bowditch curves', since the same discovery had been made some years earlier (unknown to Lissajous) by Nathaniel Bowditch (1773–1838) using a compound pendulum as a drawing mechanism. This is how both Bass and Whitney would create their respective figures a century later.

11. As Murray Pomerance puts it, rather drily: 'The recurring theme in *Vertigo* is recurring themes' (2004: 245).

12. It is easy to forget quite how radical this way of making film title sequences – inaugurated by Saul Bass's titles for *The Man with the Golden Arm* (dir. Otto Preminger, 1955) – was at the time.

13. Lev Manovich argues that the contemporary proliferation of –

effects-driven visual culture can be traced back to Whitney's film *Catalog* (1961) – a showreel of effects that he had produced with his new war surplus analogue computer apparatus – and suggests that 'it is tempting to read *Catalog* as one of the founding moments of new media' (Manovich 2001: 236).

10

The Medium Is Not the Message: Rancière, Eschatology and the End of Cinema

James A. Steintrager

Let me begin with a provocation: Jacques Rancière is *not* a media theorist. This provocation is not mine but his, and he makes it in order insist that we account for the complex genealogy of aesthetics rather than giving in to the temptations of reduction and simplification inherent in much media theory. Thus, in the prologue to *Film Fables*, Rancière remarks: 'There is no shortage of theoreticians who have attempted to ground the art of moving images on the solid base of the means specific to it. But the means specific to yesterday's analogical machine and today's digital machine have shown themselves equally suitable for filming both love stories and abstract dances and forms' (2006a: 4). He continues: 'It is only in the name of an *idea of art* that we can establish the relationship between a technical apparatus and this or that type of fable' (2006a: 4, my emphasis). A similar argument constitutes what we might call the leitmotif of Rancière's essay 'The Future of the Image'. Having posited the 'intertwining of art and non-art, of art, commodities, and discourse' – the case for complexity – Rancière remarks that it is precisely this intertwining that 'contemporary mediological discourse seeks to efface, intending by the latter, over and above the discipline that professes itself as such, the set of discourses that would deduce the forms of identity and alterity peculiar to images from the properties of apparatuses of production and diffusion' (2007a: 17–18).

Rancière objects to what we might call the materialist determinism of dominant discourses about images and mediation. Media theorists, broadly construed, choose this path because it purportedly enables you to read the nature of images directly from *things* such as cameras, projectors and screens – causality and therefore explanation grounded in 'materialities' rather than floating in the nebulous ether of ideas. Using images as our example, the standard assumption goes something like this: any difference in medium as apparatus of production or diffusion entails or induces a categorical change in the image itself, which is then differentiated according to the supposed character of a particular material substrate. Similar claims are made about the mediation of texts, sounds and so forth.

My aim is to draw out and to examine the argumentative strand in Rancière's work: his refutation of the claim that the medium is really all that matters as reductive, deceptive and misguided. I am most interested in his conceptualization of cinema at a time when *digital* media – or rather, theorists of digital media – were increasingly proclaiming the end of the dominance of film. While *Film Fables* remains Rancière's most sustained account of cinema and cinematic history, I will privilege 'The Future of the Image' because this essay most clearly, if in certain respects obliquely, addresses the digital as epochal divide. 'The Future of the Image' – 'Le Destin des images' in the original – was first presented as a lecture in January 2002. Coming less than a year after the events of 9/11, which were repeated on screens constantly, and as digital technologies such as the Internet were on their way to ubiquity, we might expect the-end-is-nigh proclamations. The portentous title, however, is rhetorical bait-and-switch. The essay begins with a shrug: the reader expecting yet another addition to the 'apocalyptic discourses of today's cultural climate' will be disappointed (Rancière 2007a: 1). Nor will she encounter any prophetic rumblings about 'the contemporary twilight of a reality devoured by media images and an art doomed to monitors and synthetic images' (2007a: 2).[1] While Rancière mentions no particular target or carrier of these 'apocalyptic discourses', the name Jean Baudrillard comes readily to mind. After all, while developing notions of simulacra and simulation since the early 1980s, Baudrillard in *Le Crime parfait* (1995) had claimed that with the abetment of digital technologies reality itself had been murdered. One finds similar arguments in theorists such as Paul Virilio, where the ever-increasing speed of information transfer points us in the direction of collapse: 'with real-time technologies, real presence bites the dust' (1995: 57).

But there is no reason to stick to theorists alone while we are attributing apocalyptic discourses. In fact, cinematic production did not so much ignore or hide from prophetic pronouncements of this sort – pronouncements in which the end of the cinematic age was figured – as stage them. Most famously, the Wachowski brothers' Hollywood spectacle *The Matrix* (1999), unfolding its own vision of the desert of the real, openly referred to Baudrillard's influence. On the side of melodrama, there was director Peter Weir's *The Truman Show* (1998), in which an entire virtual world is built around an ignorant protagonist whose life is captured and televised for entertainment until he begins to see through the ruse. And even after the Y2K bug had proven a damp squib and the dot-com bubble, having reached maximum market inflation in March 2000, had burst – events and non-events that might have tempered the apocalyptic tone – it was still easy to find hyperbolic depictions of the dystopian future of the image. A less obvious, post-millennial and French example would be director Olivier Assayas's *Demonlover*. Released in 2002, the film cannot be a target of Rancière's deflationary rhetoric, although it nonetheless confirms his take on the zeitgeist: it depicts a world in which corporations vie for rights to the latest information technologies such as 3D virtual pornography – a world where the line between reality and digitally delivered sadomasochistic fantasy relentlessly and immorally blurs. But while the films that I have mentioned are future-oriented and theorists futurologists of sorts, let us be clear: the past of the image is what Rancière's 'The Future of the Image' is primarily about. Indeed, it is an irreverent call for dispassionate historical reflection and a sceptical demand that we not wax eschatological but stick to the concrete and consider what has happened so that we might forge a path forward rather than retreading the same ground. What Rancière pinpoints and dissects in the apocalyptic rhetoric is an adherence to discourses of art that are amusingly and almost literally *passé*.

The Idealism of Mediological Materialism

The first encounter with the medium-is-not-the-message leitmotif in 'The Future of the Image' comes right at the outset, when Rancière compares the media of television and cinema using concrete examples. What is the difference between Robert Bresson's film *Au hasard Balthazar* (1966) and the television quiz show *Questions pour un champion*? Mediological discourse would like to locate the difference in the apparatuses of production and diffusion. With film, the source (projector) and the object of perception (projection) are clearly separated. For this reason, we might call cinema a medium that belongs inherently to the realm of the image proper, where *image* always implies an other, a point of origin, a reference. At least as a medium of diffusion, television lacks this distinction and would belong to the realm of the *visual*: 'the television image has no Other by virtue of its very nature . . . it has its light in itself, while the cinematic image derives it from an external source' (Rancière 2007a: 2). Again, these distinctions are not Rancière's but rather those attributed to a certain mediological *doxa*. A citation from Régis Debray's *Vie et mort de l'image* about television provides an instance of such differentiation according to medium of diffusion: 'The image here has its light in-built. It reveals itself. With its source in itself, it becomes in our eyes its own cause. Spinozist definition of God or substance' (Rancière 2007a: 2; Debray 1992: 382). The implied contrast is cinema, the light of which is not immanent but is, so to speak, transcendent.

Rancière's suggestion is that to draw distinctions in this manner is not adequate or accurate, and not only because we can invalidate such distinctions with counter-examples. What happens when a film is shown on television? Even given the different apparatuses of diffusion, is a television camera significantly different from a movie camera? What happens when both television and cinema images are captured, processed or created digitally? Mediological discourse can claim that these counter-examples are trivial and that the deeper truth has to do with dominant media at a given time: the age of cinema and projection, the age of in-built diffusion, the age of digitization, and so forth. I am oversimplifying, but there is definitely something like this in the work of a major media theorist such as Friedrich Kittler, who explicitly stated that '[m]edia determine our situation' and who bundled together the media technologies of film, gramophone and typewriter to form a particular epoch of media, history and human experience that replaced print as dominant and that was now itself being rapidly replaced by digital technologies (Kittler 1999: xxxix). I insist on the past tense, because the date of the original German publication of *Gramophone, Film, Typewriter*, the book in which Kittler makes this case, was 1986. Or consider Virilio's statement of media-underwritten epochalization and dismissal of continuities across media as ultimately insignificant: 'Each new regime remains unrecognizable when it emerges since it preserves certain traits of the preceding regime, much as a son looks vaguely like his father. We have thus, without realizing it, gone from simple statistical management to a new phenomenon of *representation*, the virtual theatricalization of the real world' (1995: 57).

Before examining the matter of epochal media history more thoroughly, let me emphasize Rancière's simple point that the distinctions most relevant to his examples from television and cinema cannot be somehow read off of the media:

> the technical properties of the cathode tube are one thing and the aesthetic properties of the images we see on the screen are another. The screen precisely lends itself to accommodating the results both of *Questions pour un champion* and of Bresson's camera. It is therefore clear that it is these results which are inherently different. (2007a: 2)

If mediological discourse can somehow not draw this obvious conclusion – that the differences at work are, in Rancière's words, 'aesthetic' rather than 'technical' – there must be a reason for it. We might simply call this reason the persistence of the McLuhanite thesis and slogan, 'The medium is the message' (McLuhan 1964: 13). And while Marshall McLuhan certainly had engaging co-formulators of the first wave of media theory in the 1950s and 60s with the likes of Walter Ong and Harold Innes, it was his gnomic formulation that was most widely diffused and that collapsed most clearly the distinction between content and apparatus, positing the former as a function of the latter by asserting their otherwise paradoxical sameness. It was to this collapse that Baudrillard would refer when claiming that high-definition reproduction in the case of digital technology is in fact a simulation that reduces the real to the merest residuum: 'The highest definition of the medium corresponds to the lowest definition of the message' (Baudrillard 1996: 31).

As the citation above suggests, the McLuhanite thesis was deeply embedded in the second wave of media theory. One can point, for example, to Mark Poster's reformulation of Marxist dialectical materialism in his prioritization of the 'mode of information' (Poster 1990) and to Kittler's addition to Foucauldian discourse analysis of the assertion of a 'technological a priori' determined by media (Kittler 1999: 117). Interestingly, both Poster and Kittler amalgamated into their versions of media studies what came to be known in North American academic circles as simply 'French theory' (Cusset 2008). Kittler's work is thus deeply informed not only by Foucault, but also by Derrida and Lacan (as different as

these thinkers otherwise are). Poster meanwhile has served as a
key disseminator and explicator of Baudrillard's interventions.
In neither Kittler nor Poster, however, is the figure who played a
major role in what might be called the first wave of French media
theory prominent: Guy Debord. And it is to Debord and his heirs
that Rancière makes glancing – and dismissive – reference when
he states that the 'exorbitant power attributed to the device itself
corresponds to a rather simplistic view of the poor morons of the
society of the spectacle, bathing contentedly in a flood of media
images' (2007a: 28). Much like the Frankfurt School version of
Adorno and Horkheimer, Debord extended Marxist analysis of
industrial capitalism into the post-war acceleration of commodi-
fied cultural production: film, television and relentless advertising,
all underwritten by technologies of mass communication. The
so-called society of the spectacle was itself envisioned by Debord
and his fellow Situationists as an almost all-encompassing trap
that could, at best, be taken on a *dérive*: disrupted, redirected,
used against itself. By the time we get to Virilio, to Baudrillard and
to the millennial moment, it is too late even for this: 'Virtuality
is different from the spectacle, which still left room for a critical
consciousness and demystification. . . . Whereas we could face up
to the unreality of the world as spectacle, we are defenceless before
the extreme reality of this world, before this virtual perfection'
(Baudrillard 1996: 29).

I sketch out this intellectual history to prove Rancière's point by
raising it to the level of second-order observation: to understand
media theory as opposed to understanding media, one must concentrate on discursive genealogies and institutional histories rather
than – or at least as well as – information technologies. Of course,
Rancière would not deny the importance of technologies such as
the printing press, telegraph, telephone, camera obscura, projector, Internet and so forth. In discussing the production, circulation
and redefinition of 'artistic images' in the nineteenth century, for
example, he remarks that it was 'thanks to mechanical presses and
the new procedure of lithography' that 'an encyclopaedia of the
shared human inheritance' made up of 'remote life-forms', 'works
of art' and 'popularized bodies of knowledge' could emerge
(2007a: 16). Rancière does not insist that we choose content and
the history of ideas instead, but rather that media materialities are
but one aspect of a complex web of relations. In this regard, an
irony to which Rancière draws our attention is that the insistence

on media as all-encompassing and determinant actually highlights the occult *idealism* of such thinking. The citation from Debray is thus reproduced to puncture the hieratic pomposity of reading metaphysical distinctions such as the Spinozist immanence of the visual versus the transcendence of the image into apparatuses. In other words, one of the problems with the materialist thesis is that its upholders do not take it seriously enough and even inadvertently subvert it: the thesis becomes the basis for a vaticinal fantasy about media history and its apocalyptic future. If Rancière advocates the explanatory force of 'ideas' or 'aesthetics' against the material and technical, it is in part to show that those who uphold the latter terms are not only reductive but also profoundly inconsistent.

Images, Operations and Programmes

If the medium is not the message, how then should we grasp the distinctions between a televised quiz show such as *Questions pour un champion* and a film such as *Au hasard Balthazar*? How exactly are 'ideas' or 'aesthetics' inscribed into the mediation of images? Anyone can readily see that the quiz show engages and amuses while the film in question provokes reflection, but how do these distinctions manifest themselves? This is how Rancière describes Bresson's film: 'The images of *Au hasard Balthazar* are not primarily manifestations of the properties of a certain technical medium, but operations: relations between a whole and parts; between a visibility and a power of signification and affect associated with it; between expectations and what happens to meet them' (2007a: 3). Shifting the ground from apparatus to operation, what Rancière locates are various relations. These can be relations between images, between image and signification, and between what a viewer expects to see and what he or she actually does see. For a certain historical strand of cinema of which Bresson's film is an example, these operations take the form of a (pretended) disruption of other, naturalized forms of communication via image and plot: 'Modern cinema and criticism claimed to interrupt the flow of media and advertising images by suspending the connections between narration and meaning. The freeze-frame that closes Truffaut's *Quatre cent coups* was emblematic of this suspension' (2007a: 27).

With his references to 'modern cinema' and to directors such as Bresson and Truffaut – Godard is another frequent point of reference in his work – Rancière tacitly introduces an important distinction: 'modern' as an adjective refers to the *types* of films to which he refers and to a certain period of the institutionalization of cinematic production in France that we can loosely characterize as the emergence of the *auteur* school. In much cinema, the story is supposed to – that is, it is expected to – flow. In so-called modern cinema, this flow and these expectations are stopped, redirected and thwarted by operations that have nothing to do with the apparatus per se. In this regard, they run parallel to what Debord put forward critically as the *dérive*. Rancière does not acquiesce in the notion that such a stoppage, redirection and self-reflection is *eo ipso* critical. He does, however, think that it is the hallmark of cinema produced according to a certain *programme* – to use the term to which Rancière frequently has recourse and that itself appears appositely taken up from the language of computing – that he elsewhere calls the aesthetic regime (as opposed to the earlier ethical and representative regimes of artistic production [Rancière 2007a]). Such a programme and the common or affiliated operations that body forth that programme may emerge, develop and fade over a given duration. However, we must proceed with caution before taking a particular programme and treating it as a general epoch – let alone as an epoch determined by media.

To grasp what Rancière has in mind with the term 'programme' – and particularly how the 'programme' of modern cinema works – I think that it is useful to turn briefly to systems theory as an account of differentiation within mass media. Niklas Luhmann proposes that mass media as a social system produce a 'background knowledge' and a 'background reality' that is highly variegated and 'not subject to consensus' (2000: 65–6). Within the mass media, however, strands have emerged – news, advertising and entertainment – that are codified and operate in different ways. As anyone who has watched Fox News will readily grasp, these strands can and do borrow from one another, but they can usually nonetheless be distinguished and are marked or framed as distinct. Advertisements take place before the film; product placement in the film tends to jar precisely because we perceive that the frame has been crossed. Entertainment works by building up tensions and relieving them *internally*. A further entailment follows:

In order to be able to generate and sustain tension, one has to have the author stepping back behind the text, because inside the text he would be someone who already knows the ending or who at any moment can make things turn out just as it suits him. Every trace of his involvement must be erased. The mechanism of generating the text must not appear again in the text itself, because otherwise it would not be possible for self-reference and other-reference to be clearly distinguished. Although entertainment texts also have an author and are communicated, the difference of information and utterance must not appear in the text – if it did, the discrepancy between the constative and performative textual components would come to light and the attention of the one engaged in understanding would be drawn to this difference and thereby diverted. (Luhmann 2000: 56–7)

Art, on the contrary, distinguishes itself from entertainment by activating in various ways the discrepancies that are suppressed in entertainment and it actively seeks the *diversion* of the reader or spectator to the other side of the frame – to communication about the object rather than within it. This at least would be one of the features of differentiated, autonomous art as it unfolds as an institution in the nineteenth century and beyond.

Luhmann privileges what we might call the classic media technology of print for his examples – and claims that it was in the mid-nineteenth century that, within this medium and with content such as Flaubert's *Education sentimentale* and Melville's *The Confidence Man*, the novel as art definitively split with the entertainment strand. He otherwise tends to concentrate on broadcast media such as television and radio. In spite of this default to texts – and primarily novels at that – as entertainment, one could easily make the necessary adjustment for cinema, where the auteur precisely inserts himself to draw the medium away from entertainment and towards art.[2] In this regard, Rancière makes explicit that the programme of modern cinema may not only run on other media platforms, but is frequently transferred from them. Thus, according to Rancière, the operations that we encounter in *Au hasard Balthazar* are not peculiar to the film image or its operations, but belong to the genealogy of modernism and aesthetic autonomy that Rancière, like Luhmann, finds epitomized in Flaubert (Rancière 2007a: 5).[3] Further, the modern novel itself is in part a product of transmedial encounters such as the reassessment of Dutch genre painting as a way to shake off the weight of history painting – with its classical themes and epic grandeur – and the transfer of the genre model from the medium of the canvas and image to press and word. The modern novel – as well as the 'new novel' and other innovative textual movements – has inhabited film history to such an extent that to treat the materiality of the medium as sole or even primary determinant appears absurd. That is, just as new digital technologies have 'remediated' older technologies – the iBook app arranges volumes on a virtual wooden bookshelf, for example – film was thoroughly penetrated with novelistic operations (on remediation, see Grusin and Boulter 2000).

For Rancière, both modern cinema and criticism need to be positioned and understood in relation to a historical genealogy or programme of aesthetics that stretches back into and remediates the operations of the novel. This programme, moreover, in many respects exhausted itself in the early to mid-twentieth century with a two-stranded project to think through the possible end of the mediation of the image: the push towards an 'imageless art' (which culminated in Symbolism and Suprematism) and a collapse of mediation as a 'becoming-life of art' (which culminated in Futurism and Constructivism) (Rancière 2007a: 21).[4] An example of the latter drawn not from static visual arts but rather cinema is Dziga Vertov's *Man with a Movie Camera* (1929), where the distinction between image-making apparatus and human eye is blurred, and with it the distinction between human perception and mediation. Rancière does treat this two-stranded programme as epochal: emerging in the 1890s, and intersecting in the 1910s and 1920s in the project to identify 'the forms of an art which was purely art with the forms of a new life abolishing the very specificity of art' (Rancière 2007a: 21). It was then discarded as irrelevant. As Rancière puts it, the programme came to an end 'when the authorities to whom this sacrifice of images was offered made it clear that they wanted nothing to do with constructor-artists, that they themselves were taking care of construction, and required of artists nothing but precisely images, understood in a narrowly defined sense: illustrations putting flesh on their programmes and slogans' (2007a: 21).

While the epoch of this programme and its strands may have exhausted itself and ended *in theory*, it drifts on in 'a minor key' in the dreams of 'architects, urban designers, choreographers' and those who work in the theatre (Rancière 2007a: 21). Modern cinema also provides examples of such atavism, as does criticism, and the two are frequently enough intertwined. For example, Rancière discusses Barthes's shift from a semiotic analysis of the images that would discover meaning – that is, ideology – everywhere in his *Mythologies* to an investment in the *punctum* – the insignificant, enrapturing detail rather than the significant *studium* – in his writings on photography (Barthes 1972; 1981). Rancière characterizes this shift as an act of mourning. Yet this is not mourning for the material world that has been lost to the multitude and virtuality of technologically reproduced images and that haunts the photograph: the reality of chemical processes in producing the image serving as a sort of ectoplasm or material trace of the once-living – the rendering present of the past. Rather, it is a threnody for a *discourse* about images that has had its moment:

> But the mourning declared for this system seems to forget that it was itself a form of mourning for a certain programme: the programme of a certain end of images. For the 'end of images' is not some mediatic or mediumistic catastrophe, to counter which we need today to restore goodness knows what transcendence enclosed in the very process of chemical printing and threatened by the digital revolution. (Rancière 2007a: 18, translation modified)

Barthes keeps alive something that has ended – should have ended – but that lingers as a sort of evolutionary survival. Likewise, while more recent mediological discourse, with its insistence on impending digital apocalypse, would appear future-oriented rather than replaying a past programme, its ideas and its operations, for Rancière the truth is quite the opposite.

Old Extremes and New Extremes (c. 2000)

The printing press can deliver Proust, Danielle Steele or *Twilight*. Gilt-edged paper and fine binding do not make pulp fiction into art, although this distinction ought not be reified, and framing does make a difference: when the Marquis de Sade made it into the nationally prestigious Editions de la Pléiade, this indicated that he should be read not for titillation, horror, or even anthropological or historical interest alone – he became an *author*. The first thing we notice about cinema qua art is that it sets up a certain parasitic relation to other image regimes such as advertising and narrative or so-called genre cinema. Reading Rancière with Luhmann, we might say that 'modern cinema' *differentiates* itself by implicit other-reference to the usual, supposedly unanalysed flow of images, and it does so by disrupting or freezing that flow, forcing us out of the frame and the coherence of internally generated and resolved tensions. For example – and as Rancière puts it – one of modern cinema's 'operations' has been to work at the level of the relation 'between expectations and what happens to meet them' (Rancière 2007a: 3). Of course, films that seek out the art strand usually have much smaller audiences and cannot rely on the distribution chains of mainstream, commercial cinema. They usually require governmental or other forms of subsidy and patronage. Interestingly, this would also appear to guarantee their 'autonomy' from commercial constraints, although it would simultaneously appear that government subsidy happens for political motives: it is important in terms of national (sometimes regional or more local) *cultural capital* to have specifically artistic film products (on cultural capital, see Bourdieu 1986). Moreover, this sort of cinema has now been reflectively labelled by critics as itself a genre: 'art house' (Wilinsky 2001).

In this regard, Truffaut's freeze-frame not only 'literalizes' the stoppage constitutive of the aesthetic regime of artistic production, it has ironically become a sort of *brand* of cinematic modernity. As devices such as self-reference, breaking the fourth wall (itself borrowed from drama) and so forth become exactly what we expect, these too must be undermined, avoided or varied. Indeed, as Rancière points out, advertising has long since taken up such operations to win over consumers-as-spectators by demonstrating that we are all on the same side and in-the-know: 'The procedures of cutting and humour have themselves become the stock-in-trade of advertising, the means by which it generates both adoration of its icons and the positive attitude towards them created by the very possibility of ironizing it' (2007a: 28).[5] Not that cinematic auteurs have given up their use of or investment in the operations that were once specific to modern cinema as carrier of an aesthetic programme strand. We see all of these techniques at work in director Michael Haneke's *Funny Games* (1997), which mimics slasher films but thwarts expectations by keeping violence off screen, by having characters address the viewer, by not cashing in on the pleasures of revenge, and the whole Brechtian arsenal.[6] Similar are those films categorized as 'New French Extremity'. This loosely defined movement in certain respects defines art cinema and particularly French cinema at the turn of the millennium. Examples include Virginie Despentes and Coralie Trinh Thi's *Baise-moi* (2000) and Gaspard Noé's *Irréversible* (2002). Assayas's *Demonlover* exists on the only slightly tamer edge of such extremes. Like *Funny Games*, these films often self-consciously copy or pastiche the most shocking or abject entertainment genres. In so doing they repeat the avant-garde dare – around at least since Duchamp's readymades – and pose that most aesthetic of questions: 'Is this art?' This move might be seen both as a reaction against the previous generation of auteurs and their now-familiar operations, and at the same time as itself familiar. Of course, the expected disruption of expectations itself creates a vicious circle that even extreme tactics can only momentarily overcome.

Moreover, the historical genealogy of the 'new extremity' is clear, and it cuts across media platforms just as reading Rancière would lead us to expect. One need only mention Antonin Artaud's theatre of cruelty and the theoretical reception of the Marquis de Sade's novels by avant-gardists from Apollinaire and André Breton to Bataille and beyond. There is something ironically very traditional – and in institutional terms very French – about this cinematic movement from the turn of the millennium. Of course, the very newness of the extremity implies an old extremity and thus a movement of return. In particular, we see a reassertion of 'immediation' or the annulment of the mediation of the image and the capture of the real that Rancière attributes to one programme strand of the historical avant-garde – the strand that Barthes was already mourning in the form of the photographic *punctum*. Interestingly, cinema itself has found itself positioned by certain upholders of drama as materially inadequate to carry out the act of immediation because lacking the bodily presence of theatre (Rancière 2009a: 16–17). Yet whereas theatre used to stake its supposedly media-specific claim against books and film, now film – as idea and aesthetic if not as technology – makes the same claim on presence in relation to the digital and to the perception of a general virtualization of reality. In this regard, one of the hallmarks of new extreme cinema generally has been unsimulated sex scenes (this extends beyond French examples such as *Baise-moi* and Leos Carax's *Pola X* [1999] to films such as Lars von Trier's *Idioterne* [1998] and Vincent Gallo's *Brown Bunny* [2003]). Some directors have quite literally enacted a discourse of the image that Rancière associates with – among others – Barthes's rejection of the reducibility of all images to the hieroglyphic/ideological sign and his embrace of the photographic *punctum* as 'senseless naked presence' (2007a: 15). Needless to say, unsimulated sex scenes are the essence of pornographic filmmaking, so the special claim to presence or authenticity in the new extremity has to be framed. It is only when claims to art or political efficacy are made that such operations become transgressive in the precise sense of *crossing over* from one frame to another. This looping backward into the discourses of theatre and photography by another medium – in this instance, film – is something that Rancière clearly marks: the past of the image weighs on the present and blocks the future from unfolding; what we witness is not the apocalypse but repetition.

In Rancière's intervention we find epochs that do not or refuse to come fully to an end, programmes that are completed or exhausted but linger as ghosts or zombies, and, if we are to go by the apocalyptic discourses of the millennial moment, prophets who grow more strident after the expiration date has past. There appears to be a fundamental paradox at work: the epoch of the end of the image is over; the epoch will not end. And what was this exhaustion? Did the discourse fail? Did it lack adequacy or correspondence? Failure and adequacy are, of course, two questions that you are not supposed to ask about a discourse, which is precisely constitutive of 'a reality' at a given time (that this statement is itself a paradox of self-reference has not escaped notice).[7] Just as a tension developed in Foucault's work between the archaeological and the genealogical, there appears an implicit tension between the epochal and the chronologically and otherwise intertwined in 'The Future of the Image'. Foucault, of course, was not the first historicist to posit discrete epochs marked by discontinuities and ruptures. There is a good bit of this already in Herder, and this fact alone points in the direction of genealogy. Foucault did break or attempted to break with dialectical accounts of historical change, where one period is present in the next and all is moving towards a final resolution, as in Hegel and Marx. These are clearly secularized – and barely secularized at that – adaptations of eschatological thinking. Rancière clearly rejects eschatology, and this rejection must be reflected into history, which cannot be heading towards any particular end (end as *telos*, utopian or dystopian perfection, or final resting point) but reveals instead the contingency of historical forms.

Still, we might wonder if there is an explanation for this survival or atavism that entails more than the unfinished work of mourning for a completed and presumably irretrievable programme. If this programme has not faded from the scene and instead repeats itself across new media and platforms, should we assume that it does so for some reason other than inertia? To suggest an answer to this question, let me turn once again to Luhmann. In the systems-theoretical account of history, the reason for this persistence – even after one would think the discursive or content side exhausted – is clear enough: it is a result or, better perhaps, *symptom* of the differentiation of social systems which for him is the hallmark of modernity. As art as a social system became autonomous and differentiated, it oscillated – and continues to do so – between a misguided assertion of such autonomy as total (art as life) and frustration that differentiation and autonomy entails a disconnection from direct, programmatic influence in politics, morality, culture and so forth. This oscillation, as Rancière notes and as Peter Bürger explored at length in his *Theory of the Avant-Garde*, is deeply embedded in avant-garde movements of the beginning of the twentieth century. As opposed to Bürger, however, Rancière tracks ramifications, interactions and intertwinings of the avant-garde, and he does so not only synchronically but diachronically, with reference to time lags, *après-coup* effects, survivals and other modes of non-linear temporality. While he still writes of epochs and endings, the past refuses to relinquish its grip on and relevance to the present – and thus to the future. It is for these reasons that we can grasp through Rancière how modern cinema as a historical type is both rejected and extended in the 'new extreme' cinema of the millennial moment of enunciation of 'The Future of the Image'. And while Luhmann's social differentiation might explain such persistence, Rancière has chosen a path that emphasizes not the differentiation of subsystems such as politics and art but areas of overlap, interaction and interference.

Notes

1. In similar anti-apocalyptic and contrarian fashion, Rancière had given a paper in New York in February 2002 that argued that the events of 9/11 'did not mark any rupture in the symbolic order'. The flipside of this assertion was that the rupture had already occurred and that the new form of the symbolic order was only brought into focus by what we might call the reception of 9/11. This new form entails the 'eclipse

of politics' as 'an identity that is inclusive of alterity' and as 'constituted through polemicizing over the common' and its replacement by an assumed or imposed *consensus* (Rancière 2010: 104).

2. While Luhmann has little to say about film as art per se, he clearly includes the medium as capable of artistic expression (2000: 231).

3. Flaubert is also central to Pierre Bourdieu's critical account of 'autonomous' art as a socio-cultural institution (Bourdieu 1996).

4. A useful point of comparison here is Bürger (1984). Like Rancière, Bürger talks about the avant-garde in historical and institutional terms, albeit not exactly as a programme for the end of the mediation of the image.

5. I might add that the freeze-frame became a gesture in, of all places, Hong Kong 'heroic bloodshed' cinema, where director John Woo in particular used it as a device to momentarily pause the otherwise frenetic action.

6. See A.O. Scott's scathing assessment of Haneke's gestures in his review of the American version of *Funny Games* (*New York Times*, 14 March 2008): 'using techniques that might have seemed audacious to an undergraduate literary theory class in 1985 or so, the film calls attention to its own artificial status. It actually knows it's a movie!'

7. See, for example, Hacking (2000) and, on a less sympathetic note, Boghossian (2006).

11

Remarks by Way of a Postface

Jacques Rancière

The editor of this volume insists that I make my contribution. The problem is that several contributors have already shown perfectly the principles that guide my approach to cinema and what consequences follow from them. Since I have no reason to contradict them and no wish to repeat them, the only path remaining to me is one of transposition. They have gone about things in an orderly way and argued with a subtlety that leaves nothing to be desired. It remains to me to punctuate in a crude and disorderly way the points that they have brought to light.

I will begin from the 'politics of the amateur'. This must be understood in a strict sense. I have never in my life given a single lecture on film theory nor have I taught in a 'film studies' department. Neither have I ever been a cinema critic. For several years I wrote chronicles for *Cahiers du cinéma*. But I remember once being reprimanded by the editor-in-chief for having expressed a judgement on a film that had not yet been released in the cinemas, something that was, according to him, the prerogative of the critic alone. Cinema was not for me first of all a scientific object or a professional matter. It was first of all a form of entertainment that I loved to go to and that I wanted to talk about because I loved it. To love cinema is firstly not to make distinctions, to love the darkness of the theatre and the flickering of the light on the screen, the emotion that the stories bear, the speed of a stampede or the slowness of a cloud, the posture of a body, the sound of a voice, a chiaroscuro, a reflection in a mirror or in a puddle of water, melancholic music and a thousand other sensory events [*événements sensibles*] which themselves echo a thousand other sensory events felt elsewhere: the rising or the setting of the sun on the sea, the lighted windows of the town, landscapes unfolding before a train window, childhood refrains, intonations of loved ones, words escaped from the pages of a book, etc. This singular combination of stories and images, of sensible immediacy and aleatory extensions, of living memory and retrospective reconstruction – it matters little whether you call it art or entertainment. What counts for the amateur, what makes it worth the effort of entering the theatre and of speaking about what you saw there – or of what you think you saw there – is this mobile composition of percepts and affects.

Here there is certainly an essential dividing line. One is interested in this mobile composition for its own sake, or one is interested in the ultimate cause of its existence, in the genre in which one can classify it, in the hidden truth of which one can make it the symptom. However opposed they may appear to be, from this point on there isn't much to choose between the criteria of appreciation. I recall the slightly disdainful astonishment of a Californian professor of cinema at hearing me evoke what was for him an unknown name: Anthony Mann. Consulting a dictionary of cinema confirmed for him that Mann was a director [*auteur*] of Westerns and commercial epics, a maker of the sort of popular entertainments that no cinéaste or professor of cinema who was conscious of the dignity of the art could be interested in. Twenty years later, the obstinate reproach repeatedly made to me by teachers of 'film studies' is exactly the inverse: I only ever talk about 'canonical' directors such as Anthony Mann or Vincente Minnelli, I speak of cinema as if it were an art when really it's an industry, a mass entertainment, a circulation of social images, and in fact is being overtaken by other more modern and more popular forms: television, the internet, etc. Yesterday's critique and today's have one point in common: neither of them needs to watch *The Far Country* or *Winchester '73*. It is enough for them to know where to classify them, that is, on the bad side: as entertainment for the old professor who thought himself modern, as art for today's professor who believes himself postmodern. This means that 'entertainment' and 'art' for them are only road signs indicating the direction in which they must not go. Nothing is more astonishing, from this point of view, than the revulsion that even just the word 'art' arouses in so many professors of cultural studies, media studies or disciplines of that kind. It is as if to consider a text, a piece of music, a performance or a collection of images as art and as a domain of 'aesthetic' appreciation were to fall into the most unpardonable sin of all, the sin against the scientific and militant spirit, that is to say, of 'elitism'. Yet this is surprising. Ordinary experience shows us that in every social milieu the word art is spoken, whether it is to designate the practice of a handyman, a cook, a rock star, a footballer, a woman who makes ceramics or a filmmaker. In every social milieu as well, individuals who are well or badly born, with or without qualifications, express judgements of taste and establish hierarchies, whether this is between popular singers, hip hop dancers or the creators of musical or cinematic works said to be experimental. Apparently one has to be in a university to see categories such as art and aesthetic judgement widely given a negative connotation. It is there above all that certain people try very hard to identify the way impressions that are the ordinary stuff of life are qualified with questions of cultural legitimacy, and to identify the fact of speaking about a film for its own sake with the shady business of the redeployment of 'cultural capital'. The fact is that this matter of legitimacy is like a suitcase with a false bottom. To denounce legitimate or 'canonical' culture can be, for an academic expert, a way of appropriating the authority that the professional militant held by virtue of speaking in the name of the humble and the voiceless [*sans-voix*]. But it is also to declare property rights over the territory of the non-legitimate, to make every popular entertainment or every ordinary practice [*manière de faire*] an object of academic knowledge. This is to institute a discipline of the non-legitimate.

It is here that, to differ from what Paul Bowman suggests in his introduction, I see an essential and persistent dividing line between the practice of cultural studies and other disciplines of the same kind and indiscipline as I understand it. These disciplines challenge or ghettoize a culture qualified as legitimate in order to be able to absorb everything that remains, every usage of everyday life and every Sunday recreation, thus delegitimized, in the empire of science. The 'either/or' – legitimate or non-legitimate – guarantees the homogeneity of the objects classed in this way. In this sense, it inherits a long normative tradition which was first embodied in sociological science: this has been and remains the science that brings the phenomena of distinction back to social facts, but is also the social norm attached to pursuing 'anomic' individuals and phenomena: those that blur the relation between (social) cause and (sensible) effect. Together, all these blurring phenomena can be summed up in one adjective: 'aesthetic'. If 'aesthetic' designates the remainder excluded from militant science, it is not, as this science might claim, because the word signifies the distinction that stamps it with the seal of legitimacy; it is, on the contrary, because it signifies the blurring of distinctions and of legitimacies.

To understand what this means, let us look at a film by one of 'my' directors: one of those films disdained as commercial yesterday by the avant-gardist guardians of pure art, today brushed aside [*écartés*] as 'canonical' by the professors of media studies; one of those Hollywood industry products that one saw first in the cinema, before the existence of the multiplex, like one novelty among others, and that one sees today as the work of an auteur in the retrospectives organized by *cinémathèques*, museums or festivals.[1] The film is called *Some Came Running*. It is firstly a story that has all the characteristics of an airport novel: a down-on-his-luck and alcoholic writer who finds himself again in the narrow-minded universe of a small town deep in the country; the impossible love that he vows to a young intellectual woman from the right circles; the desperate love vowed to him by a miserable bar hostess, herself pursued by an abandoned lover; his bourgeois brother's extramarital indiscretions with his secretary; the distress into which the adolescent who surprises her father is ready to throw herself; a series of intertwined intrigues that make us navigate between the Georgian-style villas of the local notables, the back-rooms of gambling dens filled with inveterate players and the lights of the popular fair. A perfect melodrama – good for those souls said to be sensitive (meaning by this, stupid) – whose fate for the entertainment marketplace given over to the rapid rotation of products is supposed to have been diverted by the 'aesthetes' sensitive to the power of a name, that of a director synonymous with 'distinction', Vincente Minnelli. Minnelli thus becomes a professional skilled at layering over the heaviest of melodramas or the flimsiest of comedies a glaze of harmonious colours and elegantly choreographed movement.

In fact, here is the ordinary way of understanding the word 'aesthetic': as the refinement, perceptible only to the privileged, which opposes itself directly or adds surreptitiously to montages of stimuli aimed at unrefined souls. And yet, from the first sequences of the film, one sees that this is not what is happening. Something happens to begin with that, according to proper aesthetic logic, depends on the will of the filmmaker and at the same time exceeds the limits of his power: the presence of a singular body, a female body with a round face clumsily made-up, with round eyes and a dazed look, inseparable from a strange accessory, a bag in the form of a fluffy rabbit to which she will later add an embroidered cushion bearing the word 'sweetheart'. The body of an 'idiot' then, but precisely a body that makes what the world normally calls 'idiocy' slip from being the failing of one who doesn't understand towards another idiocy, the idiocy of an art that blurs the reference points that serve ordinarily in understanding and in making understood. The body of Ginny is at once that of a child and an adult, comic and tragic, impermeable to the social play of transmitted significations and wholly receptive to the sensible affects that bear them. It is the body of a wild animal and of a doll overloaded with the signs and colours of artifice. In this, it is the carrier of a choreography, in a very precise sense: not a matter of tracery [*entrechats*] but, as Mallarmé summed it up, a way of making bodies turn around a subject rightly called 'star'. What constitutes the 'aesthetic' power of the film is the way in which characters and typical situations turn around this star of the stream and reflect its light, from the early morning which sees her land in the main street of the small town with her bag-rabbit until the night lights of the funfair which see her dying, her head on her embroidered cushion. It is this idiocy that challenges the opposition between the stupidity of a sentimental story and the 'formal' refinement of a *mise-en-scène*, and in doing so challenges the opposition between an entertainment for the people and an art for aesthetes. This invention of singular bodies that alter the normal distribution of powers attributed to bodies according to their condition, their place and their function is at the heart of cinema, by its own means and by its belonging to the aesthetic regime.

Benjamin showed how the cinema had made available to everyone the sensorial experiences that the other arts could only practise under the form of provocation, in which art, in a way, denied itself in order to stage the gap [*mettre en scène l'écart*] between its own artifice and common experience. Cinema was in a way dadaism or surrealism for everyone. I would rather evoke, for my part, the mimes and acrobats – Deburau, Tom Mathews or the Hanlon-Lees – whose performances the refined poets of the nineteenth century dreamed of importing into 'the great art' because they saw there the model of art for art's sake itself: an art unconcerned by anything other than the exact execution of its turns for the pleasure of the spectators. We know that the border crossing was made, in fact, in the other direction when artists trained in music-hall clowning like Charlie Chaplin seized the young movie camera to make their performance coincide with the lines of the new art of moving shadows. In the gesture of Ginny/Shirley MacLaine as she takes a red lipstick and a mirror out of her rabbit in order to redo her make-up before going to knock on the door of her rival, there is the memory of the gesture of Chaplin pulling on his too-tight jacket and correcting his pose at the moment of playing the seducer. In this lies the heritage to this art of phrasing in poses, in gestures and in mimicry, the behaviour of he or she who lands in a world to which they have not been invited: a comic art capable at the same time of making the most radical distresses resonate and of soothing them in graphically perfect forms. This composite art is at the heart of the 'commercial' film which puts singers and celebrity actresses (Frank Sinatra, Dean Martin, Shirley MacLaine) in the service of an airport novel intrigue, just as it is at the heart of the pure cinematographic work of Robert Bresson or of the 'elitist' cinema of Béla Tarr. Among the little sisters of the poor girl – face to face with her killer, jammed in with her bag-rabbit and her embroidered cushion – how can we not take account of two other 'idiots' transported from the pages of a book to the shadows on the screen: Mouchette, rolling towards the pond wrapped in the muslin dress that she has just torn, and Estike (*Satantango*), walking obstinately with her dead cat under her arm, over her shoulders her grandmother's cardigan, too big, and the kitchen curtain from which she has made a shawl, towards the place where she will absorb the remains of the rat poison given to the animal. Estike, the idiot who believed that one could grow a tree with leaves of gold by burying coins, and Ginny, the tart who believed that she could love a writer and even appreciate his writings, are themselves the inheritors of a long tradition first illustrated by novelists, that of the daughters of peasants who, like Emma Bovary, believed that they too had a right to beautiful things. These are, we might recall, the same daughters of peasants that Clement Greenberg accused of causing the catastrophe of great art because they – along with their brothers and husbands – had wanted, even if deprived of the leisure time of cultivated souls, to have a culture of their own, made for them.

Cinema belongs eminently to this culture made for the Emma Bovarys or the Ginnys, which transgresses all the frontiers that an imaginary modernism wanted to trace in repainting in 'modern' colours the old criteria that separated the nobility of the liberal arts from the vulgarity of the mechanical arts. Cinema is the art in which the frontiers of elite art and of popular entertainment blur, along with the distinction between the noble pleasure of forms contemplated for their own sake and the sensual pleasure of images or the idiotic emotion felt for the misfortunes of daughters of the people. This may be seen clearly in *Some Came Running* in the stunning funfair sequence where the emotion felt before the accomplishment of the unhappy destiny of the poor bar hostess is rendered exactly identical to the pleasure felt before the artificial lights and the virtuosic gestures of a well-ordered ballet on a Broadway stage. This is also another way of saying that the pure pleasure produced by cinema is created from an unstable synthesis between the emotions provoked by novels, pantomime, dance, music-hall, painting and a few other forms of emotion crossing the frontiers of the arts of narrative and the arts of form, of arts of time and arts of space, as they cross those that separate noble art from popular art, and art from non-artistic life. This pure pleasure which is a synthesis of heterogeneous emotions highlights the derisory nature of the notions of autonomy and of 'medium-specificity' supposedly characteristic of great modern art.

In this sense, cinema is an exemplarily 'aesthetic' art: an art that blurs the classification of the forms and matter of art just as it blurs the classification of artistic and non-artistic pleasures. This means as well that it is an art always swerving from its own path [*en écart par rapport à lui-même*], in relation to the fidelity to which it would wish to hold itself in relation to its 'own' principle. It is indissolubly an aleatory composition of narrations, of forms and of emotions coming from diverse arts and diverse spheres of experience and the dream of an art that would be the direct effectuation of its principle: the writing of movement, the writing of light, the alliance of an intelligence that decides and a machine that, because it wants nothing, recreates the very texture of the sensible universe, etc. I have not ceased to speak of this constitutive spacing [*cet écart constitutif*] in setting out the analyses which try to define the singularity of such and such a sensible combination of forms and emotions in relation to what are possibly polemical reflections on auteurs – filmmakers or theoreticians – who wanted to define a single vocation for cinema, even if this meant, as for Godard, that it was a vocation betrayed. At the heart of *Histoires du cinéma*, there is the denunciation of a cinema that would have betrayed its vocation in submitting itself, in the interests of industry, to the empire of stories. But the materials that Godard assembles for his demonstration and even the way in which he re-edits and restages them invalidate the demonstration right away. No vocation has been betrayed, quite simply because cinema has never had any vocation. Cinema is also an art from the aesthetic regime because it is not an art that incarnates a pure aesthetic logic but an art of mixing regimes. The very power of cinema lies in having been this assemblage of narrations, images, forms and movements, coming under contradictory logics, which lends itself to a multiplicity of modes of emotion and remembrance. Godard's 'denunciation' is in fact homogeneous with cinema's form of existence. This also means that the denunciation and its inconsistency have little importance in themselves. What gives *Histoires du cinéma* its force is to have made apparent [*sensible*] the character of the art that is not an art, or rather that is only an art insofar as it is also a world: a tissue of words, images, refrains, forms and memories available for integration into an infinity of particular lived worlds as well as for becoming the matter or providing the tone of singular new works. In this sense, the trial of cinema's responsibility or irresponsibility is only the slim pretext for a far more serious operation: to present cinema as a common world, even while the entertainment industry seeks more and more imperiously to classify the modes of production of emotion, to give to each audience or niche audience the form of entertainment or art precisely formatted for its use. In their own way, those critics who tell their readers or listeners what audience a particular film is suitable for and those academics obsessed by the opposition between the legitimate and the non-legitimate play a part in this operation. All of them contribute to fighting the only 'illegitimacy' that matters: that of the daughters of peasants who intrude on the pleasures [*jouissances*] of the refined, and that of the films and audiences that blur the normal classification of forms of pleasure.

It is to this industrial and intellectual operation that the politics of the amateur opposes itself. This is not a politics of the dilettante, on the contrary it comes close to the most rigorous seriousness in trying to bring out the type of common world drawn by the operations of an art, a science, a composition of feelings, a grid of interpretations, etc. To talk about cinema as an amateur is always to begin from certain of its singularities that allow the effects of art to be perceived, that is to say, precisely from the effects of aleatory overlap between two ideas of art: art as the result of the intentions of an artist and art as a combination of percepts and affects that belongs to everyone and no one. There is no global concept of cinema that would allow its particular forms to be analysed. There are singularities that present a certain number of features by which the power of an art allows itself to be grasped, on the condition that we grasp there precisely something other than a collection of means for producing effects (of conformity or of distinction): a way of describing the contours of a shared sensible universe, the forms of a certain community, in short a certain distribution of the sensible [*partage du sensible*]. Because, in the last instance, this is what is always in question in the singularity of an art, a discipline, a mode of discourse: the sharing and sharing out according to which certain forms of the perceptible fit with certain modes of intelligibility and certain regimes of feeling, the nature of the common world that it outlines, the chances of sharing in it that are given to such and such a person according to her or his mode of social existence. The politics of the amateur is that which is devoted to leading the analysis of singularities (a film or a map, for example, but equally the form of a strike or the slogan of a street demonstration) towards making this sharing evident. This is, in any case, the sense and direction [*sens*] of my work.

Translated by Mark Robson

Note

1. Translator's Note: The term *écart* is important for Rancière, particularly in relation to cinema, hence the title of his recent *Les Écarts du cinéma* (2011). While *écart* contains notions of distance, gap, spacing, interval or difference, Rancière draws especially on the idiom of swerving, leaping aside or shying away from in the French *faire un écart*, used to speak respectively of cars, pedestrians or horses. What is here given as 'brushed aside' – like the renderings of the other uses of *écart* noted parenthetically in the text – should thus be read with this sense of avoidance.

Contributors

Nico Baumbach is an Assistant Professor of Film at Columbia University. He received his PhD in Literature from Duke University in 2009. He is currently finishing a book on cinema in the writings of Jacques Rancière, Alain Badiou, Giorgio Agamben and Slavoj Žižek.

Paul Bowman teaches cultural studies at Cardiff University. He is author of *Post-Marxism versus Cultural Studies* (2007), *Deconstructing Popular Culture* (2008), *Theorizing Bruce Lee* (2010), *Studi culturali e Cultura Pop* (ed. and trans. Floriana Bernardi, 2011), *Culture and the Media* (2012), *Beyond Bruce Lee* (2013) and *Reading Rey Chow: Visuality, Postcoloniality, Ethnicity, Sexuality* (2013). He is editor of *Interrogating Cultural Studies* (2003), *The Rey Chow Reader* (2010) and *Popular Cultural Pedagogy, in Theory* (2014). With Richard Stamp he is co-editor of *The Truth of Žižek* (2006), *Reading Rancière* (2011) and *Jacques Rancière: In Disagreement* (2009). He is editor of numerous issues of the journal *parallax*, and special issues of the journals *Postcolonial Studies*, *Social Semiotics* and *Educational Philosophy and Theory*. He is also the founding editor of *JOMEC Journal* and founder of Cardiff University's Centre for Interdisciplinary Film and Visual Culture Research (IFVCR).

Rey Chow is Anne Firor Scott Professor of Literature at Duke University. Her more recent publications include *The Rey Chow Reader*, ed. Paul Bowman (Columbia University Press, 2010) and *Entanglements, or Transmedial Thinking about Capture* (Duke University Press, 2012). Her scholarly writings have appeared in ten languages.

Abraham Geil is a doctoral candidate in the Program in Literature at Duke University. His primary research interests centre on the intersection of cinema, philosophy and political theory. He is the co-editor of *Memory Bytes: History, Technology and Digital Culture* (Duke University Press, 2004) and a member of an editorial group working on an exhaustive two-volume collection of philosophical writings on film. He has published essays on cinematic movement in the writings of Jean Epstein and on Sergei Eisenstein's theory of *typage*. He is currently finishing a dissertation entitled 'The Face of Recognition: The Politics and Aesthetics of Facial Representation from Silent Cinema to Cognitive Neuroscience', which traces a genealogy of the human face as a privileged site of recognition in the history and theory of film and its afterlives.

Bram Ieven is an Assistant Professor of Comparative Literature at Utrecht University, the Netherlands. He has published extensively on aesthetics and politics and is currently working on a project called *The Commonality of Form: De Stijl, Modernism and the Hyperformalization of Sensation.*

Mónica López Lerma works as a researcher at the Centre of Excellence in Foundations of European Law and Polity at the University of Helsinki, funded by the Academy of Finland. She is also co-editor of the journal *No Foundations: An Interdisciplinary Journal of Law and Justice.* She received a PhD in Comparative Literature and a Graduate Certificate in Film Studies both from the University of Michigan. Her work has been published in *Revue Interdisciplinaire d'Etudes Juridiques*, *Conserveries Mémorielles*, *Southern California Interdisciplinary Law Journal* and *Política Común*. Her research interests include film and literature, with particular emphasis on aesthetics, film theory, transitional justice, cultural and theoretical aspects of law, and democracy.

Patricia MacCormack is Reader in English, Communication, Film and Media at Anglia Ruskin University, Cambridge. She has published extensively on Guattari, Blanchot, Serres, Irigaray, queer theory, teratology, body modification, posthuman theory, animal rights and horror film. Her work includes 'Inhuman Ecstasy' (*Angelaki*, 2010), 'Becoming-Vulva' (*New Formations*, 2010), 'The Great Ephemeral Tattooed Skin' (*Body and Society*, 2006), 'Necrosexuality' (*Queering the Non/Human*, 2008), 'Unnatural

Alliances' (*Deleuze and Queer Theory*, 2009), 'Vitalistic FeminEthics' (*Deleuze and Law*, 2009), and 'Cinemasochism: Time, Space and Submission' (*The Afterimage of Gilles Deleuze's Film Philosophy*, 2010). She is the author of *Cinesexuality* (2008) and the co-editor of *The Schizoanalysis of Cinema* (2008). Her most recent book is *Posthuman Ethics* (2012).

Mark Robson teaches at the University of Nottingham. His publications include *Stephen Greenblatt* (2008), *The Sense of Early Modern Writing* (2006) and *Language in Theory* (with Peter Stockwell, 2005). He edited the collection *Jacques Rancière: Aesthetics, Politics, Philosophy* (2005).

Richard Stamp is Senior Lecturer in English and Cultural Studies at Bath Spa University. He is the editor (with Paul Bowman) of *Jacques Rancière: Critical Dissensus* (Continuum, 2011), *parallax* 52 ('*Jacques Rancière: In Disagreement*', 2009) and *The Truth of Žižek* (Continuum, 2007). He has also written on different aspects of Rancière's work for *Educational Philosophy and Theory* and *borderlands e-journal* (2009). He is currently researching the development and influence of John Whitney's computer animations.

Jacques Rancière is Emeritus Professor of Philosophy at the University of Paris-VIII (Saint-Denis). Born in Algiers in 1940, he is the author of numerous books dealing with aesthetics, politics and their relationships. His oeuvre includes such diverse landmarks as *The Nights of Labour*, *The Ignorant Schoolmaster* and *The Flesh of Words*, as well as *Disagreement* and *Film Fables*. His most recent books in English include *The Emancipated Spectator* and *Aisthesis*.

James A. Steintrager is Professor of English, Comparative Literature, and European Languages and Studies at the University of California, Irvine. He is the author of *Cruel Delight: Enlightenment Culture and the Inhuman* (2004) and the forthcoming *First Sexual Revolution: Libertines, License, and the Autonomy of Pleasure* (Columbia University Press), along with articles on topics as varied as Hong Kong horror cinema, postcolonial theory and translation studies, and the theoretical reception of the Marquis de Sade. He recently edited, along with Rey

Chow, a special double issue of the journal *differences: A Journal of Feminist Cultural Studies* on sound, mediation and objectivity. In addition to sound studies, his current research focuses on the production, dissemination and reception of Hong Kong cinema at the turn of the millennium.

Bibliography

Aaron, Michele (2007), *Spectatorship: The Power of Looking On*, London and New York: Wallflower Press.

Abel, Richard (1993), *French Film Theory and Criticism: A History/ Anthology, 1907–1939. Volume 1: 1907–1929*, Princeton: Princeton University Press.

Adorno, Theodor (1967), 'An Essay on Cultural Criticism and Society', in *Prisms*, trans. Samuel and Shierry Weber, Cambridge, MA: MIT Press, 17–34.

Adorno, Theodor (1998), *Aesthetic Theory*, ed. Robert Hullot-Kentor, Minneapolis: University of Minnesota Press.

Allen, Richard (2007), *Hitchcock's Romantic Irony*, New York: Columbia University Press.

Alter, Nora M. (2006), *Chris Marker*, Champaign: University of Illinois Press.

Althusser, Louis (1971), 'Ideology and Ideological State Apparatuses', in *Lenin and Philosophy*, trans. Ben Brewster, New York: Monthly Review Press, 85–130.

Althusser, Louis, Etienne Balibar, Roger Establet, Jacques Rancière and Pierre Macheray (1971), *Reading Capital*, London: New Left Books.

Arditi, Benjamin (2008), *Politics on the Edges of Liberalism: Difference, Populism, Revolution, Agitation*, Edinburgh: Edinburgh University Press.

Arditi, Benjamin and Jeremy Valentine (1999), *Polemicization: The Contingency of the Commonplace*, Edinburgh: Edinburgh University Press.

Arnall, Gavin, Laura Gandolfi and Enea Zaramella (2012), 'Aesthetics and Politics Revisited: An Interview with Jacques Rancière', *Critical Inquiry*, 38 (Winter): 289–98.

Arnheim, Rudolph (1957), *Film as Art*, Berkeley and Los Angeles: University of California Press.

Aulier, Dan (1998), *Vertigo: The Making of a Hitchcock Classic*, New York: St Martin's Press.

Badiou, Alain (2005), *Metapolitics*, London and New York: Verso.

Baecque, Antoine de (2003), *La Cinéphilie: invention d'un regard, histoire d'une culture 1944–1968*, Paris: Fayard.

Barr, Charles (2002), *Vertigo*, London: BFI.

Barry, Keith (1997), *Film Genres: From Iconography to Ideology*, London: Wallflower Press.

Barthes, Roland (1972), *Mythologies*, trans. Annette Lavers, New York: Farrar, Straus and Giroux.

Barthes, Roland (1981), *Camera Lucida: Reflections on Photography*, trans. Richard Howard, New York: Farrar, Straus and Giroux.

Barthes, Roland (2012), *Mythologies: The Complete Edition*, trans. Richard Howard and Annette Lavers, New York: Hill and Wang.

Bass, Jennifer, and Pat Kirkham (2011), *Saul Bass: A Life in Film and Design*, London: Lawrence King.

Baudrillard, Jean (1996), *The Perfect Crime*, trans. Chris Turner, London: Verso.

Baudrillard, Jean (1998), *The Consumer Society: Myths and Structures*, London: Sage.

Baumbach, Nico (2012), 'All That Heaven Allows', *Film Comment*, March/April, www.filmcomment.com/entry/all-that-heaven-allows-what-is-or-was-cinephilia-part-one (accessed 8 March 2013).

Bazin, André (2005), *What is Cinema? Volume 1*, Berkeley: University of California Press.

Benjamin, Walter (2003), *Selected Writings, Volume 4: 1938–1940*, Cambridge, MA: Harvard University Press.

Benjamin, Walter (2008), 'The Work of Art in the Age of Its Technological Reproducibility, Second Version', trans. Edmund Jephcott and Harry Zohn, in *The Work of Art in the Age of Its Technological Reproducibility and Other Writings on Media*, Cambridge, MA: Harvard University Press, 19–55.

Blanchot, Maurice (1993), *The Infinite Conversation*, trans. Susan Hanson, Minneapolis: University of Minnesota Press.

Blanchot, Maurice (2003), *The Book to Come*, trans. Charlotte Mandell, Stanford: Stanford University Press.

Boghossian, Paul A. (2006), *Fear of Knowledge: Against Relativism and Constructivism*, Oxford: Oxford University Press.

Boileau, Pierre, and Thomas Narcejac (1997), *Vertigo [The Living and the Dead]*, trans. Geoffrey Sainsbury, London: BFI/Bloomsbury.

Bordwell, David (1985), *Narration in the Fiction Film*, Madison: University of Wisconsin Press.

Bordwell, David (1989), 'A Case for Cognitivism', *Iris*, 9 (Spring): 107–12.

Bordwell, David (2011), 'Academics vs. Critics: Never the Twain Shall Meet: Why Can't Cinephiles and Academics Just Get Along?', *Film Comment*, May/June, http://www.filmcomment.com/article/never-the-twain-shall-meet (accessed 8 March 2013).

Bordwell, David, and Kristin Thompson (2008), *Film Art: An Introduction*, 8th edn, New York: McGraw Hill.

Bourdieu, Pierre (1986), 'The Forms of Capital', trans. Richard Nice, in J.E. Richardson, ed., *Handbook of Theory of Research for the Sociology of Education*, Westport, CT: Greenwood Press, 241–58.

Bourdieu, Pierre (1996), *The Rules of Art: Genesis and Structure of the Literary Field*, trans. Susan Emanuel, Stanford: Stanford University Press.

Bowman, Paul (2007), *Post-Marxism versus Cultural Studies: Theory, Politics and Intervention*, Edinburgh: Edinburgh University Press.

Bowman, Paul (2008a), *Deconstructing Popular Culture*, Basingstoke and New York: Palgrave Macmillan.

Bowman, Paul (2008b), 'Alterdisciplinarity', *Culture, Theory and Critique*, 49(1): 93–110.

Brill, Leslie (1988), *The Hitchcock Romance: Love and Irony in Hitchcock's Films*, Princeton: Princeton University Press.

Buckland, Warren (1995), *The Film Spectator: From Sign to Mind*, Amsterdam: Amsterdam University Press.

Bürger, Peter (1984), *Theory of the Avant-Garde*, Minneapolis: University of Minnesota Press.

Burgin, Victor (2004), *The Remembered Film*, London: Reaktion Books.

Buse, Peter, Núria Triana-Toribio and Andrew Willis (2007), *The Cinema of Alex de la Iglesia*, Manchester: Manchester University Press.

Butler, Judith (1994), 'Against Proper Objects', *differences*, Special Issue: *More Gender Trouble – Feminism Meets Queer Theory*, 6(2–3): 1–26.

Butler, Judith (2005), *Giving an Account of Oneself*, New York: Fordham University Press.

Campbell, Jan (2005), *Film and Cinema Spectatorship: Melodrama and Mimesis*, Oxford: Polity Press.

Canudo, Ricciotto (1993), 'Reflections on the Seventh Art' [1923], in Richard Abel, ed., *French Film Theory and Criticism: A History/Anthology, 1907–1939. Volume 1: 1907–1929*, Princeton: Princeton University Press, 291–303.

Cartwright, Lisa (2008), *Moral Spectatorship: Technologies of Voice and Affect in Postwar Representations of the Child*, Durham, NC: Duke University Press.

Caruth, Cathy (1996), *Unclaimed Experience: Trauma, Narrative, and History*, Baltimore: Johns Hopkins University Press.

Casanova, Pascale (2007), *World Republic of Letters*, trans. W R DeBevoise, Cambridge, MA: Cambridge University Press.

Cavell, Stanley (1979), *The World Viewed*, enlarged edition, Cambridge, MA: Harvard University Press.

Chambers, Samuel A. (2011), 'The Politics of the Police: From Neoliberalism to Anarchism, and Back to Democracy', in Paul Bowman and Richard Stamp, eds, *Reading Rancière: Critical Dissensus*, London and New York: Continuum, 18–43.

Chambers, Samuel A. (2012), *The Lessons of Rancière*, Oxford and New York: Oxford University Press.

Chion, Michel (1994), *Audio-Vision: Sound on Screen*, ed. and trans. Claudia Gorbman, New York: Columbia University Press.

Chion, Michel (1999), *The Voice in Cinema*, ed. and trans. Claudia Gorbman, New York: Columbia University Press.

Chow, Rey (1993), *Writing Diaspora: Tactics of Intervention in Contemporary Cultural Studies*, Bloomington: Indiana University Press.

Chow, Rey (2012), *Entanglements, or Transmedial Thinking about Capture*, Durham, NC: Duke University Press.

Chow, Rey, and Julian Rohrhuber (2011), 'On Captivation: A Remainder from the Indistinction of Art and Nonart', in Paul Bowman and Richard Stamp, eds, *Reading Rancière: Critical Dissensus*, London: Continuum, 44–72.

Comolli, Jean-Louis, and Jean Narboni (2009), 'Cinema/Criticism/Ideology', in Leo Braudy and Marshall Cohen, eds, *Film Theory and Criticism*, 7th edn, Oxford and New York: Oxford University Press, 686–93.

Conley, Tom (1985), 'Reading Ordinary Viewing', *Diacritics*, 15(1): 2–14.

Conley, Tom (2005), 'Cinema and Its Discontents: Jacques Rancière and Film Theory', *SubStance*, 34(3): 96–106.

Conley, Tom (2010), 'Jean-Louis Schefer: Screen Memories from L'Homme ordinaire du cinéma', *New Review of Film and Television Studies*, 8(1): 12–21.

Conomos, John (2000), 'The Vertigo of Time', *Senses of Cinema* 6 (3 May), http://sensesofcinema.com/2000/6/time/ (accessed 12 February 2013).

Cusset, François (2008), *French Theory: How Foucault, Derrida, Deleuze, & Co. Transformed the Intellectual Life of the United States*, Minneapolis: University of Minnesota Press.

Dasgupta, Sudeep (2009), 'Jacques Rancière', in *Film, Theory and Philosophy: The Key Thinkers*, ed. Felicity Colman, Durham: Acumen, 339–48.

De la Iglesia, Alex (2001), 'Intrigo all'utimo piano', *Academia*, 30: 48–59.

Debray, Régis (1992), *Vie et mort de l'image*, Paris: Gallimard.

Deleuze, Gilles (1983), *Cinéma 1: l'image-mouvement*, Paris: Editions de Minuit.

Deleuze, Gilles (1986), *Cinema I: the Movement-Image*, trans. Hugh Tomlinson and Barbara Habberjam, Minneapolis: University of Minnesota Press.

Deleuze, Gilles (1989), *Cinema II: the Time-Image*, trans. Hugh Tomlinson and Robert Galeta, Minneapolis: University of Minnesota Press.

Deleuze, Gilles, and Guattari, Félix (1994), *What is Philosophy?*, trans. Hugh Tomlinson and Graham Burchell, New York: Columbia University Press.

Deranty, Jean-Philippe, and Alison Ross, eds (2012), *Jacques Rancière and the Contemporary Scene*, London: Continuum.

Derrida, Jacques (1983), 'The Principle of Reason: The University in the Eyes of its Pupils', *Diacritics*, 13(3): 2–20.

Derrida, Jacques (1992a), *The Gift of Death*, trans. David Wills, Chicago: University of Chicago Press.

Derrida, Jacques (1992b), 'Mochlos; or, The Conflict of the Faculties', in Richard Rand, ed., *Logomachia: The Conflict of the Faculties*, Lincoln, NE and London: University of Nebraska Press, 3–34.

Derrida, Jacques (2011), *Voice and Phenomenon: Introduction to the Problem of the Sign in Husserl's Phenomenology*, trans. Leonard Lawlor, Evanston: Northwestern University Press.

Dolar, Mladen (2011), 'The Burrow of Sound', *differences*, 22(2–3): 112–39.

Dronsfield, Jonathan Lahey (2010), 'Pedagogy of the Written Image', *Journal of French and Francophone Philosophy*, 18(2): 87–105.

During, Simon (n.d.), 'Postdisciplinarity', http://uq.academia.edu/SimonDuring/Papers/786180/Postdisciplinarity (accessed 12 February 2013).

Duras, Marguerite (1961), *Hiroshima mon amour*, trans. Richard Seaver, New York: Grove Press.

Edelman, Lee (1994), *Homographesis*, London: Routledge.

Eisenstein, Sergei (1988), 'The Montage of Film Attractions', in *Selected Works, Vol. I: Writings, 1922–1934*, ed. and trans. Richard Taylor, London: I.B. Tauris, 39–58.

Foucault, Michel (1997), 'The Thought from Outside', in Michel Foucault and Maurice Blanchot, *Foucault/Blanchot*, trans. Brian Massumi, New York: Zone Books, 7–60.

Fowler, Catherine (2012), 'Remembering Cinema "Elsewhere": From Retrospection to Introspection in the Gallery Film', *Cinema Journal*, 51(2): 26–45.

Gabriel, Yiannis, and Tim Lang (1995), *The Unmanageable Consumer. Contemporary Consumption and its Fragmentations*, London: Sage.

Gauny, Gabriel (1983), 'Le Travail à la tâche' [1848], in Gabriel Gauny, *Le Philosophie plébéien*, Paris: La Découverte and Presses Universitaires de Vincennes, 147–8.

Gibson, Andrew (2005), 'The Unfinished Song: Intermittency and Melancholy in Rancière', in Mark Robson, ed., *Jacques Rancière: Aesthetics, Politics, Philosophy*, Edinburgh: Edinburgh University Press, 61–76.

Giddens, Anthony (1991), *The Consequences of Modernity*, Stanford: Stanford University Press.

Godard, Jean-Luc (1972), *Godard on Godard*, ed. and trans. Tom Milne, London: Secker and Warburg.

Godard, Jean-Luc (1998), *Histoire(s) du cinema*, Paris: Gallimard.

Godard, Jean-Luc (2010), *Film socialisme: dialogue avec visages auteurs*, Paris: P.O.L.

Gramsci, Antonio (1971), *Selections from the Prison Notebooks of Antonio Gramsci*, New York: International Publishers.

Greenberg, Clement (1997), *Homemade Esthetics: The Bennington Seminars*, Oxford: Oxford University Press.

Grusin, Richard, and Jay Boulter (2000), *Remediation: Understanding New Media*, Cambridge, MA: MIT Press.

Guattari, Fèlix (1995), *Chaosmosis: An Ethico–Aesthetic Paradigm*, trans. Paul Bains and Julian Pefanis, Sydney: Powerhouse.

Gumbrecht, Hans Ulrich, and Karl Ludwig Pfeiffer, eds (1994), *Materialities of Communication*, Stanford: Stanford University Press.

Hacking, Ian (2000), *The Social Construction of What?*, Cambridge, MA: Harvard University Press.

Hagener, Malte, and Marijke de Valck (2005), *Cinephilia: Movies, Love and Memory*, Amsterdam: Amsterdam University Press.

Hall, Stuart (1992), 'Cultural Studies and its Theoretical Legacies', in

Lawrence Grossberg, ed., *Cultural Studies*, New York and London: Routledge, 277–94.

Haskin, Pamela, and Saul Bass (1996), '"Saul, Can You Make Me a Title?" Interview with Saul Bass', *Film Quarterly*, 50(1): 10–17.

Hermoso, Borja (n.d.), 'Cine-empanada mental', http://www.elmundo.es/sociedad/delaiglesia/goya/empanada.html (accessed 12 February 2013).

Irigaray, Luce (1985), *Speculum of the Other Woman*, trans. Gillian C. Gill, Ithaca, NY: Cornell University Press.

Jameson, Fredric (1973), 'The Vanishing Mediator: Narrative Structure in Max Weber', *New German Critique*, 1: 52–82.

Jameson, Fredric (1992), *Signatures of the Visible*, London and New York: Routledge.

Jancovich, Mark, Lucy Faire and Sarah Stubbings (2003), *The Place of the Audience: Cultural Geographies of Film Consumption*, London: BFI.

Johnson, Alan (2012), 'The New Communism: Resurrecting the Utopian Delusion', *World Affairs* (May/June), http://www.worldaffairsjournal.org/article/new-communism-resurrecting-utopian-delusion (accessed 12 February 2013).

Kant, Immanuel (2001), *Critique of the Power of Judgement*, trans. Paul Guyer and Eric Matthews, Cambridge: Cambridge University Press.

Keller, Sarah, and Jason N. Paul (2012), *Jean Epstein: Critical Essays and New Translations*, Amsterdam: Amsterdam University Press.

Keathley, Christian (2006), *Cinephilia and History, or, The Wind in the Trees*, Bloomington: Indiana University Press.

King, Emily (2004), 'Spiralling Aspirations: *Vertigo*, 1958', in 'Taking Credit: Film Title Sequences, 1955–1965', MA thesis, V&A/RCA, www.typotheque.com/articles/taking_credit_film_title_sequences_1955–1965_5_spiralling_aspirations_vertigo_1958 (accessed 8 March 2013).

Kirkham, Pat (1997), 'The Jeweller's Eye', *Sight & Sound*, 7(4): 18–19.

Kittler, Friedrich (1992), *Discourse Networks 1800/1900*, trans. Michael Metteer and Chris Cullens, Stanford: Stanford University Press.

Kittler, Friedrich (1999), *Gramophone, Film, Typewriter*, trans. Geoffrey Winthrop-Young and Michael Wutz, Stanford: Stanford University Press.

Kracauer, Siegfried (1997), *Theory of Film: The Redemption of Physical Reality*, Princeton: Princeton University Press [1960].

Kuhn, Thomas (1962), *The Structure of Scientific Revolutions*, Chicago and London: University of Chicago Press.

Lahey Dronsfield, Jonathan (2010), 'Pedagogy of the Written Image', *Journal of French and Francophone Philosophy*, 18(2): 87–105.

Laügt, Elodie (2012), 'Aphorismes de quelque chose de l'amour (Cioran, Godard)', *French Forum* , 37(1–2): 167–82.

Liu, Catherine (2012), *American Idyll: American Antielitism as Cultural Critique*, Iowa City: University of Iowa Press.

Luhmann, Niklas (2000), *Art as a Social System*, Stanford: Stanford University Press.

Luhmann, Niklas (2002), *The Reality of the Mass Media*, trans. Kathleen Cross, Stanford: Stanford University Press.

Lyotard, Jean-François (1984), *The Postmodern Condition: A Report on Knowledge*, Minneapolis: University of Minnesota Press.

Lyotard, Jean François (1988), *The Differend: Phrases in Dispute*, trans. Georges Van Den Abbeele, Minneapolis: University of Minnesota Press.

Lyotard, Jean François (1991), *The Inhuman*, trans. Geoffrey Bennington and Rachel Bowlby, Cambridge: Polity Press.

Manovich, Lev (2001), *The Language of New Media*, Cambridge, MA: MIT Press.

Marchart, Oliver (2007), *Post-Foundational Political Thought: Political Difference in Nancy, Lefort, Badiou and Laclau*, Edinburgh: Edinburgh University Press.

Maroto Camino, Mercedes (2005), 'Madrid me mata: Killing the Husband in Alex de la Iglesia's "La Comunidad" (2000) and Pedro Almodóvar's "¿Qué he Hecho yo para Merecer Esto?" (1984)', *Forum for Modern Languages Studies*, 41(3): 332–41.

Mayne, Judith (1993), *Cinema and Spectatorship*, London and New York: Routledge.

McLuhan, Marshall (1964), *Understanding Media: The Extensions of Man*, New York: McGraw-Hill.

Metz, Christian (1982), *The Imaginary Signifier: Psychoanalysis and the Cinema*, trans. Celia Britton, Annwyl Williams, Ben Brewster and Alfred Guzzetti, Bloomington: Indiana University Press.

Monaco, James (1978), *Alain Resnais*, Oxford and New York: Oxford University Press.

Moreiras-Menor, Cristina (2011), 'Historia(s) de espectros: "La Comunidad" de Alex de la Iglesia', in *La estela del tiempo. Imagen e historicidad en el cine español contemporáneo*, Madrid: Iberoamericana, 149–72.

Mowitt, John (2003), 'Cultural Studies, in Theory', in Paul Bowman, ed.,

Interrogating Cultural Studies: Theory, Politics, and Practice, London: Pluto Press, 175–88.

Mulvey, Laura (1986), 'Visual Pleasure and Narrative Cinema', in Philip Rosen, ed., *Narrative, Apparatus, Ideology*, New York: Columbia University Press.

Mulvey, Laura (2006), *Death 24x a Second: Stillness and the Moving Image*, London: Reaktion Books.

Nancy, Jean-Luc (2000), *Being Singular Plural*, trans. Robert D. Richardson and Anne E. O'Byrne, Stanford: Stanford University Press.

Nancy, Jean-Luc (2007), *Listening*, trans. Charlotte Mandell, New York: Fordham University Press.

Neupert, Richard (1995), *The End: Narration and Closure in the Cinema*, Detroit: Wayne State University Press.

Neupert, Richard (2002), *A History of the French New Wave Cinema*, Madison: University of Wisconsin Press.

Nichols, Bill (1991), *Representing Reality: Issues and Concepts in Documentary*, Bloomington: Indiana University Press.

Nichols, Bill (2000), 'Film Theory and the Revolt against Master Narratives', in Christine Gledhill and Linda Williams, eds, *Reinventing Film Studies*, London: Arnold, 34–52.

Nichols, Bill (2010), *Introduction to Documentary*, 2nd edn, Bloomington: Indiana University Press.

Nichols, Bill (n.d.), 'Documentary and the Coming of Sound', http://film-sound.org/film-sound-history/documentary.htm (accessed 12 February 2013).

Patterson, Zabet (2009), 'From the Gun Controller to the Mandala: The Cybernetic Cinema of John and James Whitney', *Grey Room*, 36 (Summer): 36–57.

Perkins, V.F. (1972), *Film as Film: Understanding and Judging Movies*, Harmondsworth: Penguin Books.

Plantinga, Carl R. (2008), 'Spectatorship', in Paisley Livingston and Carl Plantinga, eds, *The Routledge Companion to Philosophy and Film*, London: Routledge, 249–58.

Plantinga, Carl R. (2009), *Moving Viewers: American Film and the Spectator's Experience*, Berkeley: University of California Press.

Pohl, Burkhard (2007), 'El lado oscuro de la nación: *La Comunidad* (Alex de la Iglesia, 2000)', in Burkhard Pohl and Jörg Türschmann, eds, *Miradas glocales: cine español en el cambio de milenio*, Madrid: Iberoamerica, 119–38.

Pomerance, Murray (2004), *An Eye for Hitchcock*, New Brunswick, NJ: Rutgers University Press.

Poster, Mark (1990), *The Mode of Information: Poststructuralism and Social Context*, Chicago: University of Chicago Press.

'Project: New Cinephilia' (n.d.), *Project: New Cinephilia*, http://project-cinephilia.mubi.com/ (accessed 12 February 2013).

Rancière, Jacques (1974), *La Leçon d'Althusser*, Paris: Gallimard.

Rancière, Jacques (1989), *The Nights of Labor: The Workers' Dream in Nineteenth-Century France*, trans. John Drury, Philadelphia: Temple University Press.

Rancière, Jacques (1991), *The Ignorant Schoolmaster: Five Lessons in Intellectual Emancipation*, trans. Kristin Ross, Stanford: Stanford University Press.

Rancière, Jacques (1992), 'Politics, Identification, and Subjectivation', *October*, 61 (Summer): 58–64.

Rancière, Jacques (1994), *The Names of History: On the Poetics of Knowledge*, trans. Hassan Melehy, Minneapolis: University of Minnesota Press.

Rancière, Jacques (1995), *On the Shores of Politics*, trans. Liz Heron, London: Verso.

Rancière, Jacques (1999a), *Disagreement: Politics and Philosophy*, trans. Julie Rose, Minneapolis: University of Minnesota Press.

Rancière, Jacques (1999b), 'La Sainte et l'héritière: à propos des Histoire(s) du cinéma', *Cahiers du cinéma*, 536: 58–61.

Rancière, Jacques (2000), *Le Partage du sensible*, Paris: La Fabrique.

Rancière Jacques (2001a), *La Fable cinématographique*, Paris: Seuil.

Rancière, Jacques (2001b), *L'Inconscient esthétique*, Paris: Galilée.

Rancière, Jacques (2002a), 'The Saint and the Heiress: A propos of Godard's Histoire(s) du cinéma', trans. T.S. Murphy, *Discourse*, 24(1): 113–19.

Rancière, Jacques (2002b), 'The Aesthetic Revolution and Its Outcomes', *New Left Review*, March-April, http://newleftreview.org/II/14/jacques-ranciere-the-aesthetic-revolution-and-its-outcomes (accessed 8 March 2013).

Rancière, Jacques (2003), *Le Destin des images*, Paris: La Fabrique.

Rancière, Jacques (2004a), *The Philosopher and his Poor*, trans. John Drury, Durham, NC and London: Duke University Press.

Rancière, Jacques (2004b), *The Politics of Aesthetics: The Distribution of the Sensible*, trans. Gabriel Rockhill, New York: Continuum.

Rancière, Jacques (2004c), *The Flesh of Words*, trans. Charlotte Mandell, Stanford: Stanford University Press.

Rancière, Jacques (2005), 'From Politics to Aesthetics?', *Paragraph*, 28(1): 13–25.

Rancière, Jacques (2006a), *Film Fables*, trans. Emiliano Battista, Oxford and New York: Berg.

Rancière, Jacques (2006b), *Hatred of Democracy*, trans. Steve Corcoran, London: Verso.

Rancière, Jacques (2006c), 'Thinking Between the Disciplines: An Aesthetics of Knowledge', trans. Jon Roffe, *Parrhesia*, 1: 1–12.

Rancière, Jacques (2006d), *Politique de la littérature*, Paris: Galilée.

Rancière, Jacques (2006e), 'Politique de Pedro Costa', trans Emiliano Battista, pamphlet distributed by Tate Modern in conjunction with a retrospective of Costa's work, 25 September–4 October 2009, www.pedro-costa.net/download/TATE-PEDRO%20COSTA.pdf (accessed 12 February 2013).

Rancière, Jacques (2007a), *The Future of the Image*, trans. Gregory Elliott, New York and London: Verso.

Rancière, Jacques (2007b), 'The Emancipated Spectator', *Artforum*, 45(7): 270–81.

Rancière, Jacques (2007c), *Het esthetische denken*, Amsterdam: Valiz.

Rancière, Jacques (2007d), 'Godard, Hitchcock and the Cinematographic Image', in Michael Temple, James S. Williams and Michael Witt, eds, *For Ever Godard*, London: Black Dog, 214–31.

Rancière, Jacques (2007e), 'Art of the Possible: Fulvia Carnevale and John Kelsey in Conversation with Jacques Rancière', *Artforum*, March, http://ebookbrowse.com/artforum-art-of-the-possible-fulvia-c arnevale-and-john-kelsey-in-conversation-with-jacques-ranciere-pdf-d184714749 (accessed 8 March 2013).

Rancière, Jacques (2008a), 'Jacques Rancière and Indisciplinarity', *Art & Research: A Journal of Ideas, Contexts and Methods,* 2(1), http://www.artandresearch.org.uk/v2n1/jrinterview.html (accessed 12 February 2013).

Rancière, Jacques (2008b), *Le Spectateur émancipé*, Paris: La Fabrique.

Rancière, Jacques (2008c), 'Why Emma Bovary Had to Be Killed', *Critical Inquiry*, 34(2): 233–48.

Rancière, Jacques (2008d), 'Ce que "medium" peut vouloir dire: l'exemple de la photographie', *Revue Appareil*, 1 (February), http://revues.mshparisnord.org/appareil/index.php?id=135 (accessed 12 February 2013).

Rancière, Jacques (2008e), 'Aesthetics against Incarnation: An Interview by Anne-Marie Oliver', *Critical Inquiry*, 35(1), 172–90.

Rancière, Jacques (2009a), *The Emancipated Spectator*, trans. Gregory Elliott, London: Verso.

Rancière, Jacques (2009b), *Aesthetics and Its Discontents*, trans. Steve Corcoran, Cambridge: Polity Press.

Rancière, Jacques (2009c), 'Contemporary Art and the Politics of Aesthetics', in Beth Hinderliter et al., eds, *Communities of Sense: Rethinking Aesthetics and Politics*, Durham, NC: Duke University Press, 31–50.

Rancière, Jacques (2009d), *Et tant pis pour les gens fatigués: entretiens*, Paris: Editions Amsterdam.

Rancière, Jacques (2009e), *The Aesthetic Unconscious*, trans. Debra Keates and James Swenson, Cambridge: Polity Press.

Rancière, Jacques (2009f), 'The Aesthetic Dimension', *Critical Inquiry*, 36: 1–19.

Rancière, Jacques (2009g), 'The Method of Equality: An Answer to Some Questions', in *Jacques Rancière: History, Politics, Aesthetics*, ed. Gabriel Rockhill and Philip Watts, Durham, NC and London: Duke University Press, 273–88.

Rancière, Jacques (2010), *Dissensus: On Politics and Aesthetics*, ed. and trans. Steven Corcoran, London and New York: Continuum.

Rancière, Jacques (2011a), *Althusser's Lesson*, trans. Emiliano Battista, London: Continuum.

Rancière, Jacques (2011b), *Mute Speech: Literature, Critical Theory, and Politics*, trans. James Swenson, New York: Columbia University Press.

Rancière, Jacques (2011c), *Les Écarts du cinéma*, Paris: La Fabrique.

Rancière, Jacques (2011d), 'Re-Visions: Remarks on the Love of Cinema: An Interview by Oliver Davis', *Journal of Visual Culture*, 10(3): 294–304.

Rancière, Jacques (2011e), 'Against an Ebbing Tide', in Paul Bowman and Richard Stamp, eds, *Reading Rancière: Critical Dissensus*, London and New York: Continuum, 238–51.

Rancière, Jacques (2011f), *The Politics of Literature*, trans. Julie Rose, Cambridge: Polity Press.

Rancière, Jacques (2011g), *Aisthesis: scènes du régime esthétique de l'art*, Paris: Galilée.

Rancière, Jacques (2011h), 'What Medium Can Mean', trans. Steven Corcoran, *Parrhesia*, 11: 35–43, http://parrhesiajournal.org/parrhesia11/parrhesia11_ranciere.pdf (accessed 12 February 2013).

Rancière, Jacques (2011i), 'Questions for Jacques Rancière Around his Book *Les Écarts du cinéma*', *Cinema: Journal of Philosophy and the Moving Image*, 2, http://cjpmi.ifl.pt/storage/2/Cinema%202.pdf (accessed 8 March 2013).

Rancière, Jacques (2012), *Proletarian Nights: The Workers' Dream in Nineteenth-Century France*, 2nd edn, London: Verso.

Rancière, Jacques, and Davide Panagia (2000b), 'Dissenting Words: A Conversation with Jacques Rancière', *Diacritics*, 30(2): 113–26.

Readings, Bill (1996), *The University in Ruins*, Cambridge, MA and London: Harvard University Press.

Resnais, Alain (1960), *Hiroshima mon amour: scénario et dialogue, realization Alain Resnais*, Paris: Gallimard.

Ricoeur, Paul (1970), *Freud and Philosophy: An Essay on Interpretation*, trans Denis Savage, New Haven, CT and London: Yale University Press.

Rifkin, Adrian (2009), 'JR cinéphile, or the Philosopher Who Loved Things', *parallax*, 52, Special Issue, *Jacques Rancière: In Disagreement*, ed. Paul Bowman and Richard Stamp, 81–7.

Robson, Mark (2009), '"A literary animal": Rancière, Derrida and the Literature of Democracy', *parallax*, 52, Special Issue, *Jacques Rancière: In Disagreement*, ed. Paul Bowman and Richard Stamp, 88–101.

Robson, Mark (2011), 'Film, Fall, Fable: Rancière, Rossellini, Flaubert, Haneke', in Paul Bowman and Richard Stamp, eds, *Reading Rancière: Critical Dissensus*, London: Continuum, 185–99.

Rodowick, D.N. (1994), *The Crisis of Political Modernism*, Berkeley: University of California Press.

Rodowick, D.N. (2007), *The Virtual Life of Film*, Cambridge, MA: Harvard University Press.

Roob, Jean-Daniel (1986), *Alain Resnais*, Lyon: La Manufacture.

Rosen, Philip (2008), 'Screen and 1970s Film Theory', in Lee Grieveson and Haidee Wasson, eds, *Inventing Film Studies*, Durham, NC: Duke University Press, 264–97.

Ross, Kristin (2002), *May '68 and its Afterlives*, Chicago: University of Chicago Press.

Sarris, Andrew (1968), *American Cinema: Directors and Directions 1929–1968*, New York: E.P. Dutton.

Schefer, Jean Louis (1995), *The Enigmatic Body: Essays on the Arts*, ed. and trans. Paul Smith, New York: Cambridge University Press.

Schiller, Friedrich von (1967), *Letters on the Aesthetic Education of Man*, trans. Elizabeth M. Wilkinson and L.A. Willoughby, Oxford: Clarendon Press.

Schiller, Friedrich (2004), *On the Aesthetic Education of Man*, trans. Reginald Snell, Mineola, NY: Dover Publications.

Scott, A.O. (2008), Review of *Funny Games*, *New York Times*, 14 March.

Sellier, Geneviève (2008), *Masculine Singular: French New Wave Cinema*, trans. Kristin Ross, Durham, NC: Duke University Press.

Sellier, Geneviève (2010), 'Gender Studies and Film Studies in France: Steps Forward and Back', *Diogenes*, 57.1: 103–12.

Srebnick, Daniel Antonio (2004), 'Music and Identity: The Struggle for Harmony in *Vertigo*', in Richard Allen and Sam Ishii-Gonzàles, eds, *Hitchcock Past and Future*, London and New York: Routledge, 149–63.

Staiger, Janet (2000), *Perverse Spectators: The Practices of Film Reception*, New York: New York University Press.

Stott, William (1986), *Documentary Expression and Thirties America*, Chicago: University of Chicago Press.

Tanke, Joseph J. (2011), *Jacques Rancière: An Introduction. Philosophy, Politics, Aesthetics*, London: Continuum.

Vaughan, Dai (1999), *For Documentary: Twelve Essays*, Berkeley: University of California Press.

Virilio, Paul (1995), *The Art of the Motor*, trans. Julie Rose, Minneapolis: University of Minnesota Press.

Watts, Philip (2006), 'Images d'égalité', in *La Philosophie déplacée: autour de Jacques Rancière*, Paris: Horlieu, 361–70.

Whitney, John (1980), *Digital Harmony: On the Complementarity of Music and Visual Art*, Peterborough, NH: Byte Books/McGraw-Hill.

Whitney, Michael (1997), 'The Whitney Archive: A Fulfillment of a Dream', *Animation World Magazine*, 2(5), http://www.awn.com/mag/issue2.5/2.5frames/2.5whitneyarchive.html (accessed 12 February 2013).

Wilinsky, Barbara (2001), *Sure Seaters: The Emergence of Art House Cinema*, Minneapolis: University of Minnesota Press.

Young, Robert J.C. (1992), 'The Idea of a Chrestomathic University', in Richard Rand, ed., *Logomachia: The Conflict of the Faculties*, Lincoln, NE and London: University of Nebraska Press, 97–126.

Index